Henry, Prince of Wales
and England's Lost Renaissance

ROY STRONG

Henry, Prince of Wales

and England's Lost Renaissance

with 111 illustrations

THAMES AND HUDSON

SYLVIA LENNIE ENGLAND
In memoriam

Printed and bound in the German Democratic Republic

CONTENTS

Preface

This book has been so long in the making that I must apologize if I have omitted to thank anyone who has contributed. Those who certainly did, and whose contribution I indicate in brackets, are as follows: Dr T. D. Hobbs (the papers of Sir Adam Newton at Trinity College, Cambridge), Robin Harcourt Williams (William Cecil, 2nd Marquess of Salisbury), Professor Sir John Hale (fortifications), John Harris (architecture), Eileen Harris (Peake's edition of Serlio), Claude Blair (the Prince's armour), the late Howard Nixon (the Prince's books), Sir Oliver Millar (the picture collection), Professor K. J. Höltgen (Sir Robert Dallington and material from Landesbibliothek Kassel, MS 68), Dr Charles Avery (the gift of bronzes from Florence), Miss M. J. Poort (Abraham van Nyvelt), Dr J. A. van Dorsten (Abraham Gorlaeus and other Dutch problems), Dr Margaret McGowan (Constantino de' Servi), Professor Stephen Orgel (the masques and overall criticism), Dr Gino Corti (material from the Archivio di Stato, Florence) and Dr Alisdair Hawkyard (material on gentlemen of the Privy Chamber and early memoirs of the Prince).

Stephen Calloway has yet again provided me with an abundance of books and xeroxes of articles and organized my expeditions to the British Library. Pauline Cockrill typed nearly all of the first draft and Richard Bates the second. Finally I would like to pay affectionate tribute to the late Dr Sylvia England to whose memory this book is dedicated. It is not easy to run a national collection and sustain some programme of original research. This is the last book on which she worked for me, both in the Public Record Office and the British Library, either abstracting manuscripts or obtaining xeroxes. As the material emerged she became as obsessed with the Prince as myself. I am only sad that she did not live to read the results of her labours.

ROY STRONG
Victoria and Albert Museum
October 1984

Portrait of a Prince

Scarcely a decade after the death of Queen Elizabeth I in March 1603 the streets of London echoed once again to sounds of grief as a cavalcade bore the body of a king-to-be. James I's eldest son, Henry, Prince of Wales, was eighteen when he died on 6 November 1612. The sense of tragic loss at the time was such that he was to remain for long an ideal monarch England never had. And what a procession it was. Over a mile long, with some two thousand mourners in black, including all the members of his household and his friends, it took no less than four hours to marshal.[1] Out of the Prince's red-brick Tudor palace of St James's it wended its way to Westminster Abbey amidst an 'Ocean of Tears'. Isaac Wake, secretary to ambassador Dudley Carleton, describes the climax: a chariot drawn by six horses, preceded by armorial banners and insignia, over which knights carried a mighty canopy:

... vnder that laye the goodly image of that lovely prince clothed with the ritchest garments he had, which did so liuely represent his person, as that it did not onely draw teares from the severest beholder, but cawsed a fearefull outcrie among the people as if they felt at the present their owne ruine in that loss. I must confess never to have seen such a sight of mortification in my life, nor neuer so iust a sorrowe so well expressed as in all the spectators whose streaming eyes made knowen howe much inwardly their harts did bleed.[2]

In the Abbey stood 'a great stately hearse', six ionic pillars supporting a pyramidal structure decked with a profusion of banners, arms and mottoes. Within it reclined a slight figure, the diadem of his principality of Wales on his head, and the verge or rod of office, also bestowed on him at his investiture, in his right hand. The effigy lay enfolded in a velvet ermine-lined mantle with the chain of the Order of the Garter encircling his shoulders. Those who looked on must have remembered that day in June, two years before, when his father had invested him with these symbols of his new found rank, and pondered on the mortality of princes. After the coffin had been lowered into the vault, came that final act which, with one ceremonial gesture, wiped out a court: the breaking and tossing into the Prince's grave of the white rods of office by the members of his household. One senses their utter desolation.

A member of that vanished household was Sir John Holles, later Earl of Clare. He had been with the Prince right to the bitter end and had even escorted, bent with grief, his master's bowels to be buried. From his pen in the days and months that followed poured a series of letters that sum up the true enormity of the loss.³ Thirteen days after the marriage of the Prince's sister to the Elector Palatine on 14 February 1613, he wrote a letter to Lord Gray which is so important that I must quote it almost in full:

It is true my worthy master is no more. A jewel whom God and nature only shewed to the world, and drew in again, we being unworthy to possess him, and with him every man seems to have lost his dearest....For good men of all professions were welcome to him. He cherished the true prophets and graced with his attentive devotion and example their ministerial endeavours; those towards himself he rewarded with benefit and promotions. All men of learning, countryman or stranger, of what virtue soever, military or civil, he countenanced and comforted. He was frugally bountiful, which is true liberality....To conclude all in a word. He was respectively courteous to all, familiar with those he esteemed honest; a great, a judicious, and a silent, searcher into dispositions, wise, just, and secret, a curious observer for use of what he read or heard, constant in good things, which virtue he daily confirmed, by being not easily moved in things indifferent, in all things he affected regularity in his chapel, chamber, and household, was seldom angry, never gave foul word nor oath in his life. With ambassadors and strangers, princes, etc., he did *stare sopra di se* and usually received them with that order and majesty as they approached him rather as a king than a prince. This excellently composed inside was accompanied with as well a built outside, an able, graceful, body never wearied with labour, eminent in all princely exercises on horseback and on foot, a great sufferer of cold and heat, and in all things and to all things so framed as he promised us not only a great ableness but a long-lasting ableness...For our home preservation he held up religion and held in the presumptious papist... the industrious spirit was comforted; all actions profitable or honourable for the kingdom were fomented by him, witness the North West passage, Virginia, Guiana, The Newfoundland, etc., to all which he gave his money as well as his good word. So was he forward in all his public works which either were of use or ornament to this State: Lambeth Bridge, his intended fabrics at Richmond and St James's, the Academy, to which he had given his stables, and other helps for the better 'address' of our youth, can well witness, all which also perished in this storm: and to interpret him further in this particular, besides his entertaining the best engineers and architects of Christendom, let me tell your lordship his love to this nation that many times speech being of the glorious deeds of our ancestors both in military and civil achievements I have heard him confidently assever that there were as many as able, worthy, spirits in England as were then, who wanted but good occasions to put them to work to make them thereby as glorious as their forefathers. And as his hopes were to see those fruits, so was he so mindful and pious to the honour of times past, which he scorned to leave buried in the ignorance of merchants' quills and such like, as he stipended Doctor Hayward at 200 *l.* per annum to write the universal history of this kingdom; who, as an assay of that great labour, had not many days before his fatal sickness presented him with the first four years of Queen Elizabeth, whose memory and government this worthy prince ever much reverenced. Neither closed he his eyes from what concerned us abroad but entertained by his purse in sundry places as good intelligence as any we had: a rare vigilancy in those years commonly cast in dreams, vanities, and impertinencies. This prince we lost, this master I lost and this son the king lost....⁴

No one, he continues, exceeded him in his filial duty and yet now, only three months after his death, there are those who 'with lies and slanders endeavor to tear up his body from the quietness of his grave'.

They defile him by telling the King that such was his son's ambition that he aspired alone to 'be steersman to keep the ship from sinking, that Absolom like he might with better facility snatch the sceptre out of his father's fist'.

What an amazing youth he must have been if all this letter attributes to him is indeed true. No other document, I believe, better encapsulates the Prince's ambience or raises so many questions that need to be answered. Holles associates him with a love of learning and knowledge, with a commitment to the Protestant cause, with the maintenance of a household governed by the virtues, with colonial endeavours – from the search for the North-West Passage to the colonization of Virginia. He paints a portrait of a youth of unbelievable precocity, strong not only in mind but in body, a hero of the tiltyard and an exponent of all manly exercises. This was a Prince who was also a Maecenas of the arts, patronizing engineers and architects and who had in hand projects for mighty palaces – 'his intended fabrics' – which were never built. He maintained, moreover, a keen interest in foreign affairs, keeping agents abroad, at his own expense, to provide him with 'good intelligence'. Above all he had a patriotic fervour for England and her youth, those 'able, worthy, spirits', who would revive her fortunes and recreate the heroic golden age of Gloriana, for whose reign and government he had admiration.

Just two points in this eulogy give rise to some unease. The first is that he was 'secret', and one wonders why. The second, far more alarming, is the insinuation, denied by Holles but uttered by those close to the King, that his son desired to snatch the sceptre from him. All this is astonishing enough in a man who died before he reached his nineteenth year and whose period of independent activity extended only from January 1610 to November 1612. Holles' letter conveniently poses all the problems that this book sets out to investigate, but we must begin at the beginning in Scotland during the last decade of the sixteenth century.

Henry Frederick was the first-born child of James VI of Scotland and his queen, Anne of Denmark. He was born on 19 February 1594 at Stirling Castle and baptized six months later amidst a splendour which signalled that he was to be heir not only to the crown of Scotland but also to that of his godmother, Elizabeth I of England.[5] By his father's decree he was removed from his mother and placed in the charge of the Earl and Countess of Mar, an action which broke the marriage and left Anne an embittered woman. In their care Henry was to remain until the spring of 1603 when his father became King of England. The

1, 2

3

Prince was only nine, so that his truly formative years were to come south rather than north of the border. The same can be said of the two other surviving children, Elizabeth, who was six when her father succeeded her namesake, and Charles, who was just three.

The accession of James was to result in Anne gaining charge of her eldest son, but only after a dramatic struggle which precipitated a miscarriage. In the end a warrant was issued by the King instructing Lord Mar to hand the child over, so that Anne and Henry crossed the border together and travelled south to be joined later by her daughter, Elizabeth. It is important to grasp the huge impact that these two children made upon a kingdom that had had no royal family for over fifty years and no heir since the infant Edward VI. The flood of eulogies and engravings tells its own story of the cult of a dynasty which grew up overnight and developed on an enormous scale. The new mythology, as it affected the nine-year-old prince, is summed up in Ben Jonson's entertainment at Althorpe, in a parting speech which was to have been delivered by a youth attended by the younger sons of the county. In this the Prince was cast as the leader of a new generation with new ideals:

> O shoot vp fast in spirit, as in yeares;
> That when vpon her head proud *Europe* weares
> Her stateliest tire, you may appeare thereon
> The richest gem, without a paragon.
> Shine bright and fixed as the Arctic starre:
> And when slow Time hath made you fit for warre,
> Looke ouer the strict Ocean, and thinke where
> You may but lead vs forth, that grow vp here
> Against a day, when our officious swords
> Shall speake our action better then our words.[6]

And, as this speech reveals, those aspirations were to be militaristic; the Prince was already seen as the future leader of armies onto the mainland of Europe.

From the outset he was precocious, although to his father's despair he was not academically inclined. At the Garter ceremony at Windsor in the summer of 1603 he was noted for his 'quicke wittie answeres, pryncely carriage, and reverend peforminge his obeyance at the altar'.[7] Although from that year until the close of 1609 he rarely figured on the public stage, whenever he did he always made a considerable impression. In the state entry into London in 1604 he appeared 'smiling and over-joyde to the people's eternall comfort' and 'saluted them with many a bende',[8] a sharp contrast, even then, to his father, who 'endured this day's brunt with patience'.[9] We catch glimpses of him gravely dancing to perfection after Jonson's *Masque of Hymen* in 1606[10] and, in the same year, he made a brilliant first public appearance in the tiltyard on the occasion of the visit of his uncle Christian IV, King of Denmark.[11] But in the main these were years when he was out of the public eye, years passed in the household created around him by the King, with Sir Thomas Chaloner as his governor and Adam Newton as his schoolmaster. Initially, from 1603 to 1604 a small academy of aristocratic youths was assembled around him, but this broke up when most preceded him to the universities.[12] The Prince was left with the company of some of his closest friends: the Earl of Essex, Lord Cranborne and John Harington, heir to Lord Harington of Exton. As we pass through the years 1608 and 1609 ambassadorial dispatches begin to make more reference to him, but it was not until 1610 that he made his decisive entry onto the public stage. The year commenced with his presentation before the court in a chivalrous spectacle written by Ben Jonson, in which he fought as chief challenger; it culminated in June with the King formally creating him Prince of Wales before the assembled Lords and Commons in Westminster Hall. Simultaneously he was given his own revenues, his own household and his own palaces, Richmond on the Thames and St James's over the park from Whitehall. For the next three years he was never out of public consciousness as he gradually created around himself a dazzling court.

There are four major contemporary or near-contemporary sources which enable us to delineate the Prince, his personal appearance and character in great detail.[13] There are various discrepancies between them, but not so great as to prevent a composite picture being built up. As I shall be referring to one or the other of them throughout this book it is as well to list them at the outset. The first is a life by John Hawkins, which is dedicated to a certain Thomas Chapman. It must have been compiled in 1613, very shortly after the Prince's death. The second is a *Discourse* written in 1626 by Henry's treasurer, Sir Charles Cornwallis, and published in 1641. The third, also published in 1641, is *The True Picture and Relation of Prince Henry*. This was dedicated to his sister, Elizabeth, Queen of Bohemia, and is by a certain 'W. H.', who describes himself as having been in the Prince's service. It is not the work of a man of letters but a disconnected compilation of anecdotes lacking narrative structure and was clearly written by someone close to the Prince's circle but not cognisant of its inner political affiliations and workings. W. H. is almost certainly William Haydon, the most senior Groom of the Bedchamber. In a way more interesting than any of these is the all too short but brilliantly perceptive essay, charged with innuendo, by Francis Bacon, entitled *The Praise of Prince Henry*.

W. H. describes the Prince as follows:

He was tall and of an high stature, his body strong and well proportioned, his shoulders were broad, his eyes quicke and pleasant, his forehead broad, his nose bigg, his chinne broad and clouen, his haire inclining to bleeke, whereas before it had been of a whitish colour, the colour of his face some what swarte and scorched with the sunne, his whole face and visage comely and beautifull, looking for the most part with a sweete, smyling, and amiable countenance, and withall full of grauity, and Princely majesty, resembling much in shape of his body, and diuers actions the King of Dennemark his Vncle.[14]

Hawkins elaborates on the Prince's physiognomy in 1612 shortly before he embarks on the account of his illness and death:

... where before he was of somewhat a full round face, and very pleasant disposition, his Visage began to appear somwhat paler, longer and thinner than before, he being also more sad and retired than usual....[15]

There is no reason to share his prognostications of impending doom in the development of the Prince's physiognomy. What he is describing is nothing unusual as adolescence burgeons into manhood. The change can be pinpointed to the autumn of the previous year, 1611, when, on 6 November, John Chamberlain, the letter writer, reported to Carleton that 'the Prince in favor growes very like the Queen his mother'.[16] Bacon, also writing in retrospect, records this: 'his face long and inclining to leanness ... his look grave, and the motion of his eyes composed rather than spirited. In his countenance were some marks of severity...'. The reference to his mother's face, with its familiar angularity of bone structure and aquiline nose, provides us with all we need to identify the change of appearance. It enables us moreover conveniently to categorize the Prince's portraits, where they are not dated, to one side or the other of the time divide of the close of 1611.

On Henry's physical presence, there is, apart from W. H., a surprising paucity of documentary information. In addition to Holles' brief description mentioned earlier, there is the following from Bacon: 'strong and erect; his stature of a middle size; his limbs well made; his gait and deportment majestic', and one by Cornwallis: 'a comely personage, of indifferent stature, well and straight limmed, and strongly proportioned'.[17] On his clothes large sums of money were lavished.[18] 'Concerning his apparell,' W. H. recounts, 'he loved to goe handsome and well cloathed: yet without any maner of superfluity or excesse'.[19] In this his appearance was cultivated as a statement against the follies of his father's court. On 10 March 1611 the Venetian ambassador wrote:

The Prince has abandoned the French dress and has taken to the Italian: in this he has been followed by the Duke of York and by the larger part of their household. He says he will always wear it, as it seems to him more modest and more convenient in itself and less costly for the suite, as he cannot endure the changes in fashion which come every day from France. The Spanish ambassador, in conversation with his Highness, congratulated him on having adopted the Spanish dress, but had for his answer that it was really nearer Italian.[20]

That the change in dress was taken up by the Prince's followers is corroborated by two reports, the first also dating from March, in which Sir Edward Cecil, a close adviser, is said to be dressed *all'italiana*,[21] and the second, five months later, in which Henry himself is recorded sporting a richly embroidered Italian suit.[22]

If I had to choose the most objective analysis of the Prince's character it would have to be Francis Bacon's remarkably sharp sketch. Bacon was never part of the St James's court so that his account is observation from a distance and uncoloured by the haze of hagiography incipient in the eulogies of Cornwallis, Hawkins and W. H. Whereas they and the Venetians praise the Prince for the solemnity of his manner Bacon categorizes it as off-putting: 'and in fact raised in others an opinion of himself very unlike what his manner would at first have suggested'. What Bacon seems to be saying is that the Prince did not suffer fools gladly but only gradually responded when 'addressed and softened...with a due respect and seasonable discourse'. His conversation is described as being slow and prolonged, interlarded with hesitations, due not to incomprehension but to his methodical grasping of each point.

There can be no doubt that, unlike his parents and sister but like his brother Charles, he was basically a cold, withdrawn character. 'His affections and passions', writes Bacon again, 'were not strong, but rather equal than warm...'. There were occasional displays of temper but these were quickly succeeded by remorse and repentance. Humour and loyalty are revealed in his letters to his friends, but the only relationship that rises to the level of passion is that with his sister. Unlike his father, however, he had a dogged devotion to hard work. James was one of the great scholars of the age, an ability his son did not inherit although he thoroughly respected learning. Henry instead had a capacity for sustained application, an unremitting curiosity across a far wider spectrum than his father, an obsession with order and systems and, in addition, a rapidly expanding interest in politics and power. There was finally a strange secretive quality about him which was commented upon by a number of contemporaries. Early on in life the Prince must have learned to cultivate taciturnity as a virtue.

From the outset he was a man of action, physically tough and an assiduous exponent of the martial arts. Fiercely Protestant and a stickler for morals and good conduct he emerges as a kind of precursor of the Low Church muscular Christianity produced by the Victorian public schools. Within the context of early Jacobean England, starved of an heir to the throne since 1537, he was inevitably to become the focus of a major popular cult. His interests made him something in addition, the heir to the mantles of two late Elizabethan heroes, Sir Philip Sidney and Robert Devereux, 2nd Earl of Essex, as the epitome of militant Protestant chivalry. It was a role he unreservedly embraced and consciously developed. All the evidence corroborates Bacon's view that this aggressive young man was 'ambitious of commendation and glory'. In spite of his reserve in private he knew how to move with acclamation upon the public stage. In that ability lay one element of what was quickly to become the great divide with his father.

From the beginning that relationship was doomed. As from birth Henry was viewed as a threat to James. When he put the child in the charge of his friend Mar it was because 'if some faction got strong enough, she [i. e. Anne] could not hinder his boy being used against him, as he himself had been against his unfortunate mother'.[23] The surviving letters to the King from the Prince, in the main formal compositions in Latin, are laboured and often in draft form covered in corrections and alterations reflecting the difficulty he had in compiling them. An undated letter from the King to his son shows that the father registered the fact:

My Sonne; I am glad that by youre letter I my persave that ye make some progress in learning, althoch I suspecte ye have rather written then dyted it, for I longe to rassaue a letter from you that maye be quhollie yours, as well maitter as forme, as well formid by youre minde as drawin by youre fingers....[24]

That the Prince's letters were aimed to please there can be no doubt, listing off Latin books, which he had learnt by rote, or enclosing an oration on the subject that learning was more necessary for kings, princes and other persons of high rank.[25] Annually each New Year's Day these painful little exercises made their way to his father's unsympathetic eye.

In these private letters we sense tension between the two from childhood. The father puts the son down just as at Oxford in 1605 he refused to allow the degree of MA to be bestowed on the Prince.[26] The tension was publicly registered as early as 1607 by the Venetian Nicolo Molin, in his *relazione*, where he describes the Prince at length in what is without doubt the most perceptive pen-portrait of him as a young adolescent. It is worth quoting in full:

The eldest Henry, is about twelve years old, of a noble wit and great promise. His every action is marked by a gravity most certainly beyond his years. He studies, not with much delight, and chiefly under his father's spur, not of his own desire, and for this he is often admonished and set down. Indeed one day the King, after giving him a lecture, said that if he did not attend more earnestly to his lessons the crown would be left to his brother, the Duke of York, who was far quicker at learning and studied more earnestly. The Prince made no reply, out of respect for his father; but when he went to his room and his tutor continued in the same vein, he said, 'I know what becomes a Prince. It is not necessary for me to be a professor, but a soldier and a man of the world. If my brother is as learned as they say, we'll make him Archbishop of Canterbury'. The King took this answer in no good part; nor is he overpleased to see his son so beloved and of such promise that his subjects place all their hopes in him; and it would almost seem, to speak quite frankly, that the King was growing jealous; and so the Prince has great need of a wise counsellor to guide his steps.[27]

That this tension should register to an outsider would indicate that behind the scenes the divide was even greater. It was to colour almost every event at court after January 1610. Outwardly the Prince was, of course, deeply respectful to his father, 'albeit', W. H. writes, 'his Majestie would sometimes interlace sharpe speeches, and other demonstrations of fatherlie severitie'.[28] The Venetian ambassador records an incident exactly of this kind, when the Prince was subjected to just such 'sharpe speeches'. Henry despised his father's addiction to the chase and, when both were at Royston, the King rounded on his son on the topic. The confrontation between the two must have been on some scale, for the Prince put his spurs to his horse and rode away. Later, there was a reconciliation when Henry begged his pardon and James jokingly said, 'Well, you are no sportsman'.[29] A tiny incident but surely catching in microcosm the constant pattern of irritation that was to dog the relationship of the two courts during these three years.

Bishop Goodman is another source giving us such a glimpse when he wrote that the Prince 'did sometimes pry into the King's actions, and a little dislike them, ... and truly I think he was a little self-willed'.[30] But could one think of two more disparate characters? The bloated pedantic middle-aged father, careless of affairs of state, prepared to accept appeasement at any price, bent on the pleasures of the chase, totally unaesthetic, whose penchant for handsome courtiers was hardly becoming and whose court was certainly no model for decorum. And, in contrast, the young Prince, a man-at-arms who shone at tilt and tourney, who courted public popularity, who excelled in the art of riding, tennis and all manly sports, who, if not a scholar himself, yet was devoted to men of learning, who was an aesthete and whose court was about to be established as a model of virtue. Such polarization was intensified by a shared fatal characteristic: both were assertive and autocratic in their views. To the King, terrible though it may seem, the premature death of the Prince was to come almost as a relief.

If Henry had inherited his obstinacy from his father, from his mother, Anne of Denmark, came his love for the visual arts and those of festival. On the whole Anne lived for pleasure, passing her time moving from one of the palaces assigned to her to the next. She and her household made up what might be categorized as a second.court based on Somerset House in London and Greenwich on the Thames. In the summer there were progresses to aristocratic houses, the occasion for alfresco *fêtes*. Anne set style. Immediately on her arrival in the south, fashion changed under her aegis, as the excrescences of her predecessor's dress were jettisoned in favour of a simpler silhouette with a lavish use of ribbon rosettes in pastel colours. Although she was devoted to her brother, Christian IV, King of Denmark, who came to England twice in 1606 and 1614, she deliberately avoided politics, devoting herself instead to dancing, court entertainments and the design and decoration of her houses and gardens. She also presided over her own circle, one noted for the extravagance (she was always in debt) epitomized by her great friend, Lucy Harington, Countess of Bedford, sister of her son's childhood companion. Goodman records that 'the Queen did ever love Charles better than Prince Henry'[31] but there seems to be little evidence for this. It would probably be more accurate to say that Anne naturally felt closer to a child whose pathetic weakness would have more quickly aroused what were strong maternal feelings.

As the eldest child Henry had a somewhat embarrassing role to play as a go-between in his parents' squabbles. This cannot have been pleasant. A letter he wrote to his father in 1609 illustrates this role:

According to your Majesty's commandement I made your excuse unto the Queene for not sending her a token by me, and alledged your Majesty had a quarrell unto her for not Wryting an answere unto your second lettre Wrettin from Roisten when your foote was sore, nor making mention of the receiving of it in her next letter sent some ten days after, whereas in your Majesty's former iorney to Roisten when you tooke first the paine in your foote she sent one of purpose to visite yow. Here answere was that either she had wrettin or dreamed it, and upon that apprehension had told first my lord Hay and next Sir Thomas Somersett that she had wrettin before. I durst not reply that your Majesty was affeared least she should returne to her old byasse, for feare that such a Word might have sett her in the Way and made me a peace breaker....[32]

The Prince's reference to 'her old byasse' neatly demonstrates that even at sixteen he was keenly aware of his mother's pettiness. Cynics might and did observe that Anne made much of Henry after he was created Prince of Wales to secure her own future in the event of the King dying early,[33] but their relationship was never to enter the troubled waters of that of king and prince. This in many ways is surprising because on one thing mother and son were utterly divided: religion.

1 The Prince at the age of ten, his
robes as Knight of the Garter and
the ship jewel in his hat reflecting
his chivalrous and maritime
interests.

The Prince's Family

2   His father, King James I of England and VI of Scotland

3   His mother, Anne of Denmark

4   His brother, Charles, Duke of York

5   His sister, the Princess Elizabeth

Friends and courtiers

6 Sir Edward Cecil, later Viscount
Wimbledon

8 Robert Devereux, 3rd Earl of
Essex

7 John Harington, 2nd Lord
Harington of Exton

9 William Cecil, Lord Cranborne,
later 2nd Earl of Salisbury

10　Thomas Howard, 14th Earl of
Arundel

ÆTAT SVÆ 43

Maritime endeavour

11 The shipwright, Phineas Pett

12 The *Prince Royal* under construction

10 Thomas Howard, 14th Earl of
Arundel

Maritime endeavour

11 The shipwright, Phineas Pett

12 The *Prince Royal* under construction

13 The Prince's toy ship, the *Disdain*, presented to him by Lord Howard of Effingham in 1604

14 The *Prince Royal* launched in 1610

The child warrior

The Prince wearing the armour given him by the Prince de Joinville, 1607

15   Attributed to Rowland Lockey, 1607

16   By Nicholas Hilliard (enlarged)

Although Anne had begun her life as a Lutheran, sometime during the 1590s she became a Catholic. Her religion, covert though it was, certainly affected her views on her children's marriages. She always emerges as opposed to the Protestant Palatine match for her daughter and sympathetic to the Catholic brides mooted for Henry. To him her religion must have been anathema, but there was no *froideur* ever noted between them and, indeed, Francis Bacon records the Prince's extreme reverence towards her.

Faced with such unsatisfactory parents it is hardly surprising that the three surviving children were drawn by instinct closely together. Two years only divided Henry from his sister Elizabeth. These were the twin stars in the early Jacobean firmament, made more potent by bearing names evocative of the two greatest Tudor monarchs. Henry 'loved her alwayes so dearly, that he desired to see her alwayes by him'.[34] There was between them what Bacon describes an 'an entire affection', and the numerous notes they exchanged bear testimony to this fact.[35] The same source writes that to his younger brother, just ten in 1610, 'he was indulgent'. Charles, Duke of York, was an ailing child to whom such a brother was as a god. That Henry desired to reinforce his influence over Charles we know from the clash over the senior appointment in his brother's household in 1611. The Prince made every effort to secure the key post for his friend Sir James Fullerton, relegating the Duke of York's previous governor, Sir Robert Cary (his father's choice), to second-in-command. In spite of much spent passion he failed in reversing a decision taken by the Council under the influence of Suffolk in favour of Cary.[36]

In October 1609 this ill-assorted family was reunited at Whitehall Palace for the customary Christmas and New Year's festivities. The gathering was to serve as a preface to the series of spectacles and ceremonies in the coming months which were publicly to establish Henry as Prince of Wales. That decision was prompted, ironically enough, by the desperate financial state of the crown. This James had inherited from Elizabeth, but the situation had deteriorated even more and Parliament had yet to recognize that no monarch could live of his own. Already restless at the close of the old queen's reign over demands for money, Parliament was to become more so under her successor, and its members by no means warmed to the new king's belief in and exposition of his theory of the Divine Right of Kings. By 1609 the need for a solution to the financial problem was even more acute, and James's first minister, Robert Cecil, Earl of Salisbury, saw one whereby, through a surrender by the crown of old feudal dues, such as wardship, Parliament would guarantee in return an annual income to sustain both his own needs and those of his family, including the heir to the throne. This was the Great Contract which was to be the focal point of domestic policy in 1610.[37] The need to provide for the popular young Prince was seen to be an emotive card to play in this political game.

At the end of November 1609 Antonio Correr, the Venetian ambassador, reported that the Prince was busy forming his household. This event was accompanied by not only demands for money from the King but an intense jostling among the place-seekers. There were, he wrote, 'infinite offers from gentlemen who vie with one another in desiring admission ... for although his Highness does nothing without the King's permission, yet he is extremely particular that everything shall be the result of his own choice'.[38] I shall come later to a consideration of those who held office in a professional sense as *animateurs* of the Prince's arts policy – Oliver, Peake, Jones, de Caus, Chapman or de' Servi; they will fall into place as we embark on a study of the cultural revolution the new court represented. Here I shall confine my observations to a handful of the officers, gentlemen and servants who made up part of an establishment of over four hundred persons.[39]

In the first place the contrast in atmosphere with James's court can hardly be overestimated. Lotti, the Tuscan agent in London, wrote in code on this, for the Prince's chamberlain told him 'that His Highness did not like the court because he loves truth and hates the contrary.'[40] Henry's was to be a model of order and even swearing was to be subject to fine. Banquets and feasts, he decreed, 'should pass with decency and decorum, and without all rudeness, noise, or disorder',[41] a total novelty to those used to the scenes of chaos and drunkenness that usually attended any of the revels at Whitehall. Even more pointed was the fact that the Prince's household and circle included no Roman Catholics, whereas the King's attitude was far more tolerant, as long as there was no flaunting of the faith. The great divide came over the Howard family, most pro-Spanish and crypto-Catholic. They had been out of favour under Elizabeth but restored to honours by James. Apart from the young Thomas Howard, Earl of Arundel, and Charles Howard, Earl of Nottingham, the hero of the Armada, members of the Howard clan found no favour at the Prince's court and certainly he avoided its two most powerful and malignant members, the Earls of Suffolk and Northampton. He also had an extreme distaste for the King's favourites, in this instance Robert Carr, soon to become Earl of Somerset.

Henry's court was made up in the main of men of action, practising soldiers, or, at the least, those adept at martial sports in the tiltyard.

Their Protestant bias was overwhelming. They emerge too as men who had travelled and often resided abroad for considerable lengths of time, above all in France and Italy. Among them are those whom we can identify as the earliest connoisseurs and collectors of works of art in England: the Earl of Arundel, Adam Newton, the Earl of Ancrum and Sir Henry Fanshawe. Fanshawe, together with Sir John Danvers, was to be a major pioneering figure in the introduction of Italian garden design, with its use of sculpture and water. Lord Cranborne and Sir John Holles provide us with two of the first references ever to the use of and admiration for the work of Andrea Palladio, which was to affect the whole direction of architecture in England. And Arundel was to ensure Inigo Jones's future education as the 'Vitruvius Britannicus' subsequent to the Prince's death. Short-lived though the Prince's court was to be, the seeds of so much that we regard as the essence of Caroline civilization are present here twenty years before.[42]

At first glance it is striking how many posts went to members of the Prince's household during his minority. Chief amongst these was Sir Thomas Chaloner (1561–1615) who had been put in charge of the infant Prince in August 1603.[43] Chaloner's father had been one of Lord Burghley's closest friends and his son inherited his poetical skills in his youth. After being educated at St Paul's and Magdalen College, Oxford, he had travelled in Italy in the 1580s and served Leicester in the Low Countries in 1586. Later he became an MP and also fought in France, for which he was knighted in 1591. What strikes one most, however, is the Italian experience, for he was resident in Florence from 1596 to 1598 as an agent of Essex and in France from 1598 to 1599. He had been drawn into the Essex circle by way of Francis Bacon but by the close of the reign his family connections must have brought reconciliation with the Cecil clan as Robert Cecil sent him to Scotland, where he rapidly became a favourite of the king-to-be, actually travelling south with him in 1603. He was forty-nine in 1610 and the Prince gave him the post of Lord Chamberlain. Chaloner's main interests were philosophy and natural history, but it would be reasonable to conclude that he must have been responsible for arousing the Prince's interest in late Mannerist Florentine court culture. Chaloner was that rare phenomenon, an Elizabethan who had been resident for several years in Italy. He must have been one of the dominant forces in the Florentine influence that was to be such a marked feature of the years 1610–12.

Another key figure was the Prince's tutor, Adam Newton (d. 1630).[44] Newton was a Scot and a Greek scholar. He had not been to Italy but had taught in France in the 1580s. He was appointed Henry's tutor about 1600, and indeed it is his collection of papers that remains one of the key sources for his life. In 1605 he was rewarded with the deanery of Durham and in 1610 he became Secretary. Newton was noted for being a skilled Latinist and linguist and he was later to translate six books of Sarpi's *History of the Council of Trent*. Henry Peacham dedicates an emblem to him in his *Minerva Britanna* (1612) as 'my singuler good friend'. It depicts laurel entwined with a vine, the former in reference to 'wits diuine', the latter to those who 'swimme in health, yet want the muses still':

> This friendship should inviolate remaine,
> The rich with Bountie should rewarde the Artes....[45]

Although Newton seems not to have been in Italy he must have been interested in the arts. In 1607 he embarked on an ambitious and important mansion, Charlton House, near the palace at Greenwich.[46] Its architect is not known, but it owes much to John Thorpe and shares with Bramshill (1605–12) and Northumberland House (begun 1608) an imposing entrance piece, in this case lifted directly from an engraving by Dietterlin. The house in an H-plan of a type descending from Wimbledon (begun 1588) and has an axially-entered hall as at Hardwick. Its exterior reminds one of Hatfield but one could hardly describe it as innovatory. More important are the fragments which indicate an interest in pictures. The version of Holbein's *Richard Southwell*, now in the Louvre, has the seal of the Newton family on its reverse. On the back of their version of *Erasmus* is a paper inscribed: 'This picture of Erasmus Rotterdamus was given to the Prince by Adam Newton'.[47] It could as readily have been presented to Charles I, whose brandmark it bears, as to Henry, but the real point is that it indicates that Newton must have collected pictures. His interest in Holbein runs parallel with that of the Queen's friend, Lucy Harington, Countess of Bedford.

Sir David Murray (1567–1629) was a third survivor, being elevated from Keeper of the Privy Purse to Groom of the Stole and Gentleman of the Robes. Hawkins writes that he was 'the only Man in whom he had put Choise Trust'.[48] Like so many Scots, Murray had travelled south on the accession. Lord Roos refers to him as 'a Puritan' noted for his opposition to a Medici match for the Prince.[49] In 1611 he was to publish a volume of poetry including *The Tragicall Death of Sophonisba* and was a 'loving friend' of Michael Drayton.[50] Another Scot was Sir William Alexander (*c.* 1576–1640), later Earl of Stirling, who had been appointed a Gentleman Extraordinary of the Privy Chamber in or before 1607.[51] He too had travelled abroad through France, Spain and Italy in attendance on Archibald, 7th Earl of Argyle. In 1603 he was amongst the Scots who came south and enjoyed the King's favour and in that year published the first of his poems, *The Tragedie of Darius*. He was knighted sometime between 1608 and 1609. Besides his literary output, another facet links him decisively with the Prince's circle, a preoccupation with colonization. This must have been formed during these years but it was not to bear fruit until 1621 when Charles I granted him Nova Scotia. His efforts on behalf of colonization were to be unending and when he was created Earl in 1633 it carried the additional title of Viscount Canada.

There were others who administered the lands and estates and who went on to become part of the new household, but Chaloner, Newton, Murray and Alexander are really the only important ones who contributed directly to the creation of a cultural milieu. After them comes the influx of new blood. Among the most important was the Comptroller, John Holles (1564–1637), later Earl of Clare, a tough military man who had served in the wars in the Netherlands, Hungary and Ireland. He too had travelled and had 'viewed and observed the best Parts of *France* and *Italy*; both of which Languages he was Master of, and reasonably well of the Spanish'.[52] He was noted for his dislike of the Scottish 'invasion' of 1603, when he retired from the court. Quarrelsome and litigious, 'all his Favour at Court vanished' on the Prince's death. Holles was odd man out in another respect. He courted the King's favourite, Somerset. We know that he was interested in building because he owned a copy of Palladio's *I Quattro Libri dell' Architettura* and was in correspondence with the 9th Earl of Northumberland for the loan of a whole series of architectural works, including ones by Alberti, Serlio, de l'Orme, du Cerceau, Vignola and Dietterlin.[53] His house at Houghton in Nottinghamshire looks very old-fashioned but Kip's view of the surrounding demesne includes a rectangular lake with geometric islands, the central one circular with ascending terraces. These derive partly from Elvetham (1592) but could also reflect both the influence of de Caus's works for the Prince at Richmond and Francis Bacon's water garden at Gorhambury.

The Treasurer was Sir Charles Cornwallis (d. 1629), who came of an old Catholic family, his father having been comptroller of the household to Mary Tudor and replaced on the accession of Elizabeth I.[54] Charles was his second son and must have conformed to the Protestant faith, for he was sent in 1605 by James as resident ambassador in Spain. In March 1609 he suddenly started to write to the Prince, opening with a eulogistic letter comparing him to Alexander the Great. But by far the most interesting missive is the one describing religious ceremonies, an anti-Catholic diatribe ending with a condemnation of the splendour of Spanish churches and monasteries compared to the poverty of the rest of the kingdom: 'the temporall hath in a manner all fallen into the mouthes and devouringe throates of the spirituall'.[55] Cornwallis thus became the Prince's earliest foreign correspondent. 'I may and wish yow', he wrote to Cornwallis, 'to acquaint me further in that kynd as occasions shall be offred'.[56] Unfortunately for the Prince, Cornwallis was recalled that September. A central personage in the household, he campaigned firmly against any form of Catholic match for his master.

Wilson refers sharply to the court as adorned with 'young and Sprightly Blossoms'[57] and for these we must turn to the new Gentlemen of the Bed and Privy Chamber. The names of fourteen of the latter were listed by the Prince himself to Chaloner on 19 December 1610.[58] They include Sir George Goring, subsequently Earl of Norwich (?1583–1663), later a favourite of Charles I and a staunch royalist but, as a young man, noted as one of the 'chief and master fools' at court, a 'Mr North', probably Lord North's brother, Roger (?1585–?1652), a captain who was to sail on Raleigh's last and fatal Guiana voyage, Sir John Wentworth (d. 1631) of Gosfield, to be created a baronet the next year, Sir Ralph Clare (1587–1670), like Goring destined to be a royalist, valiant in his defence of Worcester, and Sir Philip Carey (1579/80–1631), who was later to be a member of the Virginia Company, picking up what was to be one of the major themes of Henry's policy.[59] A few names, however, spring out which deserve fuller consideration, particularly those people who like Chaloner and Holles had had experience of late sixteenth-century Italy.

The first is a 'Mr Dolington', identifiable as Sir Robert Dallington (1561–1637), later Master of Charterhouse.[60] Born in Northamptonshire he went to Corpus Christi College, Cambridge, where he enjoyed the patronage of the Butts family of Norfolk. Strongly Puritan in sentiment, they were important landed gentry connected by marriage with the Bacons. Under their aegis Dallington became a schoolmaster. Suddenly at the age of twenty-one he emerges in a surprising manner as the translator of Francesco Colonna's *Hypnerotomachia Poliphili*, which he published under his initials. In it he angles for patronage, dedicating the book to the memory of the virtues of Sir Philip Sidney, to those who survived him and to the man upon whose shoulders the mantle of the poet-knight fell, the Earl of Essex. The book is important, for it provides a vital thread which connects the Italianate interests of Prince Henry's court back with the pioneer of such taste in the 1590s. Dallington reveals, in *Hypnerotomachia Poliphili*, his fascination not only for the lascivious aspects of this romance permeated by Classical archaeology, but for visual marvels of all kinds and, in particular, architecture, to all of which he responds with such phrases as 'so great and exalted woorke', 'maruellous performance' or 'incredible charge'. Patronage did in fact come to him through Sidney's indirect heirs, for he was taken up by the Manners family. From 1595 to 1597 he accompanied Roger, 5th Earl of Rutland (who later married Sidney's daughter), through France, Italy and Germany and in 1598–1600 escorted Francis Manners, later Lord Roos, on a similar tour, one in which Inigo Jones may have been a member of the party. These tours later led to two travel books. In 1605 appeared *A Survey of the Great Dukes State of Tuscany, in the yeare of Our Lord 1596* and the year after followed *A Method of Travell: shewed by taking the view of France as it stood in the yeare of Our Lord 1598*. As in the case of his *Striue of Loue in a Dreame* there is strong interest in visual matters, referring to the new architecture of Paris and Henri IV's vast palace project, besides marvelling at the treasures and curiosities of late Medicean Florence.

All these interests fit in exactly with the attitudes of the Prince's court: the cult of Henri IV, the strongly Florentine as against Venetian bias in the case of Italy, combined with an unshakeable allegiance to the reformed faith. A letter to Salisbury from the Earl of Rutland dated 31 December 1609 states that it was he who had introduced Dallington to the Prince's service four years before and that he was one who had 'served me long'.[61]Dallington must have known Inigo Jones, who first certainly appears in the Rutland accounts in 1603 as 'picturemaker'. In 1609 he presented in manuscript to the Prince his *Aphorismes Ciuile, and Militare ... out of Guicciardine*, a text he published in 1613 dedicating it to Prince Charles. Dallington was one of the few members of Henry's household to get a place in that of his successor, who was a decade later, in 1624, to see that Dallington got the lucrative post of Master of Charterhouse, both the school (then in London) and the hospital.

One of the most interesting names, however, to appear, on the list is that of Sir John Danvers (1588?–1655).[62] John Aubrey was a kinsman and provides us with much information on him in his *The Natural History of Wiltshire* where he writes in the following terms:

But 'twas *Sir John Danvers*, of Chelsey, who first taught us the way of Italian gardens. He had well travelled France and Italy, and made good observations. He had in a fair body an harmonicall mind....He had a very fine fancy, which lay chiefly for gardens and architecture.[63]

In 1610 Danvers House with its famous gardens, together with his equally famous garden at Lavington in Wiltshire, lay in the future but they must be placed in a line of descent back to the Prince of Wales's court. Danvers also fits in tidily, as we shall see, with a number of the Prince's friends who had also travelled in France and Italy. It is not known when he went abroad but it must have been before 1608, when he married Magdalen Herbert, widow of Richard Herbert, a lady twice his age and already a mother of ten children including the poet, George. Danvers sat in the Parliament of 1610 as MP for Arundel. A young man in his mid-twenties, his Italianate aesthetic interests were to be exactly in tune with the Prince's artistic policies.

Sir James Fullerton (d. *c.* 1630), like Dallington, was to get a position in the household of Prince Charles as Groom of the Stole.[64] He was one of Henry's Gentlemen of the Privy Chamber and Keeper of the Privy Purse and with him we come into contact with one of the most extraordinary pieces of Jacobean Italianate architecture, the two-storey portico added to Byfleet Lodge, Surrey. John Aubrey writes of it as 'a noble house of brick begun by Q. Anne, who lived not to finish it: but this was done by Sir James Fullerton'.[65] The date of the original house is in fact not known but it was granted to Henry Prince of Wales in 1610 and to Queen Anne in 1616. It is unlikely that the astonishing classical appendage, which was superimposed onto the façade of the house recorded in a sketch by Aubrey, could have been done for Anne in two short years and the weight of the evidence would favour Fullerton in the 1620s. The only person who could have designed this is Inigo Jones, whom Fullerton would have first met where he would have formed such tastes: in the household of the Prince.

In a list of Gentlemen of the Bedchamber after the Prince's death occurs the name of Robert Ker of Ancrum (1578–1654).[66] Ker, later to be created 1st Earl of Ancrum by Charles I, was also to survive into the household of the next Prince of Wales. A devoted royalist, he was to die in poverty in Amsterdam during the Commonwealth. Ker, however, had possibly been in Prince Henry's service since 1603. A man of letters, he was on intimate terms with the most famous literary men of his day, including William Drummond of Hawthornden, who was to lament the demise of the Prince in his *Teares, on the death of Moeliades*, and John Donne, who was to leave Ker the celebrated portrait of the poet as a young man 'taken in the shadows'. Ker belonged to that group which had travelled abroad; we do not know where, although his acquisition of Netherlandish pictures would certainly indicate familiarity with the Low Countries. It is likely that he collected both pictures and antiquities, for van der Doort's catalogue of Charles I's collection includes no fewer than seven items presented by him to the King: three Rembrandts reckoned to be the earliest to arrive in England, a Danaë by Rottenhammer, what was thought to be a copy after Raphael of a Virgin and Child, a double portrait of the daughters of Philip II and 'a little browne Crackt Ovall Agatt Stone' of Julius Caesar.[67]

17 Sir Henry Lee's portrait of the Prince by Marcus Gheeraerts. The Prince is wearing Garter robes and has a ship jewel in his hat.

18 Armour given by Henri IV

19 Armour given by Count Maurice of Nassau, 1611–12

20 Armour given by the Prince de Joinville, 1607

21 Armour given by Sir Henry Lee, 1608

23 The Prince wearing the armour given him by Henri IV

22 The Prince exercising with the pike. Engraving by William Hole after Isaac Oliver, 1612

24   Robert Peake's group of the
Prince *à la chasse* with his friend,
John, 2nd Lord Harington of Exton,
1603

The equestrian arts

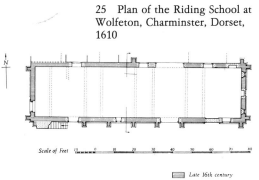

25   Plan of the Riding School at Wolfeton, Charminster, Dorset, 1610

Scale of Feet

Late 16th century

19th century, or uncertain

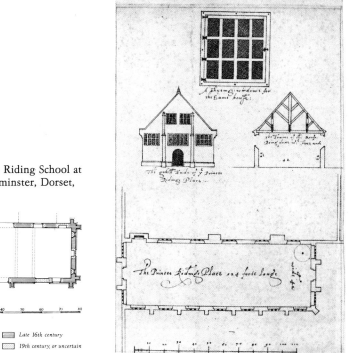

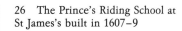

26   The Prince's Riding School at St James's built in 1607–9

27   Interior of the Riding School at Welbeck

28   Exterior of the Riding School at Welbeck, 1622

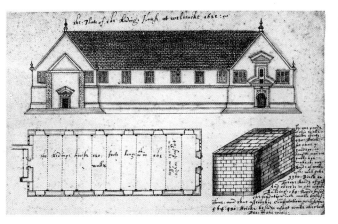

Foreign affairs

29 Frederick V, Elector Palatine

30 One of the Prince's heroes, Count Maurice of Nassau

31 Another of the Prince's heroes, Henri IV

32 The Princess Elizabeth by Marcus Gheeraerts, *c.* 1611. Portrait sent to Savoy in connection with her projected marriage to the Prince of Piedmont

33 Isaac Oliver's supreme miniature of the Prince, *c.* 1612, as a man-
at-arms with warriors *à l'antique*
seen beyond

A later addition in 1611 to the Gentlemen of the Privy Chamber was the poet, Sir Arthur Gorges (1557–1625).[68] He was a man of Devon – his mother was Raleigh's first cousin – and he had been a gentleman pensioner to Elizabeth I. In 1597 he had gone on the Azores expedition, later writing an account of it in 1607 for Prince Henry. On this he commanded Raleigh's ship and his close connection with his cousin brought him ruin in the new reign because he was suspected, though cleared, of complicity in the Bye Plot. His connection with Raleigh recommended him to the Prince and he entered the household probably in 1611. There is no evidence of any interest in the visual arts, but he lived in Chelsea, first in the Great House and later in Gorges House, which was next to Danvers House with its famous garden. Undoubtedly his attraction lay less in his role as a man of letters (he was later to translate works by Lucan and Bacon into French and English) than as an emanation of and a contact with the great man in the Tower. The steady stream of prose works is an expression of fervour for a revival of an Elizabethan policy against the old naval adversary, Spain, and the hand of Raleigh direct or otherwise is discernible in all of them: *Observations and Overtures for a Sea-fight* (unprinted), *Observations and Overtures concerning a Royall Navye and Seaservice*, *A Forme of Orders ... (for) a Fleete* and, presented in 1610 to the Prince, *A Breefe Discourse tendinge to the wealth, and strength of ... Great Brittayne*. That he was to mourn the Prince's death in a neo-Spenserian poem reflects, however, that he was responsive to the neo-Elizabethan strain that was part of the mythology. But, as H. E. Sandison has pointed out, that poem was almost certainly a reworking of an earlier one in honour of the Prince, probably begun in 1610:

Much more tangible, here in combination are practically all the themes of laudation of Henry living and lament for him dead that are reiterated, particularly after 1610: the Ars-Mars pattern of symbol and wording; the sponsorship of Bellona and of Pallas ...; the Prince's place among the nine English Henries, and his identification with other worthies, like Hector; his menace to 'Turcisme'; his courteous consideration of his household; above all, his prowess in the lists....[69]

Gorges' poem reads like a handbook to the ideas and attitudes that motivated those who made up the Prince's household during the years 1610–1612.

The Earl of Arundel's son William Howard, Lord Stafford, was to write that the Prince 'was knowne to valew none but exterordinary persons'.[70] In this, he was to form a sharp contrast with his brother, the future Charles I, whose ability to surround himself with the second-rate contributed to the ruin of the crown. A household is one thing, the ranks of servants and officers that made up the organization of the

Prince's court; but his circle is quite another. These are the people with whom the Prince had ties not only of loyalty but of genuine friendship. Two groups emerge, the first consisting of his closest friends from his own generation, young men who had all been born in the 1590s, and the second made up of an older generation, not as old as his father so much as belonging to an intermediate one born in the 1570s.

It was James himself who created a circle around the Prince by setting up on his arrival in England what amounted to an academy filled with aristocratic youths of roughly the same age as his son. Foremost amongst his appointed companions in 1603 was the heir of Elizabeth I's favourite, Essex.[71] On first coming south James I had taken the twelve-year-old Earl (1591–1646) into his arms and embraced him. As a result of the family's restoration to favour the boy was taken away from Eton under Sir Henry Saville and educated with the Prince, as was also another youth, to whom we shall come shortly, William Cecil, Lord Cranborne. These two were to become fast friends. Robert Devereux, 3rd Earl of Essex, was two years older than the Prince. The little palace academy was short lived and two years later Essex, at the age of fifteen, was to be the victim of an arranged marriage designed to make peace between the two great families of Devereux and Howard when he was married to Frances, daughter of the Earl of Suffolk. They were not, however, to live together until they were older and in the summer of the following year he was sent off on a continental tour that included France, Germany and the Low Countries (but not apparently Italy) with the Prince's riding master, Monsieur de St Antoine, in his entourage. From this tour there survive a number of dutiful letters to the Prince indicating certainly friendship if not intimacy. On his return in 1609 he caught smallpox which permanently disfigured his face; soon after his eighteenth birthday he began to live with his wife, but by 1611 the marriage had broken down. About the same period his own relationship with Henry also collapsed as a result of Frances' flirtation with the Prince. Having inherited his father's ideology, however, he fits exactly into the Prince's orbit: anti-Spanish and militant Protestant, with strong links with the reform in France, Germany and the Dutch Republic. In the Prince's funeral procession he was to walk as assistant to the chief mourner and bear his gauntlet.

John Harington, 2nd Baron Harington of Exton (1592–1614) is, owing to his early death at the age of twenty-two, like the Prince amongst the lost figures of history.[72] He is remembered today only as the subject of John Donne's *Obsequies to the Lord Harrington* dedicated to his sister.[73] Harington was the son and heir of John Harington, 1st Lord Harington (d. 1613) who was placed in charge of the Prince's sister, Elizabeth.

42

The family was noted for its strict adherence to the reformed faith and for its abhorrence of Catholicism. The young Harington's sister was Lucy, Countess of Bedford, who had established herself as the close friend and constant companion of the Prince's mother from the moment of her arrival south in 1603. The old Lord Harington was a firm believer in the virtues of learning and his son was precocious. He is recorded by Sir James Whitelock in his *Liber Familicus* as 'the most complete young gentleman of his age this kingdom could afford for religion, learning, and courteous behaviour'.[74] He was educated at Cambridge at Sidney Sussex College (his grandmother was a Sidney) and early on acquired fluency in Latin, Greek and Italian and was 'well-read' in logic and philosophy. In 1608–9, at the age of sixteen, he, like the young Essex, was sent on a continental tour which this time included Italy. Unlike the letters from the Earl to the Prince, however, this correspondence reflects a warm intimacy between the two. Henry cast the young Harington as 'Mon petit chevalier'[75] and Sir Henry Wotton presented him to the Doge as 'the right eye of the Prince'.[76] How close they were is reflected in the interchange recorded between the King and Harington before his departure:

When the Prince, with tears in his eyes, took him to the King to ask leave of absence, his Majesty said to him 'What hast thou done, John' – that is his name – 'that thou art so master of the Prince's favour – tell me what art hast thou used? Not flattery, that belongeth not to thy age,' to which he replied 'Holy Majesty, not with flattery, which I know not how to use, have I won his Highness love, but by truth, of which your Majesty's true son, his Highness, is the lover.'[77]

The tour was destined to last some five months and Harington travelled down through the Low Countries, Germany and Switzerland to Italy and returned via France. The Prince received from him a series of news letters some of which have survived.[78] The rhythm of the relationship is caught in a letter written after his return when he tells the Prince 'you will find me your better at tennis and pike'.[79] Like Henry, Harington emerges as an exemplar of Jacobean muscular Protestantism but overlaid with a love of learning.

We can expand our conception of young Harington by looking at three engravings of him.[80] One posthumously ensconces him in that Protestant pantheon, the *Herwologia* (1620), alongside his father. The other two were issued while he was yet living. Harington is the only young aristocrat of his generation to enter this popular medium, which is a fair index of how important he was regarded. The first shows him half length with two sets of verses beneath. Immediately below they read: *Religion, Learning, Language, Knowledge, Courage, Arts, Noble Parts, so Manie (at no More Age)/ Mars, Hermes, Phoebus & Chast Theseus Sonne; All mett: All made This Phoenix Harington.* Further verses develop the theme:

> *Rich Ornament, Rare Honor of our Clime,*
> *Miracle of Nature, Miracle of Grace,*
> *For all fare Pledges of a Hopefull Prince;*
> *Beyond his Yeers, before his Rank & Race,*
> *Heroik Pattern for all After-Tyme*
> *To imitate....*

Need one quote more? The second portrait repeats the head and the initial eulogy but shows him as a knight dressed for the tiltyard with his horse elaborately beplumed and caparisoned. Apart from the Prince no other youth was regarded with such expectant fervour.

Harington's cousin, John Harington, wrote an account of him that finally casts this ill-starred young man as the ideal soulmate for the Prince.[81] He dilates at length on his learning, on his fluency in both antique and modern languages and, above all, on his exemplary piety and zeal for the reformed faith (Harington makes out that he died due to prolonged poisoning by Jesuits on his grand tour). But out of this eulogy two aspects emerge which tie him in character more closely to the Prince than any other of his circle. One was his chastity. Like Henry he 'kept himself undefiled as Lot in the midst of Sodom....He spent not his time in courting of Ladies, and amorously contemplating the beauty of women, which are bellows of lust and baits of uncleanness.' The second was his central interests which again were like the Prince's, in that they were the 'study of histories, the art of war, mathematics, and navigation; wherein he attained to a great measure of perfection.'

9   The third member of this group is William Cecil, Lord Cranborne, later 2nd Earl of Salisbury (1591–1668).[82] A year older than Harington but the exact contemporary of his great friend Essex, Cranborne was heir to the foremost figure on the political stage, Robert Cecil. There must have been great hopes that one day onto his shoulders would descend the mantle of both his father and his grandfather, Lord Burghley, who had guided the realm of England for over half a century. In spite of the care lavished on his education, William Cecil was to be no scholar. In 1608 it was despairingly written of him that learning came 'by little and little, like deawe, not like a tempest'. He was to be the first of the long line of owners of Hatfield who were to represent the family in decline until its renaissance two centuries later. None of that, however, could have been foreseen in 1610. As in the case of Essex he too was to be the victim of dynastic conciliation, being married privately, in December 1608, to another daughter of the Earl of Suffolk, Catherine. And again as with Essex, the bride and groom were immediately

parted, this time to enable the young Cranborne to make the customary continental tour. A few days after the marriage his father had written to Prince Henry: 'For your servant Cranborn I humbly thank yowr Highness both for your present grace and future promises ... I have made bold to take him from Juno and to comend him yesterday to Neptune, being now gone to pass the sees.'[83] Initially his companions were two of his brothers-in-law but he went on to Italy on his own. In February he was in Paris where he witnessed a *ballet de cour* and he was still there enjoying the favour of Henri IV in March.[84] A journal survives covering the rest of the tour; it is pretty staccato in style but highlights from time to time what struck him most.[85] He notes fortifications and also where those of the reformed faith hold power. More interesting, because it is so early, is his reaction to his visual environment. Both at Nîmes and at Orange he records his admiration for the Roman ruins and both in Vicenza and in Padua he waxes lyrical on the subject of the architecture of Andrea Palladio. Of the Teatro Olimpico he writes:

Remarquez y bien le theatre fait depuis 25 ans par ce grand Architecte Palladius d'une rare invention qu'autre qui puisse estre.[86]

This is the impression of someone who must have been familiar with the theatre of Shakespeare. On his return he carried the King's train at the Prince's investiture and sat in Parliament as MP for Weymouth. If one great friend was Essex another was his cousin Edward Cecil. In November 1611 Chamberlain wrote: 'My Lord of Cranbourne used me well....Sir Edward Cecil is continually about him, very much to my Lord Treasurer's liking.'[87] Parallel with Essex his marriage began to pall and, in July 1610, it was reported that he looked 'sour upon his wife'. The letters to Henry from abroad reflect a warmth of friendship that I would categorize as midway between that of Harington and Essex. His lack of brainpower finds vivid expression in his inability to write in French to the Prince, 'knowing how able your Highness is to discover errors'.

Henry was to be denied, however, the one vital experience that these three young aristocrats shared: foreign travel. These men had experienced the court of Henri IV at its height in the aftermath of the civil wars. They would have seen the new Stable Court at Fontainebleau which is dated 1609 and the interior of the palace with its new decoration by what we know as the Second School of Fontainebleau. Both here and at St-Germain-en-Laye there were the new spectacular gardens with *parterres de broderie* by Claude Mollet and elaborate grottoes, fountains and automata by the Francini brothers. In the capital they would have seen the new developments in town planning, the Pont Neuf (1599), the Place Royale (begun 1605) and the Place Dauphine (begun 1607). All this in France alone. It was but a fraction of what they were exposed to in terms of the arts, let alone political education, as they crossed the mainland. The impact of this on the Prince must be left to the imagination; his friends acted as his eyes and ears regarding all that was new on their journeys abroad.

Although denied to him there is no doubt that travel was a major interest. In 1606 Sir Thomas Palmer had dedicated to him his *Essay ... on Trauailes into foraine Countries* and, in 1611, he and other members of the royal family were to receive copies of Thomas Coryate's *Crudities*. Coryate (1577–1617) was given a pension by the Prince and his book, illustrated with engravings by William Hole, describes just such a journey as these young aristocrats took through France over the Alps into Italy to Venice and back over the Alps by way of Germany and the Low Countries.[88]

The Prince was noted by every observer as grave beyond his years and as surrounding himself mostly with friends who were considerably older than himself. We must now turn to an examination of this group headed by Edward Cecil (1572–1638), third son of Thomas, Lord Burghley, later 1st Earl of Exeter.[89] In the 1590s he had travelled in Italy and in particular to Florence where he and William Cecil, Lord Roos, were treated with especial favour by the Grand Duke. In 1598 he began his career as a soldier in the Low Countries and in 1600 distinguished himself at the battle of Nieuport. A year later he was knighted by the Queen, returning to the Low Countries where he continued to serve under Prince Maurice until the truce with Spain in 1609 when he appealed to his uncle, Salisbury, for employment. It must have been during his period in England following this that he entered the Prince's circle. James sent him in command of 4000 troops to aid the States over the Julich-Cleves crisis in April 1610 and he took part in the siege of Julich in July. There then followed a series of letters to the Prince which place him, as one would expect, as a member of the Protestant anti-Habsburg war party. He opens that dated 21 August, with a eulogy, writing of:

> ... that grate and high favour which your Highness hath voutchsafed to cast upon me by your owne princely hand, that it hath given an n[e]we life and incoragement to all my indevors ... I hope God will add such blessinge to your Highness favore to mee that I shall gather strength and abilities in my profession, to be able in your happiest dayes to become a pore instrument in some remarkable and princely undertakings of your owne.[90]

Edward Cecil sent the Prince detailed plans of the siege defences. By 1611 he was back in England and the Florentine agent, Lotti, writes that he is 'very close to His Highness and easily influences his Highness about many things and hears from him the reasons for every thing'.[91] The year after we hear of him being one of the Prince's band in a challenge at court.[92] A month later, in April 1612, Henry sent him as his deputy to the christening of the child of Count Ernest of Nassau[93] and he again used him as his envoy in May to the dying Salisbury. Cecil was not only a man-at-arms. He was to play a key part in the negotiations for a match with a Medici princess and, more importantly, he appears to have shared the Prince's enthusiasm for the visual arts. After Inigo Jones's return from Italy in 1615, Cecil with Arundel was to give him his earliest architectural commissions.[94]

The second member of this group is Henry Wriothesley, 3rd Earl of Southampton (1573–1624).[95] Younger than Cecil by a year, he had belonged to what might be categorized as the late Elizabethan 'opposition' focusing on Essex. Like the young Essex the Earl was received back into favour in 1603 by James. The evidence that attaches Southampton to Henry is circumstantial, based on his repeated appearances in the Prince's spectacles. He was one of the challengers in the Prince's *Barriers* in January 1610, acted as his carver at his creation in June and danced as one of the masquers in *Oberon. The Fairy Prince* in January 1611. Patron of poets and dramatists, what could he and Henry have had in common? In the first place Southampton was an accomplished man-at-arms, who had graced the Accession Day Tilts throughout the 1590s and on into the new reign. During the Jacobean period he was decisively Protestant in his sympathies and his energies centred on colonial enterprise simultaneously with those of the Prince during the years 1609–12. Henry Peacham also records him as collecting pictures.[96]

Another challenger at the *Barriers* was Thomas Howard, 14th Earl of Arundel (1585–1646), who recorded his appearance at that event in a splendid full-length portrait still at Arundel Castle.[97] He, like Southampton and the young Essex, was a nobleman restored to honours by the accession of James. His marriage in 1606 to Aletheia Talbot, the Shrewsbury heiress, also restored his financial fortunes, and from 1607 onwards he seems frequently to have been in attendance on the Prince. The year after he even named his second child after him, Frederick Henry. During the years 1606–1612 his life was passed at court and, although it used to be said that he had travelled abroad in 1609, there is no certain evidence for it. He seems likely to have been among those nobles who visited the mainland in the 1590s. After Cambridge he is said to have 'travelled to see what they did either in Court, as at *France* and *Rome*; or in Camps as in the *Low Countries*; or in Universities, as in

10

St Omers, etc., from whence he returned a very accomplished gentle-man'.[98] Arundel is a shadowy figure during this period. He knew some-thing about pictures already but he did not inherit any of his great uncle, Lord Lumley's collection. Coming from an old Catholic family he was received into the Church of England in 1615, but there is little indication of his religious affiliations during the years before that date. If he was a practising Catholic he certainly was odd man out in the court at St James's. Nonetheless as we shall see he was already referred to as someone who could judge the quality of a picture. The most im-portant link with the Prince, however, was his predilection for chival-rous sports. Not only did Arundel appear in the *Barriers* but he is re-corded at the Accession Day Tilts of 1606 and 1609 and danced in the masque for the marriage of Lord Haddington in 1608. In 1611 the two princes went a-maying to one of the Arundel houses at Highgate, only a short time before Arundel's ill health led him to seek a cure at Spa from whence he travelled on to Padua. He was away therefore when the Prince died. His son records that 'Soone after the Prince lyinge on his death bed, would divers times say that hee prayed to God to send back Arundell with perfect health, which was a great expression how much hee valewed that person'.[99]

One figure is recorded in his wife's memoirs as being 'the favourite of Prince Henry'. He was Sir Henry Fanshawe (1569–1616) who was 'as handsome and as fine a gentleman as England then had'.[100] A friend of Sir Henry Wotton, Fanshawe was in every sense the virtuoso gentle-man. He was fluent in Italian (we do not know whether he had been to Italy or not), kept a noble stable and was a collector of pictures, prints, drawings, medals, engraved stones, armour, books and musical instru-ments. Above all his house at Ware Park, Hertfordshire, was famous for its garden, 'none excelling it', wrote Camden, 'in flowers, physic herbs, and fruit, in which things he did delight'. In 1606 he laid out the garden in the pattern of a Renaissance star-shaped fortress, redesigning it by 1613 in terms of water effects, reflecting exactly what was happen-ing under the aegis of Salomon de Caus in the palace gardens of Anne of Denmark and Prince Henry.

Sir John Harington of Kelston (1561–1612) was of the same genera-tion as Fanshawe and enjoyed close links with the Prince as he was cousin to the Haringtons of Exton.[101] Harington is too well known to posterity as the 'saucy godson' of Queen Elizabeth I and the author of *The Metamorphosis of Ajax* (1596), facts which tend to obscure a side which places him along with Edward Cecil, Dallington, Chaloner and Inigo Jones as one of those link figures with the early stirrings of inter-est in Italy in the 1590s. In 1591 there appeared his translation of *Or-

lando Furioso where, at the end of Book XXXIII, he follows Ariosto in listing famous artists, Leonardo, Mantegna, Giovanni Bellini, Michelangelo, Raphael and Sebastiano del Piombo. Such a listing stirs him to look for an English counterpart and he cites Nicholas Hilliard. Interestingly he draws the reader's attention to a feature 'which every one (haply), will not observe, namely the perspective in euery picture'. He then goes on to define what he believes perspective to be: 'For the personages of men, the shapes of horses, and such like, are made large at the bottome, and lesser upward, as if you were to behold all the same in one plaine, that which is nearest seemes greatest, and the fardest, shewes smallest, which is the chiefe art in picture.' Although this reflects, as Lucy Gent observes, that 'even this aficionado of painting ... did not have a working definition of perspective', it at least records his awareness of it as an attribute of 'curious painting'.[102] Harington patronized Custodis for portraits but in a letter to Prince Henry in 1608 he refers to the fact that he had a miniature painted of his dog Bungey: 'And I have an execellente picture curiously limmed, to remaine in posterity.' Harington was a minor figure, almost of fun, which accounts for the fact that he was never given proper office and nothing reveals this more than his account of the bishops written 'for the private use of Prince Henry, upon Occasion of that Proverb,

> *Henry the Eighth pull'd down Monks and their cells,*
> *Henry the Ninth should pull down Bishops and their Bells.'*

Another minor figure is Henry Peacham (*c.* 1578–*c.* 1642).[103] A Londoner by birth he matriculated at Trinity College, Cambridge, in 1592 becoming, it seems, like Dallington, a schoolmaster. Also like Dallington, it is possible that he was in Italy at the close of the 1590s, studying music in Modena under Orazio Vecchi, to whom he refers in his famous book *The Compleat Gentleman* (1622) as 'mine owne Master'. By 1606 he was back again in London seeking court patronage and three years later presented the Prince with a manuscript book of emblems based on James I's *Basilikon Doron*, of which three draft versions survive. Essentially a popularizer, his *The Compleat Gentleman*, was to make available to the aspiring classes the ideals of the gentleman virtuoso first cultivated with deliberation at the St James's court. That, however, lay in the future in 1610–12. Peacham fits into the circle on its fringes. His first book would have qualified him for entry: *The Art of Drawing with the Pen* (1606), a milestone in making drawing a respectable attribute of the gentry classes, based on Aristotle's inclusion of *Graphice* as one of the liberal arts and more particularly on its practical application for those that 'mean to follow the wars, or trauell into forreine countries'.

During the years 1610–12 he was to produce two books which deal with some of the central preoccupations of the inner ring, and which suggest that he might have had some minor position in the household. One was a reissue of his earlier book now entitled *Graphice or The Gentleman's Exercise* (1612), in which he not only strengthened the links between drawing and gentility but went on to give a longer discussion of modern painters (referring to the Prince's painter, Robert Peake, as 'my good friend'); he defines the newfangled genre of landscape and adds two chapters to appeal to the gentry, one on heraldry and the other on allegory, images necessary to comprehend *imprese*. The Prince's badge adorns this publication, as indeed it does the second which is fully dedicated to him, *Minerva Britanna, or a Garden of Heroical Deuises* (1612), which put into print many of the devices included in the earlier manuscript. It is a publication to which I shall return, for a number of its emblems are dedicated to members of the household: Sir Thomas Chaloner, Sir David Murray, Adam Newton and Sir David Foulis. The book has as its finale a vision of Britain in her role as Empress of the Isles seated beneath a mighty tree from whose branches hang the shields of her warriors, each one painted with his device. Awkward and quaint though the poem is, the vision is fully in tune with the aims of the Prince's court: imperial and aggressive in mood with a view of history that draws into one continuum (as Jonson's *Barriers* did) the martial heroes of medieval England and those of Gloriana's reign, 'some dead, some liuing still':

> Here saw I many a shiuer'd launce,
> Swordes, Battle-axes, Cannons Slinges,
> With th'Armes of PORTVGAL, and FRAVNCE,
> And Crownets of her pettie Kinges:
> High-feathered Helmets for the Tilt,
> Bowes, Steelie Targets cleft in twaine:
> Coates, cornets, Armours richly guilt,
> With tatter'd Ensignes out of SPAINE.[104]

Confined within the Tower of London there was a far greater figure, Sir Walter Raleigh.[105] His encyclopaedic mind and meteoric career cross the whole spectrum of late Elizabethan and Jacobean civilization. Due to his imprisonment any contact had to be made in the form of written advice, which gives Raleigh's pieces greater prominence than they deserve. The Prince would normally receive such advice through spoken dialogue with his entourage. Aubrey writes of this relationship:

At the end of his *History of the World*, he laments the Death of the most noble and most hopefull Prince Henry, whose great Favorite he was: and who, had he survived his father, would quickly have enlarged him; with rewards of Honour. So upon the Prince's death his first part of his *History of the World*, with a gallant Eulogie of Him, and concludes: *Versa est in Luctum Cithara mea; et cantus meus invocem fluentium* [my lyre is changed into the sound of mourning; and my song into the voices of people weeping].[106]

Well might Raleigh give way to grief, for in the Prince lay his only hope and with his death vanished not only any possibility of eventual release and restoration to favour, but also the patron for whom he had laboured on his *History of the World*.

There is no evidence that Raleigh and the Prince ever met. In 1603 the former was consigned to the Tower on a trumped-up charge of complicity in what was called the Bye Plot. There he was to remain throughout the Prince's life, although we know that there was communication by letter and probably more directly by way of Raleigh's cousin, Sir Arthur Gorges. Raleigh fits exactly into the world of the St James's court: anti-Habsburg, anti-Catholic, a pioneer and believer in colonial enterprise in the New World, a man with a deep knowledge of ships and navigation, a firm advocate of sea supremacy and a representative of the vanished glories of the old reign that Henry looked to a younger generation to revive. 'None but my father would keep such a bird in a cage' was said to have been his comment.[107]

It is likely that Henry's interest in Raleigh was aroused by his mother, who was known to be sympathetic to him. Certainly the prisoner in the Tower must have been much in the Prince's mind when he committed himself so actively to a new attempt to colonize Virginia in 1607. Raleigh, of course, had been the leading light in the initial scheme in the 1580s. The following year he wrote *The Present State of Thinges as they now Stand betweene the three great Kingedomes, Fraunce, England, and Spaine*. A reference to 'the forwardness and hope of our Prince' would indicate that the piece was inspired by someone in the Prince's entourage. Raleigh here represents the voice of the old Elizabethan war party bent on reopening the struggle with Spain.

A stream of Raleigh's pieces follow, written either for or on behalf of the Prince, starting about 1608–10 with *Observations and Notes concerning the Royal Navy, and Sea Service*, written in collaboration with Gorges. Related in subject matter but of uncertain date are the fragments of an unfinished treatise entitled *Of the Art of Warre by Sea*. Between March and December 1611 he wrote a memoir *Concerning a Match propounded by the Savoyan, between the Lady Elizabeth and the Prince of Piedmont*. In 1612 he was to do the same for the Prince himself in *Touching a Marriage between Prince Henry of England and a Daughter of Savoy*. During the same year between March and November he wrote for him another anti-Catholic paper: *A Dialogue between a Jesuit and a Recusant: shewing how Dangerous are their Principles to Christian Princes.* These were *pièces d'occasions* whose very titles tell us of their contents and how faithfully Raleigh emerges as the representative of Henry's political stance. *The History of the World* falls into a different bracket, being undertaken as a major offering to a royal patron passionately interested in history.[108] Begun in 1608 the work's *raison d'être* disappeared with the Prince's death; it became a book, as the address to the reader states, 'left to the world without a master', and so it finishes abruptly at the events of 168–67 BC. We know of the strength of Henry's commitment to Raleigh because he actually dared confront the King on his behalf over the confiscation of the Sherborne estate.[109]

Hawkins writes of the household that 'there was not one known or suspected Papist',[110] a religious bias which can hardly be overstressed. Prayers were said twice a day; the Prince was always present and those who failed to attend were docked of their food. Its atmosphere was far removed from the Catholic or crypto-Catholic undercurrents usual in the circles of his mother and father. Most important from our point of view is that the Italianate cultural milieu of Henry's court was not a vehicle for covert Catholicism or indeed incipient Laudian Anglicanism. Had he lived, the renaissance in the arts that eventually came to flower in his brother's reign would not have been tinged with the highly suspect theological overtones which made it unacceptable to the reformist populace. Hawkins wrote that the Prince was

Most ardent in his Love to Religion, to which Love, and all good causes thereof, his Heart was bent, by some Means or other (if he had lived) to have shewed, and some Way to have compounded the unkind Jars thereof....[111]

Little emerges, however, which points to a conciliatory nature and all the evidence indicates that he was a Protestant with puritan leanings. Even his Receiver-General, Augustine Nicolls (d. 1616) was celebrated for his 'noble and unshaken resolution, and mighty opposition of Popery' and in the north 'in his three yeares, he convicted, confin'd, and conform'd mor Papists than were in twenty yeares before...'.[112]

The dedications the Prince attracted were fervently anti-papal.[113] In a translation of Duplessis Mornay's *The Mysterie of Iniquitie: that is to say, The Historie of the Papacie* (1612) his sword is cast as succeeding his father's pen: 'giue me leaue ... that I may liue to march over the Alpes, and to trayle a pike before the walls of Rome, under your Highnesse standard'. Robert Abbot dedicates to him *The Trve Ancient Roman Catholike* (1611), in the hope that the Prince will 'be a terrour to that selfe-exalting Kingdome and Monarchy of the great Capitolian Priest, at length to worke the vtter ruine and coufusion thereof', and *The Fierie Tryall of Gods Saints* (1611) hails him as:

> Englands faire Hope, (borne, Downe to quell
>   the rage of Rome; That proud Babell;
> which in its swelling-madde Desires,
>   to Worlds sole Empire still Aspires;)

Of his zeal against Catholicism there can be no doubt. In the summer of 1611 he sent Sir John Holles north in order to raid the house of the recusant Countess of Shrewsbury, not, however, to much avail as the search threw up only 'an old crucifix and three or four old mass books'. None the less the letter on the subject by Holles regales the Prince with all the joys of what may be called the chase.[114] The fact that he could write in such terms vividly reflects the known preferences of the recipient.

The Prince's chaplains belong to the same ambience. One was Lionel Sharpe (1559–1631), who entered his service sometime about 1605. He had been chaplain to Robert Devereux, 2nd Earl of Essex, and had accompanied him to Tilbury in 1588 and on the Cadiz and Portugal expeditions. He was violently anti-Spanish and anti-Catholic. In 1612 he sent Henry his *Speculum Papae* which, jointly with his *Novum Fidei Symbolum* (also 1612), was to be published in translation in 1623 as *A Looking-glass for the Pope*.[115] In the same year the Prince tried unsuccessfully to recommend him to his father via Northampton for the post of Provost of King's College.[116] Northampton so phrased his letter to the King that he put to him all the reasons for not having Sharpe. Daniel Price (1581–1631) was similarly 'a frequent and remarkable preacher, especially against the papacy'. He became a chaplain in 1608 and after the Prince's death preached no fewer than four memorial sermons on him.[117] To him we can add Lewis Bayly (d. 1631), who also preached a sermon on the Prince's death, but one which caused official outrage at the time, for his devotion to his dead master went hand in hand with accusations of popery against certain members of the Privy Council! His *Practice of Piety*, dedicated to the Prince, was to be the most influential book of devotions in the puritan style in the century. It had run to three editions by 1613 and reached twenty-five by 1630.

Even better known is Joseph Hall (1574–1656), who was to end his life as Bishop of Norwich and undergo sad privations during the civil war.[118] He came from a stoutly puritan background, his family being in the service of the 3rd Earl of Huntingdon, and he was educated at that citadel of reform, Emmanuel College, Cambridge. He attracted the attention of the Prince, who made him a chaplain in 1608. Hall was to enjoy fame later for his *Meditations* (1630), but he was also known as a satirist, having published two volumes of satires in 1597–8 and a satiri-cal novel in 1605. All his writings incorporate scathing attacks on Cath-olicism, Catholic piety and the Pope. He was to dedicate to Henry in October 1607 his second volume of *Epistles* and three years later follow this with the third and final volume (many are addressed to members of both the household and the circle).

Hall, besides being a royal chaplain, was a major Protestant author, as was another, Joshua Sylvester (1563–1618).[119] He entered the house-hold sometime about 1606 and it is recorded that the Prince 'valued him so much that he made him first poet pensioner' with an annuity and intended, if he had not died, to make him a Groom of the Privy Chamber. Henry's attention must have been drawn to him in 1605, when he was eleven, when Sylvester dedicated to him his translation of *Tetrastica. Or, the quadrains of Guy de Faur, Lord or Pibrac*.[120] His most fam-ous work was the translation of the great French Protestant scriptural epic, *La Semaine*, by the Huguenot Guillaume de Saluste, Seigneur du Bartas, the first collected edition of which appeared in 1605–6 under the title *Du Bartas his Deuine Weekes and Workes*. In 1607 Sylvester first offered part of his translation to the Prince and in his role as official poet his memorial verses, *Lachrimae Lachrimarum*, were issued in no fewer than three editions.

The strongly Protestant bias of Henry's household, where attendance at sermons was obligatory, needs little more emphasis. 'HEE hated *Pop-erie* with a perfect hate', wrote Daniel Price in a sermon preached in 1613 on the anniversary of the Prince's death. He goes on to sum up in retrospect what we might describe as his religious orbit:

All the *world* were sate, to see, & harken, how his Highnesse hopefull, youthfull age should be *employed*, for HIM, a *glimmering light* of the *Golden* times appeared, all lines of expectation met in this *Center*, all *spirits* of vertue, scattered into others were extracted into him ... His *Magnetique* vertue drewe all the *eies*, and *hearts*, of the *Protestant* world....[121]

The last sentence is crucial, for Henry, had he lived, would have ef-fected in England a successful marriage of all the achievements in the arts of Renaissance Italy with an unshakeable and fiercely Protestant ethic.

During the years 1610–12 the division between the Prince's and King's courts was aggravated, owing to the increasing influence of James's new favourite Robert Carr.[122] That was to reach its peak only after the death of the Lord Treasurer, Robert Cecil, Earl of Salisbury, in May 1612. The advent of the new favourite had been in 1607. In that year Carr first attracted James's notice at the Accession Day Tilt when he carried the *impresa* shield probably of Richard Preston, later Lord Ding-wall. Carr leapt from his horse to bear the shield to the King but in do-ing so he fell and broke his leg. As a result he caught the monarch's at-tention and being, as D'Ewes wrote, of a 'bold disposition, comely visage, and proportionate personage, mixed with a courtly presence', his rise was rapid. In December James knighted him and made him a Gentleman of the Bed Chamber and, a year later, in order to bestow an estate upon him, granted him Raleigh's forfeited one of Sherborne.[123] The latter wrote to Carr on behalf of his family, beseeching him 'not to begin your first buildings upon the ruins of the innocent, and that their griefs and sorrows do not attend your first plantation', but to no avail. He appealed next to Prince Henry, who persuaded his father to cancel the grant. James gave Carr £20,000 to pacify him, but Sherborne came his way finally on the Prince's death.

Wilson casts the Prince and Carr as rivals during the years 1611 and 1612. These were the ones in which the favourite rapidly advanced. In 1611 he was created Viscount Rochester in March, a Knight of the Gar-ter in April, and Keeper of Westminster Palace in June. In April 1612 he joined the Privy Council, thanks only to Salisbury's absence due to illness, and after his death was made Acting Secretary. By then he had formed an alliance with Sir Thomas Overbury and already embarked on the *amour* that was to be his undoing, that with the wife of the Prince's friend, Essex, the notorious and beautiful Frances Howard.

In this Wilson indeed implies that the Prince preceded Rochester but she 'grounding more hope upon him, than the uncertain and hope-less *love* of the *Prince*', abandoned the affair. He retaliated by publicly slighting her during a court ball:

For dancing one time among the *Ladies*, and her Gloue falling down, it was taken up, and presented to him, by one that thought he did him acceptable service; but the *Prince* re-fused to receive it, saying publickly, He would not have it, it is *stretcht* by another, mean-ing the *Viscount*: This was an aggravation of hatred betwixt the Kings Son and the Kings Friend.[124]

D'Ewes also records that Henry 'doth utterly dislike him, forbears his company' and 'falls flat at odds with him, not once giving him any countenance or vouchsafing him his company'.[125]

It is impossible to know whether the Prince had an affair with Lady Essex. No other source directly records the fact and all the evidence in-dicates a sexual abstinence positively abnormal for the period and cer-tainly out of key with the promiscuity of the court. There may, how-ever, have been some truth in it, for it may have upset the relationship of Henry to his boyhood friend, Essex. They quarrelled on the tennis court when the Prince called Essex 'the son of a traitor' and the Earl, 'full of fire and courage', struck the Prince on the head with his tennis racquet drawing blood. The King acted his usual role of peacemaker, pardoning Essex but (as usual) admonishing the Prince.[126] More interesting, however, are the allusions to political trials of strength, what Wilson refers to as Rochester's 'grapling often with the *Prince* himself in his own *Sphear*, in divers contestations'.[127] Unlike the instance of Frances Howard there is evidence of this from another source. It must always have been distasteful for the Prince to have to witness his father's infatuation with the young Rochester, who was not much older than himself, but one senses real gall only when the favourite, who was not intellectually bright, gained admittance to the Privy Council. In June 1612 Thomas, Viscount Fenton, wrote that Rochester was 'exceiding great with his Majestie' but he had 'not find the rycht waye to pleis ather the Quein or the Prince.'[128]

We get another instance of this resentment in an anecdote in Robert Johnston's *Historia Rerum Britannicarum*.[129]Johnston (1567–1639) was a Scot who had migrated south and was appointed Clerk of the Deliveries of the Ordinance. The incident he records must have occurred – if it did at all – sometime between the admittance of Rochester to the Privy Council on 22 April 1612 and Salisbury's death on 24 May. Prince Henry had requested the King that he might be appointed to preside at the Council. In this he was apparently seconded by Rochester, but the proposal was defeated by Cecil who 'thought it dangerous to divide the government, and to invest the son with the authority of the father'. Salisbury, however, blamed this decision on Rochester, which made the Prince resent him even more. Rochester tried in vain to explain the truth of the matter to him but Henry turned away in great indignation and refused to listen. So bitter was Henry's dislike of Rochester, records Wilson, that:

Sir James Elphington, who (observing the *Prince* one day to be discontented with the Viscount) offered to kill him: but the *Prince* reprieved him with a gallant Spirit, saying If there were cause he would do it himself.[130]

What are we to make of all this? There is no doubt that what we are reading is posthumous embroidery of a reality written with the hindsight of the fall of Somerset and all the revelations of the terrible trial resulting from Overbury's murder. Whatever Henry felt about Rochester he was no real threat until the summer of 1612 when suddenly he began to wield political power and influence, with Overbury behind him as the brains. This became significant because after the death of Salisbury in May the Prince's court was cut off from the lively line of communication with the King's chief minister. St James's Palace became a real 'opposition' court to the one at Whitehall, and Rochester would inevitably have been viewed as the one who had contrived this new order of things in which the Prince found himself, for the first time, left in total isolation from the affairs of government. Perhaps Sir Anthony Weldon's comment is correct when he recorded that Henry had said 'if ever he were King, he would not leave one of that family to piss against the wall'.[131]

On 6 March 1604, a few days prior to his father's coronation entry into London, Charles Howard, Lord Howard of Effingham and recently created Earl of Nottingham, presented the ten-year-old Prince with a small ship.[132] It had been designed by Phineas Pett (1570–1647), the   13, 11 shipwright, and built in the Chatham dockyard. The ship was brought to the Tower where, we are told, Henry viewed it with 'great delight'. A fortnight later, on the 22nd, it was carried down by Pett to Whitehall and on to it stepped not only the young Prince but Nottingham, Worcester and other great lords who then sailed as far as Paul's Wharf where the Prince baptized it the *Disdain* with a great bowl of wine. Next day Pett was sworn in as his servant. The little ship was only twenty-eight feet in length and adorned both within and without with much carving and painted decoration. One can imagine few more entrancing gifts for a ten-year-old boy. This initial attraction of the Prince to ships and the sea was reinforced three years later with a model ship which was presented by Pett and placed in a room off the gallery in the Prince's palace at Richmond.[133] The navy was to become for Henry a major obsession. In 1603 England was supreme at sea and James had inherited the finest navy afloat, manned still by the remnants of an heroic generation of Elizabethan sailors renowned for their daring and bravery.[134] But they were ageing. Nottingham, the Lord High Admiral, was already sixty-seven in 1603, but this was not to deter him from clinging on to power until 1618 with, needless to say, catastrophic results. Mercifully, as the King's foreign policy was one of peace and mediation, the navy was never put to the test and the fact that it was in reality crumbling away never had to be faced.

Ironically the Prince remained passionately loyal to Pett, who was one of the men who typified the navy's corrupt administration. On 20 October 1608 the keel was laid by Pett of the ship that Henry regarded as his own, the *Prince Royal*, the first three-decker ever built for   12, 14 the English navy and the largest ship constructed during the reign.[135] Pett estimated that 775 loads of timber would be required to build it, but 1627 loads were used. Meanwhile Pett built himself a handsome country house out of the proceeds. That maladministration was taking place was recognized in high places and although Nottingham and the Prince consistently protected Pett, in 1609 an inquiry was set up under the aegis of the Earl of Northampton with the Earls of Nottingham, Suffolk, Worcester and many others. The findings were favourable to the last three but were unacceptable to Northampton, with the result that both King and Prince came to Woolwich to hear and see the evidence themselves on 8 May 1609.[136] Pett was acquitted of all blame, owing much to the blind loyalty of the Prince to his servant. During the hearing before the King he entreated that Pett be allowed to rise from his knees and, when he was finally cleared, he cried. 'Where be now these perjured fellows that dare thus abuse his Majesty with these false informations, do they not deserve hanging?'[137] As the Prince left, Pett wrote,

Then I presented myself upon my knee to the most noble Prince my Master who, taking me from the ground, did so affectionately express his joy for my clearing and the satisfaction that his father had received that day, that he protested he would not only countenance and comfort me hereafter, but care to provide for me and my posterity whilst he lived.[138]

The Prince epitomized honesty of conduct and he would have been appalled had he known that his personal loyalty to an old servant was maintaining a far from satisfactory *status quo*.

The ship was in fact to end up a curiosity, for its hulk rose far too high above the water-line and ignored all the advances being made at the time by both the Dutch and the Spanish. The *Prince Royal* represented all those criticisms which Raleigh made in his *Observations*, dedicated to the Prince. He wrote that a man-of-war should be strongly built, swift, stout-sided, able to carry her guns in all weathers: 'it were also behoofeful that his Majesty's ships were not so overpestered and clogged with great ordnance ... so that much of it serves to no better use but only to labour and overcharge the ship's sides'. In spite of this the progress of the *Prince Royal* was followed intently by the court and there was a grand launching attended by the King, Queen, Prince Henry and Princess Elizabeth on 24 September 1610. The occasion was a disaster as the dockhead was too narrow to permit the ship to pass. The Prince returned, however, later and at 2 am the following morning it was successfully launched and named by him the *Prince Royal* amidst fanfares of trumpets.[139]

Whatever its faults (and they were to be fully recognized only in the future) this was to all intents a spectacular addition to the navy. It was a magnificent, elaborately decorated vessel, £868 being spent on its gilding and painting, including the Prince's badges and his own cabin which was 'very curiously wrought with divers histories'.[140] Correr, the

Venetian ambassador, records that it had been built and supervised throughout by the Prince and that the number of guns had been reduced – in response to Raleigh's views, it seems reasonable to conclude – from eighty to fifty pieces to ensure ease of handling.

The *Prince Royal* was not the only ship to be constructed under Pett's auspices at this period. He was also responsible for two of the largest merchant ships built, *Trades Increase* and the *Peppercorn*, for the East India Company.[141] These were launched on 30 December 1609 when the latter was named by the Prince. Pett himself constructed one more ship specifically for the Prince on which he began work in the middle of June 1612. This was to be a pinnace, a small light vessel to act as a tender or scout to the *Prince Royal*; its keel was laid at the end of that month. The boat was not to be completed until after the Prince's death, being launched by Pett on 27 February 1613 and called the *Phoenix*. It was designed, he records, for the Prince 'to solace himself sometimes into the Narrow Seas'.[142]

Pett's autobiography is a mine of information on Henry's maritime preoccupations during 1611 and 1612. Without doubt the reform of the navy seems to have been at the forefront of his thoughts. Hawkins states that the Prince saw that sea power was essential and sought 'to advance the Affairs of the Navy, to his Power, now and then got Leave of his Majesty to go in Person to view the Ships, and Store-Houses, which divers Time he did'.[143] This began in April 1611 when Pett was summoned to St James's, where the Prince informed him of his decision to make a tour of Chatham 'giving me strait charge I should acquaint none with it'.[144] Henry made the tour accompanied by the Earls of Shrewsbury, Arundel and Mar, amongst others, and began with the *Prince Royal*:[145]

... and so from ship to ship of the lower reach, taking particular private information from Sir Robert Mansell and myself (none else suffered to come near) of the state and condition of each several ship in his own table book....Dinner done, his Highness proceeded again in viewing all the ships and pinnaces in the upper reach, not leaving out any one which he was not on board of....[146]

This must be the occasion Hawkins records. He describes the diligence of the Prince in examining each ship in detail, its structure, its strengths and weaknesses, his application in carefully noting each defect and checking the availability in the naval stores of what was needful 'to make them serviceable and useful'.[147]

About a month later a new Surveyor of the Navy was appointed. Initially Pett refused to co-operate and join in the survey he ordered. Subsequently he agreed:

... whereby I incurred great blame and a sharp check from the Prince's Highness, which I had much ado to pacify by the help of the best friends I had about him, being sent for on purpose to Richmond to give his Highness satisfaction therein.[148]

Even then Pett reiterates that the Prince had taken his behaviour as 'an affront'.

In January 1612 Pett describes the Prince summoning all the royal shipwrights to Greenwich 'about a resolution of building ships in Ireland'.[149] At the same time Pett assisted Thomas Button in the choice of a ship for his North-West Passage expedition under the Prince's patronage[150] and the last time that he ever saw his beloved master was at the beginning of August prior to the Prince's departure on his summer progress.

These skirmishes between Pett and the Prince fit in with the other evidence we have. Goodman records: 'A knight told me the tale that he was privily sent by Prince Henry to see how the royal navy was ordered; what defects there were, and to be a spy for them...'.[151] More interestingly Foscarini reports in October 1611 the Prince's aspiration to be Lord High Admiral, stating that he had got the King's agreement and that 'with his diligence and authority [he] will regulate many abuses which the present Admiral, who is decrepit, can hardly do'.[152] He further reports the Prince pressing the Council in November to sanction the construction of eight galleons and in December outlining massive navy reforms.[153] Nothing however came of this and Nottingham, by now seventy-five, was not dislodged.

All this points to the conclusion that the navy was the principal focus of Henry's interest during the period following his creation, that he wished to revive the old Elizabethan tradition and rescue it from decline and corruption. Like Raleigh, upon whose advice he leaned, the Prince saw maritime might as central to the country's power and prosperity. It could not only vanquish the forces of Catholic Spain but also be a means of Britain's expansion into new worlds. Edward Wright, his librarian, in the dedication to the Prince of his famous *Certaine Errours in Navigation* (1611), writes of these voyages of colonization:

... for the discouerie of strange and forraine lands and nations vnknowne, whereby the poore people living in darknesse and in the shadow of death ... may in short time grow to some acquaintance and familiaritie with this our Christian world, and in the end come to the saving knowledge of the true God....[154]

Viewed in this light a mighty navy was to be the vanguard of the new Protestant chivalry of England bearing across the seas the light of the Gospel to new horizons.

This interest in things maritime extended naturally, therefore, into an active role in the two major enterprises of the early Jacobean period:

the renewed attempts at the colonization of America and the search for the North-West Passage (a route to India avoiding the Cape of Good Hope). Without doubt the most astonishing of all the letters to find in the two volumes of incoming correspondence that survive is one from a Robert Tindall in Jamestown, Virginia, dated 22 June 1607. The Prince was then only thirteen, and to him Tindall sent 'a dearnall of our voyage and draughte of our Riuer hearinclosed by us discovered where never Christian before hathe been'.[155]

The early years of James I's reign witnessed a vigorous revival of the colonization projects of Raleigh in the 1580s.[156] This was an immediate consequence of the peace with Spain in 1604 which inaugurated a new phase of English activity in the New World. The Prince, as we know, was a fervent admirer of Raleigh and the other prime mover, Southampton, was also a key member of his circle. It was under the latter's aegis, together with Lord Arundell of Wardour, that an exploratory voyage was made in 1605. As a direct result of this letters patent were granted by the King on 10 April 1606 to the Virginia Company for the foundation of two colonies, one a revival of the former Virginia, the second in the area we now call New England. The expedition left on 19 December and sighted Chesapeake Bay the following April, naming its southern promontory Cape Henry. In May they founded Jamestown and on 22 June they set sail for England. Captain Newport, who had been in charge of the expedition, was carrying, amongst other things, Robert Tindall's letter to the Prince.

Two years were to pass, however, before the topic of Virginia rose to new heights of public interest, resulting in the big expedition of 1609.[157] There was a second far more important charter which separated the two original enterprises and it was launched amidst what reads like a vast public relations exercise: tracts, sermons and appeals. In April, in a sermon at court, the project was presented as a revival of the Elizabethan ideal: 'this land was of old time offered to our kings. Our late sovereign Queen Elizabeth (whose story hath no peer among princes of her sex) being a pure virgin, found it, set foot in it and called it Virginia'. The Prince's poet, Michael Drayton, celebrated the event with an ode:

> You brave Heroique Minds,
> Worthy your countries Name;
>   That Honour still pursue,
>   Goe, and subdue,
> Whilst loyt'ring Hinds
> Lurke here at home, with shame.[158]

Sir Thomas Dale (d.1619) was sent in his capacity as High Marshal of

Virginia, with men and provisions, to alleviate the distress of the new colony. Shortly after his arrival Dale decided to found a second town seventy miles up river on a less marshy site and this he called Henrico. It consisted of three streets of well-framed buildings and a church.

Sir Thomas Dale had been a soldier in the Low Countries and it was to be under his stern governorship that the infant colony began to prosper. He was to be relieved by Sir Thomas Gates in August 1611, succeeding him again in 1614, returning finally to England in 1616 bringing back the exotic Princess Pocahontas. Dale interestingly referred to the Prince in retrospect as his 'glorious Master', one 'who would have enammelled with his favours the labours of God's cause'. Since his death, he lamented, it seemed that the 'whole frame of this business' had fallen 'into his grave'.[159] From the beginning the Virginia enterprise would have appealed to the Prince as an expansion of the Empire of Great Britain both in a political and religious context. The charter speaks of 'propagating of the Christian religion to such people as yet live in darkness and miserable ignorance of the true knowledge and worship of God'. William Crashaw's sermon before the court casts both King and Prince in an imperial messianic role as *'new Constantines or Charles the Great'*. The Governor General of the colony, Lord de la Warr, is represented in terms of Jacobean chivalry as a Protestant knight about to embark on a venture whose end was 'the destruction of the devel's kingdome, and propagation of the gospel'. A Huguenot, Pierre Erondelle, dedicated his edition of Marc Lescarbot's *Nova Francia* (1609) to the Prince in the same terms: 'And lastly your poore Virginians doe seeme to implore your Princely aide, to helpe them to shake off the yoke of the divel, who hath hitherto made them live worse then beasts'.

Colonial expansion may be seen as an extension of the chivalrous tradition, of which the Prince's exercises in the tiltyard were also a part. Likewise connected with the cult of chivalry was the search for the North-West Passage. An undated letter to Anne of Denmark refers to both these enterprises and goes on to seek her to use influence with the King for the establishment of a new order of chivalry headed by Prince Henry:

... there being diverse knights and esquires of the best sort and great livings, who desire this society and to be adventurers under the Prince at their own charge.[160]

This was not to be, but it is important for us to realize that the great upsurge that was to result in the creation of America sprang out of the chivalrous tradition. This went back to the old Queen's reign when at the Accession Day Tilts, for instance, a knight could arrive disguised as an Indian (i.e. American) prince come to pay tribute and, as a result, have his sight miraculously restored.

The new reign saw a renewed series of attempts to find the North-West Passage.[161] The Prince took a keen interest in the voyages of Henry Hudson, of which that of 1610 led to the formation of the Company of the Merchant Discoverers of the North-West Passage, with Henry as its Supreme Protector.[162] Chamberlain reports this in a letter early in December 1611[163] and, later in the same month, the Venetian ambassador adds: 'there are those who tell the Prince of the discovery of a continent much more handy and much richer than Virginia. The Prince listens graciously and guides all his actions towards lofty aims'.[164] More reports follow in the spring of the next year when the expedition set sail under the Prince's auspices: 'To the ears of the Prince, who is keen for glory, come suggestions of conquests far greater than any made by the kings of Spain.'[165]

His instructions to his servant Thomas Button (d. 1634), dated 5 April 1612, open with exhortations to devotion: 'Let there be a religious care throughout your shippes...'. They run on, reminding one of the rules governing the household, to condemn all quarrelling, swearing, drunkenness and lewd behaviour. Strict instructions are given that an exact navigational-geographical record be kept to present to the Prince on his return.[166] Alas, he was never to live to read it. Button was in fact to be the first navigator to cross the Hudson Bay from east to west. The crews passed a winter amidst appalling cold and losses but at last, on 5 April 1613, the ice broke. In June they sailed back to England to learn the tragic news and Button, initially let down, was rewarded with the post of admiral of the King's ships on the coast of Ireland.

As in the case of the sea, horsemanship became a major preoccupation of the Prince early on. It is reflected in the dedication of books: Gervase Markham's *Cavelrice; or the English Horseman* (1607) and Nicholas Morgan's *The perfection of horsemanship* (1609). It was also widely recognized in the long series of gifts of horses and horse caparisons that begin as early as 1604 with a richly caparisoned pony presented by the Constable of Castile.[167] It was not, however, Spain but France that was the main focus of the Prince's attention in relation to developments in the art of horsemanship. There Antoine de Pluvinel, who had been an equerry to Henri III, introduced the new Italian style of riding and kept an academy. This was precisely the type of training which the Prince required and to achieve it Henri IV sent over one of Pluvinel's star pupils, Monsieur de St Antoine, in the train of the Duc de Sully in 1603.[168] The French King introduced him to James I as 'ung escuier choisy de ma main pour ayder à monter à cheval mon cher nepueu vostre filz' and presented the Prince at the same time with a 'lance and a helmet of gold, enriched with diamonds; together with a fencing master and a vaulter or tumbler'. St Antoine was not only to train the Prince in this newfangled horsemanship but to spend a certain amount of time travelling to and from his own country with horses for the Prince's stables.

The new horsemanship was of the kind we know today only through the Spanish Riding School in Vienna, the artificialities of *haute école*, the *ménage* or *dressage*, with its techniques, *capriole* or *courbette*, *volte* and *demi-volte*, *levade* and *passade*, added to the related questions of the breeding, training and veterinary care of horses. The origins of this were Italian, where Pluvinel had learned the art at the Pignatelli school at Naples, and resulted, for example, in Florence in the revival of the horse ballet in emulation of the ancient Greeks and Romans. The Medici stables were famous and it was little wonder that heavy hints were made that should the Grand Duke wish for the Prince's favour he should send him a horse able to caper.[169] Horsemanship of this kind presupposed a special building, a riding school, and to meet his needs the Prince erected the first ever in England, to the west of St James's Palace's Office.[170] Built between 1607 and 1609, it measured 128 ft by 43 ft (39 m × 13 m) internally and its groundplan together with a section and a detail of a window were recorded by the architect Robert Smythson on a visit to London soon after its completion.

26

It must have made an enormous impact at the time, for the Prince gave it over, as Holles records in his letter, as a school or academy for training young men in the new horsemanship of *haute école*. Amongst the young men who saw it and conceivably used it was an MP from Dorset, George Trenchard II (*c.* 1575–1610) who died in the summer of 1610 having got badly into debt in London to the despair of his father. One of the reasons for that debt must have been the prodigal extravagance of building, at his family seat at Wolfeton, Charminster, Dorset, what is virtually a duplicate of the Prince's riding house.[171] A unique survival, it perfectly evokes the milieu of the Prince's Riding House. It is slightly smaller, measuring inside just over 100 by 35 ft (30.5 m × 10.5 m), and is seven bays long, with end gables and large, square, three-light windows, in alternate bays. It can be dated only by its style, which is closely related to nearby Lulworth Castle, a monument to Jacobean romantic neo-Gothicism in the vein of the *Masque of Oberon*, which was nearing completion in 1607.

25

Twelve years later Smythson's son John was to model the riding school at Welbeck on the Prince's building and drawings for that pro-

28, 27

ject survive both of the exterior and interior.[172] The Welbeck riding school was built for Sir William Cavendish, later 1st Duke of Newcastle (1593–1676), the greatest horseman of his age and author of *La Méthode Nouvelle et Invention Extraordinaire de Dresser les Chevaux* (1658).[173] Cavendish, son of Sir Charles Cavendish, was one of the twenty-five well-born youths who were made Knights of the Bath on the occasion of the Prince's creation in 1610. His interest in horsemanship, however, began with his training by St Antoine. 'I have practised', he wrote in old age, 'ever since I was ten years old, have rid with the best masters of all nations...'. We must therefore imagine the royal riding school training the youths of the Prince's circle in this new art. The young Earl of Essex is likely to have been another pupil, for it was St Antoine who accompanied him to France in 1608. The last service rendered the Prince by his riding master was his escorting in of the mourning horse at his funeral. After Henry's death St Antoine became part of the household of the new Prince of Wales and we see him gazing up at his royal pupil in admiration and devotion in the vast full length of Charles I riding through a triumphal arch by Van Dyck.[174] He looks a cheerful, sinewy, masculine soul, with a face not unlike that of his former master, Henri IV.

The diary of a gentleman in the train of Otto, Landgrave of Hesse, who came to England in the summer of 1611, refers not only to the St James's School but also to another one at Richmond Palace, which was situated in 'an old monastery called Sheen'. This must have been an adaptation of part of the Carthusian house suppressed by Henry VIII in 1534 and leased subsequently to various tenants. The visitor describes witnessing Prince Henry and Prince Charles receiving instruction there at the hands of St Antoine.[175]

This passion for the art of riding demanded the creation of a fine stable. On this topic W. H. writes as follows:

He tooke great delight in ryding of great horses, and laboured to have of the best and rarest horses that were to be found, and had such care of them that he went often to stables to see them and accounted them to be a part of his best jewels....[176]

Hawkins also records this obsession and how horses were sent 'unto him from all Countries'.[177] The accounts record Polonian and Barbary horses, and gifts of others come from donors as varied as the Prince de Joinville, the Count of Embden, the Landgrave of Hesse, the Comte de Vaudemont and Lord Salisbury.[178] In addition there was a purchasing policy. In 1609 the Prince sent Robert Douglas (?1574–1639), later Viscount Belhaven, to Italy to buy horses.[179] Sir Henry Wotton presented him to the Doge in July and he was later in Florence. On the formation of the household in December he was appointed Master of the Horse.

Shortly after, the Prince was petitioning Salisbury for a letter of exchange for £600 for 'fair horses' purchased by Douglas in Italy. At the foot of the letter the Prince scribbled in his own hand: 'My Lord, I thank you for the little nag you sent me, which though he be little, yet he wants no mettle as all little things have.'[180] In August 1611 the Venetian ambassador describes the Prince talking of the breeds of various countries and extolling the virtues of Barbary horses which he himself rode.[181]

Such grounding presupposed that this Prince was to be an adornment to the tiltyard. As we have noted, his earliest public appearance there was at the tender age of twelve on 5 August 1606; it was at Greenwich, on the occasion of the visit of his uncle, the King of Denmark, and he took part in a tilt 'gallantly mounted, and a hart as powerfull as any, though that youth denyed strength'.[182] Three years later he was issuing a challenge for running at the ring as part of the court's Shrovetide revels. Exercises in the tiltyard were still practice for the realities of war; that this was central to the Prince's ambitions is reflected in Molin's observation that it was unnecessary for him to be a professor but 'a soldier and a man of the world'. From his childhood Hawkins records 'no Musick being so pleasant to his ears, as the sounding of the Trumpet, the Beating of the Drum, the Roaring of the Cannon, or any sort of Armour'.[183] That reminiscence may well be tinged by optimistic hindsight but it also embodied truth. As early as 1601 Sir Richard Preston (d. 1628), one of the King's most favoured Gentlemen of the Bedchamber and later Lord Dingwall, was appointed to instruct the Prince in the use of arms.[184] That he was an adept pupil we can gather by a description of the Prince in a letter by La Boderie, the French ambassador, dated 31 October 1606:

None of his pleasures savour the least of a child. He is a particular lover of horses and what belongs to them; but is not fond of hunting; and when he goes to it, it is rather for the pleasure of galloping, than that which the dogs give him. He plays willingly enough at Tennis, and at another Scots diversion very like mall [i.e. golf]; but this always with persons elder than himself, as if he despised those of his own age. He studies two hours a day, and employs the rest of his time in tossing the pike, or leaping, or shooting with the bow, or throwing the bar, or vaulting, or some other exercise of that kind....[185]

His predilection for arms is amply reflected in two boyhood portraits, both miniatures, one by Nicholas Hilliard, *c.* 1607–10, and the second attributed to Rowland Lockey, dated 1607, in which he poses wearing the suit of armour given him in that year by the Prince de Joinville.[186] Indeed its arrival must have prompted the sittings.

16
15

The obsessions of the Prince awakened the immediate interest both of the old Elizabethan war party and of those who had graced the tiltyard in Gloriana's reign. The two groups were, of course, not mutually exclusive. Foremost amongst the latter figured that ancient knight, Sir Henry Lee, who came to court in the summer of 1608 from Woodstock specifically to present the Prince with a suit of armour valued at £200;   21 that armour is still at Windsor Castle. So great was the impression made by this visit that Lee resolved to 'have one more fling at the Court before he die'. Sir Henry Lee (1533–1611) was Ranger of Woodstock and Master of the Armoury but, more particularly, he had been Queen Elizabeth I's Champion at the Tilt.[187] It was his challenge right back at the opening of her reign, half a century before, that had inaugurated the long series of ceremonial jousts held annually on her Accession Day. Lee, who in 1608 was the enormous age of seventy-five, must have viewed their sharp decline in the new reign with concern, and the emergence of a young Prince able to revive the flagging chivalry of England would have been infinitely appealing to the old knight in his dotage. Henry must have seen quite a lot of Lee when the court went to Woodstock hunting, but we have additional evidence in a touching letter which the knight wrote to the Prince. Undated, it reads as follows:

'The Fa(rther) burthen of my songe is to bestowe the remnant of my tyme all I may to please you. Your Highnes aptenes to horsemanship, and matters of armes is such, that a meane dyrector may make you most perfect in that exercise, on whom my duty shall never fayle, when it shall please so greate, so devine, and so mightie a Prince to command me....[188]

Lee had found a new cult figure to replace the Faerie Queene. In the gallery of his house at Ditchley used to hang a portrait of Prince Henry by Lee's favourite artist, Marcus Gheeraerts. The Elizabeth was his   17 grandest concept of her, the divine cosmic vision we know as the Ditchley Portrait, her feet atop the globe of the world, her very presence evoking a golden dawn. The young Prince is depicted in his robes as Knight of the Garter, that valiant symbol of Protestant chivalry of which Lee himself was also a member.

The resulting image of the Prince was inevitably a martial one. He is depicted on horseback as a knight in armour in Henry Peacham's *Minerva Britanna* (1612):

> THVS, thus young HENRY, like Macedo[n]'s son,
> Ought'st thou in armes before thy people shine.
> A prodigie for foes to gaze vpon,
> But still a glorious Load-starre vnto thine....[189]

A French Huguenot, d'Esdiguières, makes the same equation: '*Voicy L'Alexandre de la grande Bretaigne....Le voicy les armes à la main, face et pointe tournées ver L'ennemy de Dieu....*'[190] And, as in the case of Peacham, the eulogy is accompanied by a portrait of the Prince as an armed knight on horseback. His portrait iconography was, as a consequence, quite different from that cultivated by his father.

This image, that was to become a *leitmotif* in all eulogies, was rooted not only in the arts of horsemanship and the exercises in the tiltyard but also in their eventual fulfilment in active service in the field. Such things were recognized as necessary training for war:

> ... he did also practise Tilting, Charging on Horseback with Pistols, after the Manner of the Wars, with all other the like Inventions. Now also delighting to confer, both with his own, and other strangers, and great Captains, of all Manner of Wars, Battle, Furniture, Arms by Sea and Land, Disciplines, Orders, Marches, Alarms, Watches, Strategems, Ambuscades, Approaches, Scalings, Fortifications, Incampings; and having now and then Battles of Head-men appointed both on Horse and Foot, in a long Table; whereby he might in a manner, View the right ordering of a Battle....Neither did he omit, as he loved the *Theorick* of these Things, to practise the same, entertaining in his House a Dutch Captain, sent unto him by his Excellence (Grave Maurice) a most excellent Engineer, in all manner of Things belonging to the *Wars*; causing also, from Time to Time, new Pieces of Ordnance to be mace, learning to shoot, and level them right to the Whiste....[191]

In this account by Hawkins, Prince Henry's martial preoccupations far exceed any other aspect of his portrait. It also presents us with problems in terms of relating it to what little evidence survives.

We can begin by identifying the 'Dutch Captain'. He was a certain Abraham van Nyevelt, who is first referred to in a letter from Maurice of Nassau to the Prince dated 8 December 1611.[192] Van Nyevelt had supervised Maurice's restructuring of the defences of Deventer and other places in 1606. The letter is one of introduction on his behalf and Maurice tells the Prince that Nyevelt intends to publish shortly a book on the subject of military fortifications and to dedicate it to Prince Henry to whom he wishes to present it in person. That he came we have no doubt for he was accorded a salary equalled only by that of the Italian polymath, Constantino de' Servi, of £200 p.a.

His arrival must have been early in 1612 and hence his activities can only have covered the last few months of the Prince's life. One would conclude that his presence explains a payment in the household accounts for the 'Making of patterns for fortifications'.[193] It must remain purely speculative as to what those were. Two possibilities arise, however, one that the Prince was contemplating updating the fortifications of Kenilworth Castle, the negotiations for the purchase of which from Sir Robert Dudley were nearing completion;[194] the second that the Prince was aiming at some long-term reconstruction of the defences of the realm, the garrison forts built by Henry VIII in 1539–42 which were now hopelessly old-fashioned. These had not been radically re-built under Elizabeth, although for the first time the Italian system of fortification with the use of angled bastions began to be introduced.[195]

As in the case of every other area of activity we register the Prince's desire to recruit into his service someone abreast of the latest develop-ments. His interest went back as early as the age of fourteen when in June 1607 he had sent an engineer to France in the train of the Prince de Joinville to study the fortifications of Calais.[196] In August 1611 he talked to the Venetian ambassador about the fortifications of Venice, especially admiring the fort of Palma, 'the finest in the world as far as the art of fortification goes'.[197] This must refer to that landmark in Ren-aissance fortification, San Michele's San Andrea. The Dutch were amongst the most advanced exponents of military engineering at the opening of the seventeenth century when what we can term their school emerged under the aegis of Maurice of Nassau, who had stud-ied mathematics and fortress engineering under Simon Stevin (1548–1620). As a result a new generation of Dutch military engineers arose whose main attention was focused on refining the Italian tech-niques in response to water defences and dealing with the construction and operation of dams and sluices. Van Nyevelt was no doubt in-tended to be the introducer to England of these advances.

In addition to new systems of military fortification Maurice was cele-brated as the virtual creator of the Dutch army along quite original lines. Part of his reforms included the introduction of the drill deve-loped by his cousin, Johann of Nassau, and printed in a famous book il-lustrated with 117 engravings by Jacob de Gheyn entitled *Wapenhande-linghe* (1607).[198] After being published in Dutch it was swiftly translated into French, German, Danish and English. *The Exercise of Armes* (1607) was dedicated to the Prince with a eulogy by Gheyn in honour of one who 'doth yet give such a lustre to this Armes, by the continuall famil-iaritye he hath with them in his often practise'. We have only to refer to the famous engraving of the Prince practising with the pike to know   22 the truth of that statement, besides the evidence of Hawkins's account. In addition there are the many suits of armour that were either pre-sented to him or commissioned.[199] In 1607 he was given suits by both the Prince de Joinville and Henri IV. The latter is etched and gilded   20, 18 and bears an *impresa* of a fireball. It was presented to the Prince by La Boderie in July and we can see it in a half-length portrait at Dunster   23 Castle. In October 1609 the accounts refer to 'a new sute of Armer', now unidentifiable, and in 1611–12 there is a payment to Maurice of   19 Nassau's armourer. This probably connects with an armour recorded as still in the possession of Sir Edward Cecil in March 1613 and is probably identical with a suit of Dutch type bearing the Prince of Wales's feathers at Windsor.

His practice of discussing the tactics of battle in model form set out 'in a long Table' relates to a letter written in October 1612 from his friend Edward Cecil in Utrecht describing his discovery of a set of models of engines and artillery valued at £1,000 and ideal for the Prince to show him 'the verie practice of everie thinge either defensive or offensive'.[200] Just such a collection of items is recorded in the armoury of St James's Palace in the Commonwealth sale. It is a huge list of pieces, running through '15. peeces of brass ordinance', each twenty-two inches long, 'one modell of a becon', 'one modell for a brige', 'an Ingin for driveing piles', 'one scailing lader', '17, boards wth foot companies', '16, small boards wth carrages', 'one table wth a Campe of horse. & 3. pavillions', to 'one table wth 3 boates on a Cart 2 Carrages for mortar peeces one sledge'.[201]

Given all this it was inevitable that the court at St James's should become the focal point of the hopes of the old Elizabethan war party. About 1609–10 a group of these military men manoeuvred for the Prince's favour presenting him with a paper 'Inciting him to affect arms more than Peace'.[202] The King countered by asking Sir Robert Cotton to write a reply. Henry's 'foreign policy', if we may call it such, shows a total commitment to the Pan-European cause in Europe, in which England should manifest its leadership in acts of assertion and not ones of passive mediation. Although English troops had fought in Ireland, France and in the Low Countries under Elizabeth, no monarch had led his troops since Henry VIII. The circle around the Prince was peppered with those who had fought in the Netherlands and all of them were keenly to watch the strategy of the war ensuing from the Julich-Cleves crisis of 1609.

Princely Policy

Henry came of age when the lull that had followed the treaty of peace between France and Spain in 1598 seemed on the verge of being shattered. It was a Europe dominated by the twin branches of the Habsburg dynasty. The head of the Austrian branch was Rudolf II, who reigned in Prague as Holy Roman Emperor, and whose territories embraced Upper and Lower Austria lying either side of the middle reaches of the Danube, the principalities of Styria, Carinthia, Carniola and Tyrol with, to the west, lands and provinces in Alsace. The Spanish branch was an equally formidable landmass bringing with it Portugal, the kingdom of Naples, Franche-Comté and the southern Netherlands. It was a vast empire kept going by the wealth still pouring in from the New World and the Asiatic colonies. To secure their hegemony, however, now that the sea route north by way of the channel was denied them by the twin maritime powers of the English and Dutch, the domination of Italy remained crucial, for it provided the land route whereby resources and above all troops passed from south to north. And this depended on the subservience not only of the papal states but also of the Italy of the princes. It is too easy for us to read back into the era around 1610 what happened subsequently, but no one at the time quite believed the grip to be as inexorable as it was soon to prove. In general the Italian princes were held in allegiance because they owed their titles to the Empire, and by way of marriages with Habsburg princesses, but as a group they remained what was categorized as *stati liberi*, that is, countries which could be grouped along with England, the Dutch and the German Protestant states, whether of Calvinist or Lutheran persuasion, as capable of action independent of the might of the Habsburgs. All across Europe, on both sides of the religious divide, during the years down to the holocaust that followed 1618, there were those who waited and watched with a hope that some tremendous event would trigger off the shattering of the twin might of Spain and Austria.

The position of England was, of course, crucial. As the leading Protestant state her forces had defeated Spain and Catholicism in 1588; in the aftermath of the Armada she had sent soldiers to France in support of the Huguenot King, Henri IV, in his struggle against the Catholic League; and she had aided the Dutch in their long battle against Spain.[1] All that changed, however, with the accession of James I, who made peace with Spain in 1604 and whose policy was epitomized in his motto, *Beati Pacifici*. In terms of the state of crown finances and in those of trade the decision was a wise one, but it was also a position which had an ideological basis, for James belonged to that broad spectrum of educated opinion within western Europe which, after the bloody wars of religion of the late sixteenth century, sought to find some kind of *via media*. As a leading example himself of late Renaissance humanism there was more than a degree of nostalgia for putting the clock back to the lost halcyon days of the *respublica litterarum* before the theological divide. In the King's case his policy was expressed in the academic battle of words, to which he was a notable contributor, in his role as a mediator and in his belief that cross-marriages could heal the rift. In this last objective his children were each to be victims.

In the light of this it was natural that the old Elizabethan war party should focus its attentions on the heir to the throne, who certainly did nothing other than encourage them. If his father had abdicated his role as the leader of Protestant Europe, his son was more than willing to accept it when the time came. In what might be described as the cold war atmosphere of the opening years of the seventeenth century James was viewed by the war party as a monument to appeasement. That his son was cast in a quite different mould is reflected in his cultivation of a fiercely militaristic image. Cornwallis rounds off his account of Henry's supervision of the fleet with the statement that all this was done in preparation for 'a naval war with Spain, whensoever that King shall give cause of a public hostility'.[2] The Prince had even worked out the strategy that should be employed when war broke out, the fleet in part to be sent to the West Indies, in part to blockade Spain. Moreover he 'himself (if so it should agree with his Majesty's pleasure) would in person become the executor of that noble attempt for the West Indies'.[3]

Henry also differed from his father in his attitude to the French king, Henri IV. The latter had deliberately cultivated the Prince from a very early age via his ambassador, sending the child armour and horses and Monsieur de St Antoine.[4] The Prince's friends were made much of when they visited the French court. In the Prince the French king evoked what can only be described as a kind of hero-worship. His portrait and that of a second hero of a similar type, the soldier Maurice of Nassau, were the only ones to adorn the walls of the Prince's gallery at St James's Palace.[5] As the Prince grew to manhood Henri IV was by far the most important figure on the European scene, a ruler whose career was extraordinary both as a soldier, who had to fight to gain his kingdom, and as a figure in the *politique* tradition, who began as a Protestant but who converted to Catholicism in order to reunite his people.[6] There always remained an ambiguity about his theological stance and

31

no ruler attracted such messianic prognostications as the old century crossed into the new: he was regarded alternately as the monarch who would shatter Habsburg domination of Italy, who would unite Europe and lead a new crusade against the Turk or who could succeed Rudolf II as Holy Roman Emperor. As the young Prince grew up the French king represented an ideal to which he aspired, that of the warrior-king leading his people in the field of battle.

His second hero was the Stadtholder of Holland, Maurice of Nassau, 30 whose election to the Order of the Garter he was to work for and which Maurice was eventually to receive after Henry's death. Maurice, like Henri IV, was a military commander and had led the forces of the Dutch Republic in the war against Spain which drew to a halt in 1609 with the Twelve Years Truce. Overtures were made to Maurice on the subject of the Garter as early as May 1611 when, in a remarkable letter to Adam Newton, Sir Edward Conway described how he had told Maurice of Henry's admiration of him:

... I toke occassion to tell the cownte, that if he knew the gallant and actiue composition of the Princes minde, how properly and naturally he loued worthy actions and those that did them, he wolde easily beleve that the Prince did especially favour and affecte his person; that those that hade the honor to be some times abowte the Prince did obserue by the mayny questions his Hyghnes did make towcheing the cownte Moris his person, his great actions, his recreations, his paseing of his time, that the Prince did take delight to heare Honnor of him and to approue hit....[7]

These two heroes of Henry help us to see his own ambitions and aspirations within a European context.

Henry belongs to that period of history which stretches from 1598 to 1618, when the Thirty Years War broke out. From the outset there is never any doubt as to where his commitment lay, and it is evident in the three great international incidents in which he was to a varying extent involved: the rupture between Venice and the Papacy over the Servite friar, Paolo Sarpi; the crisis provoked by the succession to the tiny German state of Julich-Cleves; and, finally, the negotiations between England and the League of German Protestant Princes, an alliance which was to be sealed in 1613, after his death, with the marriage of his sister, Elizabeth, to Frederick V, Elector Palatine. The last might be said to be the culmination of his policy.

The Prince's intense interest in foreign affairs can be attributed to two things. One was his relatives. Through his mother he had as uncles the King of Denmark, the Landgrave of Hesse, the Duke of Holstein and the Duke of Brunswick. Through his great-grandmother, Mary of Guise, he was related to the Guise family, Dukes of Lorraine, and through them to the Medici, Grand Dukes of Florence. Few things are more striking in the volumes of correspondence than the quantity of letters within this large European family network. Even more important, however, was the attitude of the leading figure on the home political stage, Robert Cecil, Earl of Salisbury. His approach to the heir to the throne was quite different from his father's.[8] James looked to the child only to prove himself academically; his sole contribution to the Prince's political education had been his treatise, the *Basilikon Doron*, which he had written specifically for Henry's instruction and which dealt in abstract with the idea of kingship by Divine Right. Salisbury's approach, in sharp contrast, was both pragmatic and practical. From as early as 1607, when Henry was only thirteen, he had kept the Prince and his tutor, Adam Newton, abreast of political events. Ambassadorial dispatches were even sent for his perusal: 'I have sent to you with the last dispatch from Ireland', he wrote, 'the reading whereof will evry day prove more proper for the Prince of Bretany then Aristotle or Cicero...'.[9] As we have seen, Salisbury's son William was a close friend of the Prince's and there was an equally affectionate relationship between Henry and the father. They had much in common: both had a passion for building – for Hatfield House was arising during these years – and an interest in the new gardening, patronizing Salomon de Caus; they were simultaneously assembling picture collections and both employed Inigo Jones. It is significant that it is only after May 1612, when Salisbury died, that the St James's court found itself cut off from direct knowledge of affairs of state, and the Prince sought to establish his own network of agents abroad.[10]

The securing of direct information from such agents became a preoccupation early on. As we have already noted, the Prince had asked Sir Charles Cornwallis in 1609, when he was only fourteen, to write to him from Madrid of events in Spain. France, owing to its large and militant Huguenot minority, was, however, of even more interest to him. In September 1610 Adam Newton reminded Sir Thomas Edmondes, ambassador in Paris, of his promise to write 'unto him [i.e. the Prince] such occurences, as that country yieldeth'.[11] Edmondes was cautious, fearing to offend Salisbury if he found out that the ambassador was sending a separate set of reports direct to the Prince, and declined. By then a solution had been found. Newton was patron of a certain Reverend Thomas Lorkin, tutor to Sir Thomas Puckering, who was being educated in Paris. Lorkin wrote for over a year, until in February 1612 he was able to secure an agent at the French court for £80 p.a. who wrote regular reports (still extant) which were sent via a different network of postmasters to avoid falling into the hands of Salisbury. The letters deal in the main with the activities of the Princes of the Blood and with the Huguenots. The agent's exact identity was concealed under the pseudonym of 'Forboyst'.[12]

Reflective of the period of peace following the Treaty of Vervins in 1598, Venice reopened diplomatic relations with England in the last year of the old queen's reign. In 1603 James responded by sending Sir Henry Wotton as ambassador to the Serenissima. Wotton made much of the young prince and a portrait of him was hung in his *palazzo*, which became almost a finishing school for young gentlemen and which was certainly seminal for the introduction to England of Italian culture, whether it was the architecture of Palladio or the painting of members of the Venetian school. Wotton, like so many, was anti-papal and anti-Habsburg, but saw that the only way of breaking this hegemony was by way of an alliance of 'liberal' Catholic and Protestant powers against the Pope, Spain and Austria. In this scenario, the two Italian states of Venice and Savoy were designed to play a crucial part, for Wotton believed that through one of them Protestantism could gain a foothold once more in Italy.

The rift between Venice and the papacy in 1606 excited great attention throughout Europe and above all in England. Venice, a republic which was foremost among the *stati liberi* in Italy, had a long proud history of independence from papal intervention, reflected, above all, in its own Patriarch.[13] The quarrel arose over laws passed by the Senate which were seen to infringe, in the eyes of the Curia, ecclesiastical prerogatives. The Venetians on their side had a notable spokesman in their official theologian, the friar, Paolo Sarpi. He was a man of liberal persuasion, maintaining a correspondence with Protestants north of the Alps and later writing his famous *History of the Council of Trent*, in which the blame for the present disunity of Christendom was not laid solely at the door of the reformers. Later in life the Prince's tutor was to translate it into Latin. That lay in the future but in 1606, as the result of a deadlock, Pope Paul V placed Venice under an interdict, an act which the Venetians promptly ignored, they, in their turn, expelling the Jesuits. This Wotton viewed as his golden opportunity to introduce Protestantism. The Venetians began to observe the Anglican liturgy in his *palazzo* and both it and Jewel's *Apology*, a cornerstone of the Anglican theological position, being both Catholic and reformed, were translated into Italian and distributed. Sarpi's *apologia* was sent by the Doge not only to James I but also to Prince Henry in September 1606.[14] He would have been thirteen at the time and it must have made a profound effect on him for in May of the following year Wotton told the Doge how the young heir to the throne had written offering his services to the Republic against the Pope if only he were old enough.[15] A

year later Wotton was writing again in response to the Prince's desire
to know the 'state of things here'.[16] He also wrote of impending
princely marriages, ending with how there would be princesses enough
left for the Prince to choose from when the time came. By then the
Sarpi affair was over and Wotton's mind had moved on to his second
ploy for an erosion of Habsburg power in the peninsula by way of a
Catholic–Protestant marriage. Sarpi, however, ought to have the last
word as an acute observer of the European political scene. In 1609 he
wrote perceptively:

... from all sides one hears about the great *virtu* of the Prince, son to the King of England. But the world must wait a great while to reap benefit therefrom: for the King of
England, however accomplished in the reformed religion, appears for the rest not to be
worth much: *he* would like to do everything with words.[17]

The Prince's interest in the Sarpi affair shows how intently he studied foreign affairs and how closely he watched, even at such an early
age, any developments that might undermine Habsburg domination.
These were to reach a climax in the month leading up to his creation as
Prince of Wales in June 1610, in the events triggered off by what is
known as the Julich-Cleves crisis.[18] In broad terms the death of the ruler of this tiny German state in March 1609 sparked off preparations
for a major European conflagration in which the Prince's hero,
Henri IV, allied with the United Provinces, the Union of German Protestant Princes and, it was hoped, England, were to confront the Habsburg armies in the Empire, while a second army, allied with Savoy, was
to reopen the Italian wars and invade the Duchy of Milan. Both Julich-
Cleves and Milan were crucial to the geographical supply-line through
Europe which sustained the Habsburgs. In spite of numerous delegations James kept out of the dispute. The diplomatic correspondence
pouring into England mounted to a fever pitch of excitement as vast
armies were seen to mass on the French borders, all to be as dust early
in May when the French king was assassinated, an event which delayed
a major European war for a decade.

There is no doubt of the Prince of Wales's enthusiasm for this anti-
Habsburg crusade. As we shall see, it was a decisive factor in providing
the political context of Ben Jonson's *Barriers*, whereby Henry presented
himself as a direct successor to the warlike kings of England, thirsty for
blood and glory. On hearing of the news of the French king's murder
he is said to have taken to his bed for several days repeating the words,
'My second father is dead'.[19] Foscarini, the Venetian ambassador in Paris, supplies us with the interesting comment passed on by the Secretary of State at the English embassy that when Henri IV died 'one of
his [i.e. Prince Henry's] chief projects, which he never communicated

to anyone, was now destroyed; for he had resolved to fight under his Most Christian Majesty whenever he marched on Cleves'.[20] Although James I would never have allowed it, this has the ring of truth and squares with all that we know of the martial aspirations of this fifteen-year-old youth. When Henry carried to the altar Henri IV's banner and helm as a Knight of the Garter in May a year later his face was described as being one of sorrow and pain.[21]

France now entered a period of regency under Henri's widow, Marie de' Medici, and the crown found itself faced with the problem of internal dissension, which it responded to by a reversion to late Valois policies, those of vacillation, conciliation and compromise. A French force did in fact take part in the capture of Julich in September but already, by the following month, news reached England of the Queen Mother's policy of appeasement with Spain expressed in the initiation of negotiations for a double marriage between the two houses. This reached its climax at the opening of 1612 when the matches were declared public and in March Paris was *en fête* in celebration. In the eyes of the court at St James's, the anti-Habsburg crusade henceforth depended on England in alliance with the United Provinces and the German Protestant princes. And that too was expressed in the negotiations for another marriage which runs almost as a counterpoint to the Franco-Spanish alliances, that of Henry's beloved sister to the Elector Palatine. This was to be a project in which his father's and his own interests were uniquely to coincide.

Through his mother Henry had an abundance of German Protestant relatives. Anne of Denmark's mother was sister to Ulric III, Duke of Mecklenburg. Her three sisters were married respectively to the Duke of Brunswick, the Landgrave of Hesse and the Duke of Holstein. Although Anne loved her regal brother of Denmark she certainly looked down on her other in-laws as inferior. Nonetheless not until the accession of the House of Hanover in 1714 was the relationship of England and northern Europe to be so close. This is a forgotten aspect of late Elizabethan and Jacobean civilization, for these tiny courts dotted across the Holy Roman Empire looked to the courts of Elizabeth I and James I as their cultural mecca. Starting in the 1590s a long stream of visits to England by German princelings occurs. Although it has been argued that the marriage of the Princess Elizabeth to the Elector Palatine led to the establishment of an outpost of Jacobean civilization in Heidelberg, this was the culmination of a movement that had been going on for almost two decades. The cultural interplay between these courts has never been studied, but certainly deserves to be, for the journals and diaries alone (still largely unpublished) kept during these tours form our major source of information for the appearance and contents of the palaces, great houses and gardens as they appeared before the deluge of the Civil War.

For Henry these princes, who were his first cousins, were his only real family. One with whom the Prince struck up a close friendship was Frederic Ulric (1591–1634), son of Henry Julius, Duke of Brunswick, and his wife, Anne's sister, Elizabeth.[22] A long series of letters from 1604[23] onwards to the Prince culminated in his visit to England in the spring of 1610.[24] Frederic Ulric was three years older than Henry and lodged with him at St James's Palace. They shared a passion for the martial arts and the Accession Day Tilt was ordered to be especially elaborate that year to honour him. The visit included the usual tour, taking in Oxford, where he received a volume of eulogistic verse, and we find him in May in Bath, from which he wrote to the Prince expressing his horror at the assassination of Henri IV – 'abominacion d'un si méchante acte'.[25] He was back in Carlsburg sometime in June and only reappears to any point in the Prince's correspondence in the middle of 1611 when he makes a direct overture for the hand of Elizabeth, stating that if Henry knew what his family knew about the son of the Duke of Savoy, he would be the last person he would wish to have as brother-in-law![26] Although Henry approached his father, it was to no avail. At about the same time letters appear from Frederic Ulric's younger brother, Christian, who was to figure during the Thirty Years War as the romantic champion of the Winter Queen.[27] An example of the strength of Henry's friendship for Frederic Ulric is the magnificent gift of a superb suit of Greenwich armour, the last recorded, decorated with bands of Tudor roses interlinked by double knots, with the arms of Brunswick-Wolfenbuettel etched on the armour for the horse. It was not to reach Germany until after Henry's death.[28]

A second cousin who made a more forceful bid to marry the Princess Elizabeth was Otto, Prince of Hesse (d. 1617).[29] He came during the summer of 1611, specifically seeking her hand, accompanied by a train of some thirty, which included Henry, Count of Nassau. Otto went on the usual tour (the account is a mine of information on Jacobean palaces and gardens) 'and demeaned himself in all things very princely and bountifully'. On 3 August he left England, however, empty-handed.

The trouble with these German Protestant princelings is that none was thought to be grand enough for a daughter of Great Britain, none that is save one. Frederick V, Elector Palatine of the Rhine, was the senior Elector of the Holy Roman Empire who counted emperors in

29

his lineage and was descended from Charlemagne. In addition, the mantle of the head of the League of Protestant Princes also descended upon him at the same time as James I was desiring to enter into open alliance. In this instance James's policy of conciliatory matches for his children was to have the support of his eldest son in one aspect. That was the King's decision that his daughter should be bestowed on the leader of Protestant Europe. The complementary aspect, that Henry should marry a Catholic princess, was totally unpalatable to him. But that did not happen immediately for there were a number of offers for her hand on the Catholic side, including Philip III, which came to nothing, and more importantly a double match with Savoy which can be more conveniently touched upon in the discussion of the Prince's own marriage.

There can be no doubt, however, that from the outset Henry was pledged to support a Protestant match for his sister.[30] The marriage had been mooted as early as February 1610: 'nor is there wanting a certain inclination to take the Palatine's daughter for the Prince of Wales'.[31] There is a degree of evidence that would support the view that Henry would have liked his own and his sister's marriages to be a Protestant riposte to the Catholic Bourbon – Habsburg alliances soon to be simultaneously in negotiation. Although much talked of,[32] it was in fact not until October of the following year that the princes of the Protestant Union petitioned James for the match as an expression of the alliance.[33] In the meantime, the King had dabbled with the proposed double marriage for his two eldest children with the Duke of Savoy and it was only from January 1612 onwards that he seems to have made up his mind that he should proceed definitely with the Palatine project.[34]

In his attitude to the delegations from Germany during the spring and summer of 1612 there is abundant evidence of Henry's deep commitment, expressed both in the entertainment of the envoys sent to settle the terms and, above all, in his efforts to persuade his mother to withdraw her opposition.[35] In this he was successful, although Anne was never wholly reconciled. The marriage treaty was formally concluded in May when a double embassy came, headed by the Count of Hanau and the Huguenot Duke of Bouillon.[36] On 6 July the old Electress Palatine, daughter of William the Silent, put pen to paper to express her gratitude to the Prince for all the support he had given.[37] And it was to be the Prince who set about ordering what he conceived to be a great set of festivals that were not only to inaugurate England's role as the leader of the anti-Habsburg crusade in Europe, by way of the Palatinate, but also to reaffirm his own as the heir to Henri IV.

James's *via media* marital policy was characteristic: with his daughter allied to Protestant Germany and his son married, preferably to a Catholic Habsburg princess,[38] the British Solomon could mediate across the political and religious divide. In retrospect there is no reason to condemn a policy whose only alternative was to increase the polarization of faiths amongst the ruling houses of Europe. Henry, of course, was never consulted and although the identity of the bride changes, her faith remains constant.

Of the Prince's interest in women there seems to be no evidence at all before the summer of 1612. 'With regard to that of love', wrote Bacon, 'there was a wonderful silence, considering his age, so that he passed that dangerous time of his youth in the highest fortune and in a vigorous state of health, without any remarkable imputation of gallantry.' Cornwallis naturally adds chastity to the list of the Prince's virtues and describes banquets to which the ladies of both the court and the City had been bidden but one 'could neither then discover by his behaviour, his eye, or his countenance, any show of singular or special fancy to any'.[39] This supports the view that the atmosphere of the palaces at St James's and Richmond was more like that of a puritan monastery than what we recognize as a Jacobean court. There seems to have been a thaw, however, in the summer of 1612, when we get hints of some kind of liaison, probably with Frances Howard.

Although a Spanish marriage had been mooted as long ago as 1605, it was not until 1611, when a match with Savoy was under negotiation, that an offer was made.[40] James was immediately flattered and sent one of his favourites, Sir John Digby, to pursue the matter. He was not long at the Spanish court when he discovered about the Franco-Spanish marriages and that only one of Philip III's younger daughters, aged six, was on offer. James was insulted not only by this but even more that such an alliance presupposed Henry's conversion to the Catholic faith. There it fortunately languished for surely nothing could have been more distasteful to the Prince than marrying a daughter of his arch-enemy, the King of Spain, thus being instrumental in bringing Britain into the Habsburg orbit.

Salisbury was never in favour of the Spanish match and his view was that if the King was absolutely set on a Catholic bride a marriage into the Medici family would cause the fewest international complications.[41] There would also be a large dowry, which would help to solve royal finances after the collapse of the Great Contract in 1610. Even the sale of baronetcies in 1611 had hardly ameliorated the situation. Although there was a long history of close connections between James and the Medici court, including offers of marriage, it was not until the spring of 1611 that the project was treated with any seriousness. Salisbury worked on the Prince by way of two major figures in the St James's court, his nephew, Sir Edward Cecil, and another old family friend, Sir Thomas Chaloner. Both, as we know, had been in Florence in the 1590s. In March 1611 Edward Cecil, doubtless acting as Salisbury's mouthpiece, made overtures on the subject to the Tuscan Resident, Ottaviano Lotti, and requested that portraits of the Medici princesses be obtained. These arrived in August but it was not until the autumn that the negotiations entered a significant phase, prompted by both the knowledge of the Franco-Spanish double marriages and the duplicity of Philip III in offering only a young infanta. In October it was reported that the Catholic party in the Council, led by Northampton and Suffolk, began to say, 'Behold our Prince turns to Tuscany for a bride.'

The moving spirit at the Florentine end was the Duke's mother, Christina of Lorraine, but the match soon ran into difficulties with Rome, so much so that Lotti had to be recalled to present the case to the Pope, and one of the ducal secretaries, Andrea Cioli, was sent to England to replace him. Lotti carried with him not only a letter of support from the Catholic lords but also one from Anne of Denmark admitting her Catholicism and telling the Pope that the marriage would result in the conversion of her son. While things went from bad to worse between Rome and Florence, the main proponent of the match in England, Salisbury, died. Henry declared against it publicly, while privately he sent his own messenger to Florence to make sure, via the exiled Robert Dudley, that if it did go through he would obtain some of the dowry money. The project was, however, dead from May 1612 onwards when negotiations with the Duke of Savoy entered a serious phase.

The key figure this time was Sir Henry Wotton, who believed that if a double match could be achieved it would be a means whereby Protestantism could be introduced into Italy.[42] For Wotton the project was an ideological continuation of the Sarpi incident in Venice a few years before. Savoy, like Tuscany, was one of the *stati liberi* and the Duke, Charles Emmanuel, had been an ally of Henri IV in 1610 and was to have assisted in reopening the Italian wars by invading the duchy of Milan. In the aftermath of that collapse he was left politically isolated and proposed to James the marriage of the Prince of Piedmont, then aged twenty-four, to the Princess Elizabeth and that of his third daughter, Maria, to Henry, the two being of the same age. Early in 1611 Wotton travelled back to England via Turin where the proposal was made. By February the news had reached England and in March an ambassador, the Count of Cartignana, actually arrived with the offer. Cecil, then deep into the Medici offer, expressed surprise and turned down the Savoy princess for Henry but promised to consider the second. In fact, he was in favour of neither (the international complications of an alliance with the bellicose Duke could have been catastrophic), a view also held by Prince Henry.

The affair cooled until the close of 1611 when Cartignana returned and was surprised to find James reopen the offer of Henry (the Spanish match had collapsed) and dismiss that of Elizabeth (by then he had virtually come down in favour of the Palatine alliance). The King decided to send an embassy to Turin and Wotton left for Savoy in March. Once again the course of events was changed by Salisbury's death. In June the Palatine marriage was officially concluded, at which point Chamberlain, the letter writer, records, 'some new matter is abrewing in Savoy for that Infanta for our Prince'.[43] The negotiations then suddenly accelerated for two reasons: mounting royal debt could be reduced by a vast dowry, and both James and Anne wished the Prince to be married, 'as his Highness has begun to show a leaning to a certain lady of the court' (Frances Howard?).[44] The negotiations were carried out by a Savoyard banker resident in London, Gabaleone, who pursued both King and Prince to Belvoir Castle during their summer progress. By then Wotton had returned and presented the Savoy case in its most favourable light with astonishing assurances that the Infanta 'was so far from being superstitious as that she had always about her a lady of the religion, and would desire them [i.e. Catholic services] only in her chamber as privately as could be wished, promising likewise to accompany the Queen to our sermons at times when she should be called.'[45] He even added that he had hopes of the Duke turning Huguenot! Rome would have been appalled had these terms been known but Savoy was in a stronger position, due to its geographical location, to ignore papal fury.

Marie de' Medici, getting wind of the Savoy match, reopened marriage negotiations with the offer of her nine-year-old second daughter, Christine.[46] This proposal was conveyed to the Prince by Carr, now Rochester, at the end of July. Henry, however, would hear of it only if the princess were handed over at the same time as her sister went to Spain, thereby increasing the hope of her conversion. At the close of September Henry's response on the topic was nothing if not a frosty one, apologizing via Rochester to the King for his indifference and adding tartly that his role 'which is to be in love with any of them, is not yet at hand'.

The French match never seems to have been taken seriously owing to the age of the bride and to the size of the dowry because, as Henry remarked, if it depended on the latter the match with Savoy was inevitable. All the surviving evidence points to the presumption that James actually intended to go through with this marriage and that it was to be formally concluded in October 1612, thus revealing to the world his plan of double conciliatory matches. It would have reaffirmed his *via media* policy and eliminated any possibility of the Palatine alliance implying his acceptance of the role as the leader of an anti-Habsburg pan-Protestant league. That was how both the Prince and the war party would have liked to have viewed it. Overnight what seemed to herald their triumph would have been as dust when it was announced that the future leader of Protestant Europe was literally to be sold by his father to a Catholic bride. On 26 October the Council declared in favour of the marriage, the very day that the Prince took ill to his bed. By then he was being influenced by Henry of Nassau and sent messages imploring that the decision be delayed until he was better. References after his death refer to the marriage as settled. James knighted Gabaleone and, in a letter of May 1613, he is casually referred to as the man 'who negotiated the late Prince's marriage'.[47]

Obedience to the King was a central facet of the Prince's make-up and whether he liked it or not he was to marry a Catholic. It is fascinating to speculate how different the course of early Stuart history would have been had this marriage actually taken place. There is no doubt that the problem of how to avoid a Catholic marriage or, if forced to make one, how to nullify its effect occupied a large part of the Prince's thoughts during 1612. This is supported by the existence of a whole series of treatises arguing about the matter. Raleigh was called upon to write against the Spanish match. The document was in the main a rerun of the arguments used against the marriage of Elizabeth into Savoy. He ends, however, with a prophetic vision of what was to come in 1618:

Seing therfore wee have nothinge yet in hande, seing ther is nothinge moves, seinge the worlde is yet a slumber, And that this longe Calme will shortly breake out in to some terrible tempest, I would advise the Prince to keepe his owne grounde for a while and no waye to ingage or intangle himselfe....[48]

Raleigh came out in favour of waiting for a French marriage (the princess in question was only six).

More interesting and surely closer to the Prince's thoughts is the tract by Cornwallis in which he marshalled the objections of the St James's court to the Medici match. This closes with a forthright statement that a marriage into Protestant Germany was the only right one:

Your conjunction with those of your owne Religion will demonstrate your clear, and un-doubted resolution not to decline in the cause of GOD. This will fasten unto you throughout all *Christendom* the professors of the reformation, and make you dear to the subjects of this kingdom: out of whose loves you may expect a permanent and continual treasure, not to be equalled by many decrees greater than can be hoped; and whose con-trary conceite upon a marriage in so high a degree distasteful unto them is likely to breed and increase those obstructions which have lately been shewed upon the demands of supply in Parliament by the King your father.[49]

If Raleigh's advice prognosticates the Thirty Years War, Cornwallis's focuses on the breakdown of the relationship of King and Parliament which was to result in the Civil War.

What a moment to die, at the very time when the Protestant chivalry of northern Europe had converged on the New Jerusalem of London. How the alarm bells must have rung at the thought that their future destined leader, the 'heir' of Henri IV, was to be sacrificed to a Cath-olic bride. The Venetian ambassador states that if Henry had appeared before the Council on 20 October he would have argued against the marriage. Later Isaac Wake records Adam Newton's evidence that 'He was resolved that two religions should never lie in his bed.'[50] After his death it was rumoured that he intended to escort his sister to the Palat-inate and choose a Protestant bride.[51] In this we see the clash of two ideologies. The King's was still within the framework of a humanist *pol-itique* tradition derived from the previous century that believed in reli-gious conciliation through mixed marriages, in this instance Calvin-ist – Anglican and Catholic – Anglican. In the case of the Prince it was a policy of intensifying the polarity, of drawing together by means of marriage and political alliance the forces of the Reformation as a pre-lude to some vast European conflagration in which Catholicism and the Habsburgs would be defeated and Rome with its Antichrist Pope laid low. Four centuries later one's sympathies inevitably lie with the idealism of the father.

Bacon wrote: 'There were indeed in the Prince some things obscure, and not to be discovered by the sagacity of any person, but by time only, which was deinied him.' Chamberlain reported after his death that 'His papers showed him to have had many strange and vast con-ceits and projects.'[52] The reports of the Venetian ambassador record papers being burned and talk of schemes and ambitions, all of which focused on an active intervention in the affairs of Protestant Germany and Huguenot France.[53] There is no doubt that within the context of the opening years of the seventeenth century this taciturn youth was cast as the hoped-for leader of liberal Europe in its battle against Habs-burg and papal domination. And yet 'liberal' in his religious views he was not. Henry Prince of Wales was no Henri of Navarre. At no point does he ever emerge as anything other than violently anti-Catholic. Those liberal Catholics, like Paolo Sarpi, who looked to him were misplacing their hopes. What they needed, ironically, to lead them was a man who was part the father and part the son, a liberal tolerant exponent of an ideological *via media* expressed not in words but in actions. In that respect James I and the future Henry IX fell equally short.

Art and Artists

Nothing could be more remarkable than the greatly enhanced status enjoyed by artists during the Mannerist phase as it dominated the courts of Europe, down to the outbreak of the Thirty Years War. Painters, sculptors, architects and designers became central and respected contributors to the intellectual quest for a new universal order of things. Artists, poets, philosophers and scientists by means of inner vision and insight, experimentation and intellectual speculation could make equally valid contributions and the lines of demarcation between these spheres of activity were not as yet tightly drawn. In general, such people tended to be polymathic. At the court of Prince Henry, the visual arts were to play this greatly ennobled role and thus occupy a position quite unparalleled in England before 1610. In tandem with a neo-Elizabethan revival, there was a passionate preoccupation with the recruiting from abroad of artists who would be able to surround the Prince, and present his public persona, with all the trappings and marvels of the Mannerist age, from the splendours of illusionistic scenery to the surprises of a garden grotto.

This importance attached to artists can only be understood within a European context, and it is late Medicean Florence and Rudolfine Prague which will give us an essential point of reference. Both courts were of interest to the Prince and from both he recruited members for his own household. The key figure at the Medici court for over thirty years was Bernardo Buontalenti.[1] Architect and interior decorator of palaces, churches and villas, designer of the scenery for the spectacular *intermezzi* and the décor for dynastic ceremonies, mastermind behind the conceits of the gardens of the Villa Pratolino with its grottoes and automata, no aspect of the presentation of the Grand Dukes went untouched by his genius. And each of these manifold activities sprang from the nature of the magic universe of the late Renaissance as the marvels of nature were revealed and harnessed, platonic truths made visible and the central role of man the microcosm confirmed. A grotto with automata was at once a demonstration of revived Alexandrian School pneumatics and an emulation of antique technology, but it was also a moving tableau with subject matter bearing layers of symbolic allusion that could be interpreted at various levels: literal, figurative, allegorical and anagogical. An *intermezzo* was also in one aspect scientific, a demonstration of the optical principles of perspective allied to developments in Renaissance engineering derived from Vitruvius.

And, as in the case of the grotto, it presented to the onlooker a symbolic tableau in which music, singing, poetry, mime and the dance united to reveal to man the cosmic harmonies, confirming the reigning dynasty in its right to rule as virtue triumphed over vice and peace vanquished war. In this sense an artist such as Buontalenti had powers which were literally supernatural.

Such powers were enhanced by the repertory of images that he used, for the artist expressed himself through the mind in symbol. The latter may, of course, be drawn from reality – a landscape, a portrait or a still-life – but its role was essentially that of an artistic symbol. As a result of the mythological encyclopaedias and hundreds of emblem books, that visual repertory had, by 1600, reached a flood; the language it spoke in was that of Renaissance hermeticism and the occult. The artist was drawn in as an agent purveying its ideas; through such a repertory alone was he able to construct his representations of abstract thoughts and notions. In monarchical terms, as the century drew to its close, these artists were essential to a court, not only as overt political propagandists through image, masque and portrait, but also as interpreters of messianic hopes, as aspirations, in that uncertain age, were focused on prophetic figures, whether Elizabeth I, in the aftermath of the defeat of the Armada, or Henri IV after his conversion.

A parallel to late Medicean Florence was Rudolfine Prague, where artists occupied a major role in a court dedicated to the occult sciences and mystical epiphanies of the Habsburg Emperor through court festival, allegorical painting and sculpture, architecture and gardening.[2] The key figures here were Giuseppe Arcimboldo, who orchestrated court ceremonial as well as painting his strange esoteric grotesque fantasies; Bartholomaeus Spranger, who again designed for festivals and painted mythological canvases apotheosizing Rudolf with hints of astrological and alchemical symbolism; and Adriaen de Vries, the sculptor. All these artists occupied a privileged position at court. They were friends and cronies of the Emperor; one was even ennobled as Count Palatine. In other words, they enjoyed a status equal to that of the humanists, scientists and other men of intellect.

Florence and Prague are perhaps the best points of reference for the long-term objectives of the Henrician era. The Jacobean court, like the Elizabethan, offered no place of prestige to the artist. The architect in the Renaissance sense as *uomo universale* did not exist, the painter was a humble tradesman plying his craft, the hydraulic engineer and garden designer had not arrived, and Inigo Jones was just fitfully establishing himself as the creator of the visual apparatus of the court masque. Stylistically England was a backwater, for Gloriana's reign had been a rock against change. It had almost glorified in its own insularity, producing during its last two decades a unique and archaic visual culture which had little to do with the mainstream of Renaissance art. The only Italian artist of international renown who came to England was the painter Federigo Zuccaro and he soon left. Elizabethan England fostered a neo-medievalism of style: in its architecture as the great houses arose as castles of glass; in its painting, which was flat and iconic, totally oblivious of Renaissance principles; and in its decorative arts, which cultivated flat two-dimensional pattern and gothic sinuosity of line. The advent of a new dynasty brought no radical change in concept.

All this throws the events of the year 1610 and after into dramatic relief as we see the new court of the Prince of Wales embark on the deliberate recruitment of artists of the type that graced the courts of Florence and Prague. The implications of such a programme were momentous. The Prince needed an architect for his palaces which were to be built in the new style; a designer for his court festivals, for they were to emulate those of the Medici; a court portrait painter, for the Prince must be presented both at home and abroad as a man-at-arms and the perfect *cortigiano*; an expert on hydraulics, for his gardens must outshine Pratolino and Saint-Germain-en-Laye; and even an engraver, for the visual arts of his court must be taken to the people through the art of mass reproduction. The search for each of these or a combination of them was to occupy the years 1610 to 1612. Three figures emerge as occupying major positions. They are Constantino de' Servi, Salomon de Caus and Inigo Jones. In the long run it was to be the last who was to dominate the stage and become an enduring and towering figure in the history of the arts in England. But no one in 1610 could have predicted this. As we shall see, all the evidence points to the fact that had the Prince lived the other two might have been of even greater importance and influence. And it is with restoring these two lost major figures to the canvas of the arts of Jacobean England that I shall begin.

Of all the figures in the history of the arts in early Stuart England whose importance needs to be re-examined, the Florentine Constantino de' Servi (*c.* 1554–1622) must rank as potentially the most important. Up until recently, we have known little about him beyond some references by students of the court masques as to his role as the designer of the scenery and costumes for Campion's masque for the marriage of the Earl of Somerset in 1613, the stage mechanics for which failed to work. Sir John Summerson has provided a little detail, payments from the accounts and snatches of information from the Medici archives which indicate that de' Servi was also a painter and a garden designer and that he was, for instance, working on a huge giant for Richmond Palace three times the size of Giovanni Bologna's Mount Apennino at Pratolino. The fact is that de' Servi was in England for almost five years from 1611 to 1615, and that he was a polymath in the tradition of servants of the Medici court, one who was deliberately chosen by Cosimo II to act in all those capacities for the Prince of Wales. De' Servi was an international figure and his English period is one phase of an immensely complicated and totally uninvestigated nomadic career which deserves to be investigated in full.

De' Servi was born in Florence in about 1554 and trained initially as a painter under Santi di Tito (1536–1603).[3] Santi had returned to Florence from Rome in 1564, bringing with him the style of the Roman School based on Siciolante and Taddeo Zuccaro. During the next thirty years, responding to the influences of both Bronzino and Andrea del Sarto, he developed a style whose naturalistic tendencies ran counter to that favoured by the court of Francesco I, as typified by the other artists who contributed to his *studiolo*. More to the point is that de' Servi's earliest experiences were of grandducal Florence in the 1570s under the *principe dello studiolo*, whose polymathic court architect was Bernardo Buontalenti.[4] This unpopular Grand Duke was in many ways a prototype late Renaissance ruler in his obsession with the occult and the hermetic. The magical properties of nature were explored, harnessed and released in activities as varied as the grandducal workshops' manufacturing of objects of crystal and precious metals, the botanical and zoological drawings of Jacopo Ligozzi, or the *periaktoi* that achieved scene changes on the stages erected in the *gran salone*.

In 1579 de' Servi was in Rome, after which he was in the service of the Cardinal of Austria, at Innsbruck, then in that of Emperor Rudolf II, at Prague, followed, more surprisingly, by a year in Persia. We know that he was in Rome again in 1585, as Pope Sixtus V commissioned him to make a statue of St Paul to go on top of the Antonine column, for which he did a *modello*.[5] In 1586 he was in Naples. He is next recorded in Florence in 1602 attending a meeting, in his capacity as a specialist in the Florentine art of *pietre dure*, that pronounced in favour of Don Giovanni de' Medici's new *modello* for the Capella dei Principi. At that gathering there was also present Giovanni Bologna, Caccini, Francavilla, Santi di Tito, Cigoli, Allori, Passignano and the Grand Duke Ferdinand himself incognito. This implies that he was an important figure at the Tuscan court. In 1604 de' Servi was back in Prague again and wrote, at the request of the Duke, a report on the arts at the Rudolfine court. He wrote of Velvet Brueghel, Bartholomaeus Spranger, Hans von Aachen, Aegidio Sadelaer and Dionysio Miseroni.

De' Servi's presence there was due to the Emperor's passion for tableaux, mostly landscapes, made out of mosaics of stone, the so-called
commessi in pietra dura. The centre for this activity was Florence, and Rudolf had attracted to Prague Giovanni and Cosimo Castrucci. One of
these two was more than alarmed at de' Servi's appearance, and we get
a glimpse of the jealousies between rival artists jostling for imperial
favour which anticipated what was to happen in England. Under Cosimo II, who succeeded in 1608, de' Servi was appointed *Sopraintendente
della manifattura dei mosaici*.

His nomadic career has had the unfortunate result that no one until
now has ever produced a single work of art that we can assign to de'
Servi.[6] Although it has been suggested that he had a hand in the décor
for the *entrées* of Marie de' Medici into Avignon and Lyons in 1600
there is no evidence to support that hypothesis. In the book describing
the Avignon entry he is described as *ingenieur du roy*, which presupposes a period in the service of the Prince's hero, Henri IV.

At the end of September 1610, Ottaviano Lotti, the Tuscan Resident
in London, went to see Prince Henry's Chamberlain, Sir Thomas Chaloner. The latter had been instructed by the Prince to ask whether the
Grand Duke would release the two brothers, Tommaso and Alessandro
Francini, then in the service of the French crown, to come to work for
him. They would be better paid, he indicated, but, if it were not possible to get them, he asked the Duke to provide His Royal Highness with
a man who, like them, would be able to introduce into England *si belli
artifizii*. All of this was communicated in complete confidence because,
as Lotti wrote, the Prince feared being stopped.[7]

Tommaso (1571–1648) and Alessandro Francini went to France at
the close of the sixteenth century, at the behest of Henri IV, who was
recreating a new court life after the long years of religious civil war had
destroyed late Valois civilization.[8] They took with them from the Medici court all that was new both in the visual arts and in technical advance. Tommaso, or Thomas, was in charge of the design and layout of
the royal gardens, introducing both at Fontainebleau and Saint-Germain-en-Laye spectacular fountains and grottoes with symbolic automata on the lines of those at Pratolino. He was also responsible for the
mise-en-scène of the *ballets de cour*, which were rapidly developing into a
highly sophisticated art form ideally suited to expressing the political
outlook of the French monarchy. As in the case of the gardens, the
Francini were to introduce from Florence complex machinery on the
lines of that evolved for the spectacular *intermezzi*, above all abandon-
ing the theatre-in-the-round principle in favour of single-point perspective. The Francini could also, as easily, turn their hand to working

on a state entry, and in 1610 had been busy on that for Marie de' Medici into Paris. Prince Henry's request for the Francini brothers is therefore infinitely revealing of the programme he had in mind for the reform of the visual arts in England. It also suggests that, by the autumn of 1610, he had reached the conclusion that his own Surveyor, Inigo Jones, was incapable of producing what he wanted.

The Francini brothers, as it happened, could not be released (Thomas had in fact been naturalized as a Frenchman as early as 1600) but de' Servi, who was also in France in royal service at that moment, could be made available. In November he was in Paris, where he said he would be for the next seven or eight months until he had finished the task in hand, a portrait and a medal, which were ready for dispatch to Florence in April 1611. This meant that he did not reach England until early June, an unfortunate delay because Henry had by then made extensive use of the Huguenot hydraulic engineer, Salomon de Caus.[9] In spite of this he was well received by the Queen, an ardent promoter of all things Italian, who summoned both Lotti and de' Servi to Greenwich and ordered a portrait of someone so far unidentifiable, 'Signor Deonior', after which she agreed to sit herself.[10]

On 9 June, de' Servi wrote that he had left Greenwich for Richmond, where the Prince was to lay out a garden with grottoes and fountains, but the times were not propitious because there was a great dearth of money.[11] He records that the Prince was fascinated by such things and by pictures. Six days later Lotti reports of the high favour in which de' Servi stood with the Queen, 'who takes pleasure in the portraits from life he has painted for her', and with her first Lady of the Bedchamber, Jean Drummond. The architect and painter had been assigned a room in the palace, but now the Prince 'has ordered him to make designs for constructing fountains, summer houses, galleries and other things'.[12] He must have worked up his initial scheme with vast speed because, on 23 June, de' Servi was able to write to Florence that his *concetti* for the surrounding of Richmond Palace had delighted the Prince in contrast to those by '*questo franceze*' (Salomon de Caus) – the first hints of de' Servi's customary megalomania and desire to eliminate any form of competition. The Prince now desired that he work only for him, but de' Servi said that he would attempt to serve both Prince and Queen.[13]

Ottaviano Lotti wrote on 13 July:

And with one project in hand [the surroundings of Richmond Palace] and with other designs and schemes drawn up he [i.e. de' Servi] has greatly pleased His Highness, of whom he is now executing a life-sized portrait and he is so disposed towards him that he comes to see him in his lodging. He also willingly obeys him in painting life-size a horse that His Highness greatly loves; so from this point of view he has reason to hope that he has fallen on his feet. To me it is sad that Her Majesty the Queen, who wanted her portrait painted, was abandoned, but Signor Constantine could not divide himself in time and will rectify this in due course.[14]

A fortnight later his progress was such 'that others of his profession [Inigo Jones and de Caus?], that at first sought to impede him now pay him court'.[15] De' Servi's designs for the buildings at Richmond, being better than any of the others, were to go ahead. De' Servi tells us something about these in a letter five days later in which he informs Cioli that the Prince wishes him to make a giant three times the size of that at Pratolino (Giovanni Bologna's Appennino) with many rooms in it, a great dovecot in the head and two grottoes in the base.[16]

38

At the end of August de' Servi himself wrote at some length to the Grand Duke's secretary, describing his meteoric rise in princely esteem, achieved, us he put it, 'in spite of the interference of rivals'.[17] He petitions the Grand Duke that he be allowed to remain in England two years and dilates on the Prince's enthusiasm and judgment in matters of design, which were such that 'bad influences' would be eliminated. De' Servi was highly impressed by him, such was his kindness, goodness and knowledge, 'you would marvel at it'. There then follows a postscript with contents as remarkable as those in the letter of 13 July:

> I wish that you would approach their Most Serene Highnesses regarding something which the Prince has suggested to me. He desires that I should make some designs for *balletti* on the first occasion they are given here, and as I have not yet seen the manner and style of their contrivances for that reason I wish you to beg their Most Serene Highnesses to permit me to have a number of the sketches of the different designs formerly made by Bernardo delle Girandole [Buontalenti], or by others, either for masques, barriers, or *intermedii* from the time of the Grand Duke Francesco up to now. And though I could make them by myself, you know very well that everyone seeks to compose and improve according to his own ideas, I shall see what their customs are and shall use my own judgement in adding the rest as to give full satisfaction to the Prince and everyone.
>
> It seems to me in any case these things [the designs] are lying idle in the wardrobe and they are not things of great account as they have already been seen and used. And also they will be equally well kept in the Prince's wardrobe.

This is a request to send to England designs for the court festivals of the Medici by Buontalenti or Parigi. Within three months, de' Servi had progressed from painting portraits to designing the palace gardens to being commissioned to design the Prince's court festivals. Salomon de Caus and Inigo Jones were fast becoming redundant.

This rise in favour continued unabated into September when Lotti and de' Servi were summoned to Woodstock in order to look at the Prince's palace there.[18] On 22 August de' Servi wrote that he had now overcome every opposition and had been entrusted by the Prince with complete authority to carry out his designs,

... with the knowledge of the King, to whom two days ago, the Prince showed my solutions of the plan and disposition of the gardens, fountains and grottoes which I have prepared; so that there is no more danger of anyone else getting in front of me; and I am now making all the models of the statues and fountains aforesaid.[19]

Also at Woodstock, the Prince asked Lotti to petition the Grand Duke to allow de' Servi to stay.[20] Orders had been given at Richmond that he was to be obeyed in the building work, the designs for which had been seen by both the King and Salisbury.

The period following the establishment of de' Servi as the Buontalenti of the Prince's court can be treated as a single entity running from the autumn of 1611 to the Prince's death a year later. Having scored a tremendous success and vanquished all rivals, de' Servi, who, if the Prince had lived, would probably have taken architecture in England in a different direction, found himself confronted by that perennial misery besetting the Stuart kings, lack of money. De' Servi's letters give hints of this early on and in order to refund his travelling expenses Sir John Holles, Comptroller of the Household, had to borrow £102.10. from a merchant to meet the gift of £200 which the Prince had made at the beginning of August.[21] The sum of £200 was to be the architect's salary, which was four times that of Inigo Jones, indicating the prime position he occupied in the Prince's artistic policies.[22] In December Holles wrote to the Prince that trees had arrived for the Richmond garden and he indicated that de' Servi – who was a permanent troublemaker whose reactions to everything were characteristically volatile and Mediterranean, and who was now lodging in the Tower – 'will bring forth no models' without further payment, nor could the architect be brought closer to St James's without money.[23] De' Servi's own correspondence is depressingly preoccupied with money problems; he is forever harping on about his poverty, his exile from the Medici court in foreign lands, the necessity to provide for his wife and family and, periodically, for he was Catholic, the inability to attend to his devotions in a Protestant country. One of his sons, Gian Domenico, was indeed brought over and placed in the house of the Venetian ambassador, Antonio Correr. And, just to make things even more complicated, de' Servi fell out with Lotti, who became jealous of the influence the architect was gaining over the Prince. That the finances were an echo of reality we know only too well, for in the summer of 1612, subsequent to Salisbury's death, the Treasury was put into the hands of commissioners. Both Henry and his mother blamed the prodigality of the King and both were hampered in their patronage of the arts by a crippling lack of funds.

In spite of this there are astonishing references to the rebuilding of

Richmond Palace. These first appear in a letter of 24 July in which it is stated that de' Servi is spending all his time at Richmond with the Prince: 'where he [the Prince] untertakes to the designs of Signor Constantino de' Servi the great work of a new palace saying he wished to begin as soon as possible so that his wife would find it built'.[24] This is reiterated five days later in a second letter, which speaks of 'una gran fabrica d'un nuovo palazzo' which Henry wishes to be built immediately in time to receive his bride.[25] It is last referred to in a letter from the architect himself dated 9 August:

His Serene Highness keeps me occupied daily in diverse projects, and in particular for a palace that would be built from plan [*levar della pianta*], and every hour he is with me, having exhibited various demonstrations of his great taste....[26]

He then goes on to ask for his recall to Florence on various grounds and proceeds to list a few of them, including the persecution of Catholics, the fact that he had not been paid for a year, and 'the scarcity of money at this court'. In spite of this, within this correspondence, we have evidence of the first major royal building project since the 1530s, the rebuilding of Richmond Palace in the new classical style.

Throughout 1612 de' Servi was determined to be, if anything, reforming and was highly critical of the disorganization and waste in the management of the Prince's works operation which was characteristically a hydra-headed machine leaving plenty of opportunities for pickings to be made. Tuscany was one of the best run states in Europe and when it came to building administration that too was a model of efficiency. Needless to say, this did not endear de' Servi either to those previously in charge, or to the workmen and artificers. He was clearly horrified that he would have to carry through a major project of a new royal palace with what appeared to him such an inefficient and wasteful administrative machine. In a letter to the Prince he wrote on the matter at length.[27] In the spring, presumably of 1612 (the letter is undated), a *provveditore* or purveyor should be appointed to keep records of the architect's orders and see that nothing contrary to his wishes was done. He should keep proper day books and accounts and watch the progress of the work, seeing that no delay arose through lack of materials. Weekly or monthly he should present a report to the Comptroller. A tight watch was to be kept on prices and materials to avoid overcharging. He was to see that if two of anything were wanted four should not be ordered. In all, the *provveditore* was to be site manager, the architect's right-hand man, replacing all the people that at present he had to deal with. In short de' Servi asks to be an architect in the Renaissance sense, totally in charge of a building project run '*secondo lo stile di Fiorenza et altri luoghi di Italia in simili affari*' (according to the style of Florence and other places in Italy in similar undertakings).

De' Servi was particularly friendly with Sir Edward Cecil, a strong promoter of the Tuscan match, and was intending to take a house close to his 'for the convenience of working the models for the Prince and for being close to the men who would work on them'.[28] In October 1612 work was also in hand for the great series of fêtes to celebrate the marriage of Elizabeth to the Elector Palatine; this was the apogee of the Prince's policies, and to his period surely belongs another undated letter which sheds fascinating light on what was intended. As in the earlier one he requests the loans of

... two or three books of various inventions for masques, *intermezzi* and architecture to be sent to me for the time being.... The reason is that I may have to do something for the wedding, and I should then be able to borrow some ideas from them in addition to what I propose to do myself.... Once you have obtained them, do not tell anyone that they are for me, so as to avoid people finding out what I am copying and all the difficulties that would follow from that. Say instead that His Highness wants to see them in his private room, and tell nothing more.[29]

Although instructions were given that these were to be sent in bales of cloth to Burlamachi we have no way of knowing whether they came or not. We shall never know, for the wedding festivities as initially conceived never happened.

The intention before the Prince's death was that de' Servi was to return to Italy to arrange for materials to be sent for the Richmond palace project.[30] This did not happen and, as with other members of the household, he was left in a highly unsatisfactory state of suspense for some months. We know, however, that when at last the wedding of Elizabeth and the Elector Palatine did take place, in February 1613, de' Servi was responsible for the naval battle on the Thames,[31] and in March he is heard of as being in the house of Lord Hay working for him but hoping to get recalled to Italy to enter the service of Cosimo II's sister who had just become Duchess of Mantua. James, Lord Hay, later Viscount Doncaster, was a great favourite of the King's and noted for his extreme prodigality. While he was in his house de' Servi not only ran up debts but damaged the furniture. He also wrote that he was to act the part of a deaf man in a play and that he continued to paint portraits, including one of Prince Charles and another, commissioned by the King, of the Princess Elizabeth before she embarked for Heidelberg.[32] At the close of 1613 he reappears as the designer of the masque by Thomas Campion that marked the marriage of the notorious Frances Howard to Somerset.

With Thomas Campion's *Masque of Squires* we are actually dealing with the one major festival event at the Stuart court which de' Servi certainly designed.[33] What is so striking is that no fewer than three quite unconnected sources record that it was a disaster, the reasons for which could be laid firmly at the door of this arrogant Florentine architect. One source, inevitably hostile as he had seen his concept ruined, was the poet. He wrote of de' Servi:

… he, being too much him selfe, and no way to be drawne to impart his intentions, fayled so farre in the assurance he gave, that the mayne invention, even at the last cast, was of force drawne into farre narrower compasse than was from the beginning intended.[34]

On the English side there was the inevitable Chamberlain recording the general view of it of those who had been present: 'I hear little or no commendation of the mask made by the lords that night, either for device or dancing, only it was rich and costly.'[35] More interesting is the recently discovered hostile account by the agent of the Duke of Savoy.[36] He wrote:

The festivities turned out differently from people's expectations and the great preparations, they say, through the shortcomings of the architect, a Florentine who was in the service of the late prince. He has disgraced himself, if truth be told, and mis-spent much of these gentlemen's money....

He then goes on to tell us what happened. In the first case everything was unfinished, corroborating Campion's lament that the masque had had to be drastically revised and cut down at the last moment. Apart from the poor costumes and melancholy music, the main cause for complaint was the wretched cloud machine in which the masquers arrived. After the miracles of Jones's engineering in the poet's *Lords Masque* at the beginning of the year this machine 'turned out to be … a lowering device behind the cloud just like one used in dropping a portcullis … when it came down one could see the ropes that supported it and hear the pulleys, or rather wheels, making the same noise as when they raise or lower the mast of ship'. Worse still, the cloud descended with none of the customary 'loud music', so that all the audience heard was 'the screeching of the wheels'.

Catastrophe indeed! It looks as though the Prince had in his employ an Italian who was all sound and fury but incapable of producing concrete results. The crudity of this engineering certainly bears little relation to sophisticated effects attained in the Florentine *intermezzi*. Was the disaster due to a breakdown of communication between the designer and the workmen? It is difficult to dismiss the Somerset masque totally, for whatever its shortcomings the court had been looking at a series of scenes and machines designed and supervised by a man who was familiar with all that had been achieved at the Medici court.

INIGO·IONES·ARCHITECTOR
MAGNAE·BRITANIAE

F·VILLAMOENA·F

34 The Prince's Surveyor, Inigo
Jones

The Prince's architect, Constantino de' Servi

35 Knight masquer perhaps in
Campion's *Masque of Squires*, 1613

36 The car of Venus in the *Sbarra*
of 1579

37 The Harmony of the Spheres,
the first of the 1589 *intermezzi*

38 The giant Appennino at
Pratolino

The Prince's tutor
in perspective,
Salomon de Caus

39   Project for a giant with a grotto within

40   Project for a fountain adorned with Tudor roses

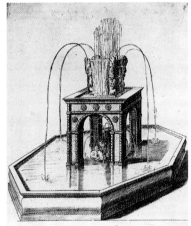

41   The Prince's palace of Richmond

42   The warrior Prince, a portrait
sent to the Duke of Savoy

43   Hendrik Goltzius's *Manlius
Torquatus*

The Prince's portraiture I

Portraits by Robert Peake

44   Clouet's equestrian portrait of
Henri II

45 The Prince seizes Opportunity by the forelock (picture in the process of restoration)

The Prince's portraiture II

Portraits by Oliver and Boel

46 George Clifford, 3rd Earl of
Cumberland, by William Rogers

47 Unknown man *à l'antique* by
Marcus Gheeraerts, *c.* 1610

48 Isaac Oliver's miniature of the
Prince *à l'antique*

49 Robert Devereux, 2nd Earl of
Essex, by William Rogers

HENRICVS PRINCEPS WALLIÆ MAGNÆ BRITANNIÆ REGIS PRIMOGENITVS.

ICH DIEN

C. Boel fecit. Petrus de Iode excudit

Rege ſub hoc, iunctis quem viribus alma Minerua
Et Natura parens ad meliora trahunt;
Anglia composito fiet noua Græcia bello,
Inque quiete artes, quas colit ipse, colet.

50 Boel's engraving of the Prince
flanked by Minerva and Nature,
c. 1612

Drawings as works of art:
Isaac Oliver

51   Moses striking the Rock

52   Nymphs and Satyrs

It is also important to remember that de' Servi's audience was a relatively unsophisticated one as far as his visual sense was concerned. The proscenium arch Campion admits was 'an Arch Tryumphall, passing beautifull' and the stage had steps to the dancing arena 'made exceeding curiously in the form of a Schalop shell'.[37] Scene change was by way of the *Scena ductalis*, the withdrawal of wings and back-shutters, and the scenes must have been in terms of perspective in the true Renaissance sense. The first scene was a garden leading to 'a Sea in perspective with ships, some cunningly painted, some arteficially sayling'.[38] The second was quite original, a view of 'London with the Thames'. This must have been within the tradition of known topographical locations such as Pisa or Siena usual for *commedie* at the Medici court.

De' Servi had written on 27 November that he was to be responsible for the *invenzioni* to celebrate the marriage, so that there is no need to exclude from his likely contribution another major event, the Tilt.[39] This was marked by a strongly Florentine input for it has been pointed out that the theme was directly lifted from the tilt staged in the Teatro Mediceo nine months before, on 11 February, only that one, on the subject of Eros and Anteros, had been considerably more complex.[40] The Somerset tilt was *alfresco* and its décor consisted of 'two handsome chariots or pageants'. The text was by Jonson, who gives no detailed description of them, but we can establish that one was drawn by swans and one by doves, and that on one rode Persuasion and the Graces and on the other Mercury, Youth, Audacity and Favour. *Carri trionfali* were a distinctive feature of Medici *fêtes* and there was a long tradition stretching through Vasari, Buontalenti and Parigi for processions and *sbarre*.[41] Those for the *sbarre* of both 1579 and 1589 had been engraved and published so that we cannot exclude the possibility that something like, for example, the chariot of Venus in the 1579 festival wended its way across the tiltyard at Whitehall.

36

This account of de' Servi ends with a question mark hanging over it. There is amongst the masque drawings at Chatsworth one which may be de' Servi's design for one of the masquers. It is feeble in quality. Nonetheless we should not underestimate the impact of this man's presence for nearly five years in England embodying, however inadequately, the Renaissance concept of the architect as *uomo universale*. At the least it must have been a contributory factor to Jones's second Italian visit. De' Servi's English period came to its close by 8 February 1615 when he wrote to Cioli from The Hague where he was in the service of Prince Henry's friend Maurice of Nassau and the States of Holland.

35

As we have seen, during the summer of 1611 de' Servi was systematically trying to deprive two men of the Prince's favour: Inigo Jones and *'questo franceze'*. That Frenchman, celebrated in his own time, was Salomon de Caus (1576–1626), an hydraulic engineer and garden designer, also well trained in the Vitruvian disciplines. As I have already dealt elsewhere with his contribution to garden history, what now follows must inevitably be a recapitulation but set in a quite different perspective and taking into account subsequent scholarship.[42]

De Caus came of a Huguenot family and was born in Normandy in 1576. There was a strong English connection because members of his family are recorded as worshipping at the French Reformed Church in London in 1600. To this we can add a new fact, that Salomon himself actually appears on the register of aliens for 1598.[43] That means he had been in England during the late Elizabethan period. Sometime during the late 1590s, however, like so many other figures that make up the fabric of this book, he had travelled in Italy. There he was influenced in particular by the gardens of the Villa d'Este, by those at Frascati and, above all, by the Medici villa of Pratolino, which was famed throughout Europe for its fabulous water effects in the form of huge fountains and cascades, extraordinary grottoes and miraculous automata constructed in emulation of those of Hero and the School of Alexandria. De Caus also kept abreast of garden developments in the palaces of Henri IV brought about by the Francini brothers and Claude Mollet. He first worked for the Archdukes Albert and Isabella from about 1603–4 and appears to have come to England in a fit of pique in 1607–8.

His initial work came from Anne of Denmark and the accounts indicate this starting in 1609. At Somerset House he built a huge fountain in the form of Mount Parnassus with Apollo and the Muses on its summit and four rivers reclining at its base, imagery prefiguring that of the creation masque, *Tethys' Festival*. As a whole it was almost a copy of the famous Parnassus at Pratolino. Simultaneously he reordered her garden at Greenwich and supervised a second fountain with a reclining river goddess, this time inspired by the *Fontaine du Tibre* at Fontainebleau, and a grotto-aviary. De Caus includes engravings of these with slight variations of detail in his book *Les Raisons des Forces Mouvantes* (1615–24).

We need to consider in greater detail his work for the Queen's son, Prince Henry. On the creation of his household in 1610–11 it was de Caus and not Inigo Jones who was appointed his 'Architect' at £100 p.a., twice what Jones was paid as Surveyor, and half what de' Servi was to get a year later.[44] But the relationship went back earlier, because in his book on perspective de Caus states in the preface, dated 1 October

1611, that he had given lessons to the Prince in this subject for two or three years, which would take us back to 1608 when the Prince was fourteen.

De Caus's work for Henry was only at Richmond Palace.[45] Unlike   41 that for Anne of Denmark, we have very little idea of what it actually looked like because it was never finished and no one at the time bothered to describe it. One thing, however, is clear and that is that it was on a far larger scale than either of Anne's projects. Between June 1611 and November 1612 not less than £10,000 was spent on Richmond Palace. Work began in 1610 with the building of a cistern house which was apparently never finished. This was to convey water by means of lead pipes to three islands which had been created between the palace and the Thames, to which access was had by way of a system of bridges and steps.[46] It is likely that de Caus did not design this layout, for payments exist to Mountain Jennings, Robert Cecil's gardener, for 'drawinge sundrye plattes of the orcharde howse, ffriers, and the three Islandes', with charges for commuting to and from Hatfield (where de Caus also worked).[47] This would make sense as the arrangement belongs in sequence to a whole series of gardens created more or less simultaneously in the form of islands, rivers and fountains making use of water: Francis Bacon's Gorhambury, for which a 'plat' was made in 1608, Cecil's Hatfield begun in 1609 and the remodelled garden at Ware Park, the country house of the Prince's devoted friend, Sir Henry Fanshawe, which was in the making in 1613.[48] De Caus's work at Richmond was to be an elaborate series of grottoes, what one of the accounts refer to as 'the devises of the Frenchman which cannot be valued because unknown'.[49]

What also remains unknown is what happened after de' Servi began to be employed for the garden projects during the summer of 1611. Were de Caus's designs abandoned, as his correspondence implies? We have no evidence to guide us as to what happened. There is a reference to the fact that work stopped at Richmond in August 1611, owing probably to lack of money but perhaps also to the fact that de' Servi was preparing his great schemes. But de Caus was back there in 1613 after the Prince's death, so we are no nearer a solution.[50]

Two sources give us an impression of what was planned. One is purely atmospheric, a view from a landing to the water and what looks like an island in the background of a portrait of the Prince. The second is the series of engravings in *Les Raisons*, the second part of which is dedicated to the Prince's sister, Elizabeth, and dated 1 January 1615/16.[51] In it he states that he is printing the designs he made while he was in Henry's service, some of which were for Richmond and others '*pour satisfaire à sa gentille curiosité qui desiroit touriours voir & coignoister quelque chose nouveau*'. One which was certainly for him is a simple fountain adorned with Tudor roses, with jets falling into an octagonal basin. This he had already published in his *La Perspective*. Others are far more strange: one is a reclining river god giant, seemingly an island, and there is another giant sitting, perched also on a mountain but this time having a grotto within it. Both derive from Giovanni da Bologna's Apennino at Pratolino. There is a *tempietto* for the centre of a garden or a labyrinth, a fountain of Cupid, a nymph playing an hydraulic organ, a grotto with automata depicting Pan and Apollo before Midas, another with a triumph of Neptune and a design for a rectangular hill, 55 feet high, with a walkway up to a recreation of the Alexandrian speaking statue of Memnon.

Regardless of what happened, the drift of his work is clear. The Prince was creating a kind of Stuart Pratolino or Villa d'Este in which the Mannerist alliance of science and art in garden terms would be manifest. It would have been filled with statuary and automata which would have subjected visitors not only to the experiences of wonder and surprise but also to knowledge as they comprehended the emulation of the mechanical marvels of the Alexandrian school and understood the symbolic content of each tableau. The Prince's garden mania should therefore be seen in conjunction with his scientific preoccupations.

We can perhaps appreciate better the intellectual context of de Caus's Richmond by going forward in time a few years and studying his masterpiece, the Hortus Palatinus, created for Elizabeth and Frederick, as Count and Countess Palatine of the Rhine.[52] De Caus published in 1620 a series of engravings of this vast project which was never completed owing to the outbreak of the Thirty Years War which was eventually to destroy it. Richard Patterson has made an important, if highly speculative, analysis of its meaning.[53] He draws attention to de Caus's grotto mythology, which makes 'repeated allusions to music as an aspect of universal harmony, and to the mechanical-rational-harmonic powers of music to effect satisfaction through the just delineation of proportion'. De Caus's later book, *Institution Harmonique* (1615), dedicated to Anne of Denmark, firmly places him in that stream of 'reform' stemming from the French Academies and the *pléiade* at the Valois court who attempted to revive ancient music in order to recapture its ethical effects on the listener. De Caus's view of the cosmos therefore derives from the tradition of Euclid, Pythagoras and Plato in their Renaissance guise: the structure of the universe and man's ability to tune himself to it being dependent on number. The development of music he regards as the progressive imposition of number upon an unconscious musical practice. In his instance the numerological – musicological – cosmological analogies extend into mechanical and technical matters. The garden and the grotto are thus expressions of the reformation of nature as well as means whereby nature might be studied in the Baconian sense as a path towards knowledge: 'much more of nature under constraint and vexed; that is to say, when by art and the hand of man she is forced out of her natural state, and squeezed and moulded'.

How far all this found expression in the plans for Richmond it is impossible to say. For Henry there is no doubt that the garden would also have vividly fulfilled another aspect of the Hortus Palatinus, one familiar from Tudor palace gardens: a eulogy of the ruling house. But this time it would not have taken the simple form of the traditional vocabulary of coats of arms and symbols but the wider encyclopaedic reference which is implicit in all the great palace gardens of the period, that is of giving visible form to the idea of the ruler as the source of all political, cultural and material largesse and patronage by drawing within its orbit all flowers, trees, plants, fruits, together with the cycle of the seasons, with water as a flowing, serpentining, spouting, unifying element.

One aspect more of de Caus calls for elaboration and that is his book on perspective. In it he bills himself as '*Ingénieur du Sérénissime Prince de Galles*'.[54] The dedication states that he had taught Henry perspective, a startling novelty in itself, which of all the sciences dependent on mathematics is that most essential to those who practise painting and architecture. He quotes Vitruvius's definition of architecture as being concerned with order and proportion and writes that such works and buildings that the Prince shall erect need to be governed by such principles. He adds that he is including in the book a section on shadows for the benefit of painters, 'for one cannot depict anything well in painting if the shadows are not done with some reason'.[55] This is the first treatise ever published on the subject in England, issued in the same year that Henry Peacham refers to 'a discourse of perspective I will shortly publish' – which he never did.[56] Books on perspective were not uncommon in libraries, although it is noticeable that they are found in those of people whose passion was building. Interest in perspective and chiaroscuro as essential attributes of the art of painting began to be understood and referred to in earnest only in the 1590s; thus the standard Renaissance means of perceiving pictured surfaces were received into England somewhat belatedly.[57] De Caus works from a Renaissance concept of the architect as the purveyor in building terms of the microcosm – macrocosm analogy. The inclusion of painting moves from the same premise, its participation in the mathematical arts. That all this should appear in London in 1612 in a lavishly illustrated book whose dedication is signed as from Richmond Palace is a rich monument to this late Renaissance court and an index of the Prince's interests, explaining his visual demands for his festivals and his quest for a painter in the new style.

De Caus left England in 1613 to work in Heidelberg, where his career was again cut short by the war. Later he worked for Louis XIII and he died in Paris in 1626. By then his younger brother, Isaac, was in England working for the sister of the Prince's dearest friend, Lucy Harington, Countess of Bedford. In this work was to be revived one of the major themes: the new gardening.

34   Inigo Jones (1573–1652) was even younger than de Caus. In 1610 he was thirty-seven. As we have noted, his salary was half that of the Frenchman and a quarter of that of the Italian, facts which neatly reveal the pecking order at the Prince of Wales's court. He was a figure of diminishing importance, increasingly overshadowed by the two foreigners and confronted by the cruel reality that when he became Surveyor to the Prince he had never actually erected a building. These two years were almost his ruin. We are so used to seeing Jones as the 'Vitruvius Britannicus', the Vitruvian architect–engineer who dominated the artistic policies of the Stuart court in the years after 1615, that we have lost sight of Jones as he was in the years before.

His background was very different from that of de' Servi.[58] Born in London in 1573, the first fact that we have for certain about him is a payment in the accounts of Roger Manners, 5th Earl of Rutland, in 1603 as a 'picture maker'. Two years later he was referred to as 'a great Traveller' and the reason why he accompanied Lord and Lady Arundel on their Italian tour of 1613–14 was 'by means of his language and experience in those parts'. These fragments would suggest an early life something along the lines of an apprenticeship to one of the painters of the day in the 1590s, perhaps Gheeraerts or more probably Peake. Soon after his father died in 1597 he must have travelled abroad and the most likely way would have been in the train of Lord Rutland's brother, Francis Manners, later Lord Roos, who left England in 1598 for a tour through France, Germany and Italy. In 1603 Jones the painter was back in England but he left it shortly after in the train of Rutland, who was sent to Denmark to invest Christian IV with the Order of the Garter. In Danish records he appears as 'M. Johns'.[59] And it was perhaps through the Danish king that he was brought to the notice of his sister, the new queen, Anne of Denmark. By the close of 1604 he must have been working on the scenery and costumes of the revolutionary production of Ben Jonson's *Masque of Blackness*.

In the years that followed up to 1610 he designed certainly two more masques and possibly more. The certain ones are *Hymenaei* (1606) and the *Masque of Queens* (1609). In addition to this he designed the scenery for the plays performed during the visit of the court to Oxford in 1605 and a series of entertainments given by Robert Cecil at Theobalds (1606 and 1607), Salisbury House (1608), and for the opening of the New Exchange (1609).[60] And it was Salisbury who seems to have been responsible for his first essays in building. In 1608 Jones prepared a design for Salisbury's New Exchange, called Britain's Burse, and about the same time did a project for the completion of the tower and spire of Old St Paul's Cathedral, a project under the auspices of a commission on which Salisbury sat.[61] Both belong to the fantasy world of the masque rather than to that of reality. Britain's Burse was built by Simon Basil according either to his own design or to an interpretation of Jones's. There is no way of knowing, but one thing is more definite. In 1610 Jones seems to have revised Robert Liming's design for the south front and clock tower of Hatfield House.[62] It is a hesitant essay, in the main French in inspiration with Italianate detail. In this instance Jones was taking part in the typical process whereby a great Elizabethan or Jacobean house arose. The instigator was always the patron, who called on one or many people for what he required, and who would certainly alter anything as he pleased as he went along. It is also important to remember that there was no lack of building enterprises during the opening years of the new reign, either by the crown or by the aristocracy, which indicates that few people as yet associated Jones with building or perhaps even regarded him as capable of doing it.

In this light it becomes the more surprising that he was appointed Surveyor to the Prince's court at all.[63] One can only surmise as to what led to the decision. In the first instance, Henry would have been familiar with Jones's work for court masques, and festivals were an integral part of his policy. In the second, the Prince would have known that he worked for Salisbury, whom he respected. In the third, there was no one else in England at the time who could have offered an alternative to the traditional Office of Works style, that of the Surveyor, Simon Basil, which was the usual late Elizabethan neo-Gothic with a Netherlandish Mannerist overlay. Given Prince Henry's reverence for Henri IV, Jones's eligibility would have been strengthened by his visit to France in 1609; there he certainly studied French court art and architecture of the school of Fontainebleau.[64] In addition he toured Provence studying the antiquities: the Pont du Gard, the Maison Carré and the temple of Diana at Nîmes, the Roman theatre at Orange and antique sarcophagi at Arles. Gordon Higgott has recently established these facts,[65] experiences which Jones would have undergone some time after 11 April 1609, when his entertainment for the opening of the New Exchange on the Strand was staged, but before he was paid for having delivered 'Letters for his majesty's service into ffraunce'. What has not been pointed out is that this precedes by only a few months the tour of Lord Salisbury's son, Prince Henry's friend, Lord Cranborne, in September to the same sites. Surely Jones must have been an influence on determining the young lord's route? He was then working virtually full time for Salisbury. From the moment of his return we find constant references to this French experience.[66] Jones was a bold choice, made in the immediate aftermath of his spectacular décor for the *Barriers*, for his appearance on the payroll of the household dates from just a week after that event, 13 January 1610.

Prince Henry's Office of Works existed for so short a period of time that its organization and effectiveness cannot be judged and certainly it led to confusion with the King's Office. We know of no specific commissions to Jones in the way of building and it seems doubtful that the Prince ever thought of him as an 'architect'. De' Servi occupied that post; it is referred to both in the accounts and by Thomas Campion, who specifically acknowledges him as 'Architect to our late Prince Henry'.[67] After his arrival there is no evidence that Jones designed any of the Prince's festivals and the indications are that he was not, at the time of Henry's death, thought of as designer for those for the marriage of the Princess Elizabeth. Jones must have been made to feel how very inferior a surveyor was and it must have sharpened, if not initiated, his desire to be an architect. It is surely significant that the earliest reference we have to Jones as an architect occurs just three months after de' Servi's arrival. Thomas Coryate, the traveller who was patronized by the Prince, on 11 September asked eleven of his cronies to a 'philosophical feast' at The Mitre, Fleet Street. They included Lionel Cranfield, later Earl of Middlesex, Sir Henry Nevill, John Donne, Sir Robert Phelps, Richard Cannock, the Prince's auditor, John Hoskins, lawyer and poet, Sir Henry Goodyere, poet and emblematist, Hugo Holland, Arthur Ingram, the merchant, and Inigo Jones, described as

> *Nec indoctus nec profanus*
> *Ignatius architectus.*[68]
> (Neither unlearned nor uninitiated,
> Inigo the architect.)

May one speculate that native feathers had been ruffled? In 1613 George Chapman almost goes out of his way to refer to him in his

Memorable Masque as 'our kingdom's most artfull and ingenious architect'.[69] Was this a riposte to the foreigner? Inigo Jones was *our kingdom's
architect* although he had never actually put up one building! Here was
no arrogant, troublesome foreigner and a Roman Catholic to boot.

In the event his masques for the great marriage were so successful
that he obtained the reversion of the Surveyorship of the Office of
Works. With that in the offing and with the unnerving experience of
the previous two years, suddenly, at the age of forty, he had to learn
about architecture in detail. Without the inadequacy that he was made
to feel under de' Servi it is probable that he would never have gone
again to Italy. And even if he had he would not have worked with the
passion that he did, for he had to return this time not a picture maker
but the 'Vitruvius Britannicus' who would eliminate any question of
future foreign competition.

By 1610 the purveyance of official portraits of the royal family had become the prerogative of three artists: John de Critz (1553–1641) and
Robert Peake (*fl.* 1576–1616), who in 1607 were appointed joint Ser-
jeant Painters to the King, and de Critz's brother-in-law, Marcus
Gheeraerts the Younger (*fl.* 1561; d. 1635). In European terms, by the
opening of the second decade of the seventeenth century they were all
decidedly old-fashioned. The formal state portrait and its mass manu-
facture in the court painter's studio were to become a problem of increasing importance for the absolutist monarchies. Royal portraiture
transmuted the physical reality of a ruler into a metaphysical idea. The
acquisition of a portrait painter able to meet and express those ideals
and capable of running a studio that could maintain the production of
copies of quality occupied the mind of every European ruler. In England the eventual solution was Van Dyck, but it was a problem that was
pondered twenty years before by Prince Henry.

The Prince swiftly recognized the inadequacy of his portrait painters
in large (he was always aware of the genius of Oliver). Of John de
Critz's *oeuvre* little is known.[70] He is recorded as having painted a full-
length of the Prince in 1606 but what little we can disentangle of his
work suggests an extremely pedestrian painter turning out flat decorative icons of king, queen and court in the formalist style of the late Elizabethan era. Of the three, Gheeraerts was by far the most avant garde,
having risen to prominence in the 1590s under the patronage of Sir
Henry Lee, for whom he painted a portrait of the Prince.[71] Gheeraerts's   17
style is akin to that of Isaac Oliver but in large, and betrays knowledge
of developments in the Antwerp school in the era of Pourbus. As an
artist he was extensively patronized by the Queen, but curiously there

is no evidence of any interest by Prince Henry, and no portrait by Gheeraerts, whose style is fully established, can be identified from the years 1610 to 1612.

The role of painter to the Prince fell to Robert Peake, whose work was entirely in the tradition of the old Queen's reign and who was decidedly tired and past his prime.[72] It is difficult to know why Henry chose him, although the Prince had a strong sense of loyalty and Peake had produced images of him consistently since his arrival south, paint-

24   ing the strikingly original portraits of him *à la chasse*.[73] The Prince was eleven when these were painted and already they represent a quite unprecedented innovation in royal portraiture, the placing of the sitter into a landscape setting, something first essayed by Gheeraerts in the 1590s in his *Captain Thomas Lee* (1594). The subject, *Le Roi à la Chasse*, was also new for formal portraiture, although Peake would have been familiar with the woodcuts in Turbervile's *Book of Hunting* (1575), which were reissued in the new reign with the figure of Elizabeth replaced by that of James I. The format, for which there is likely to emerge an engraved source, is of a figure kneeling in adoration, and the Prince's pose is based on Holbein's famous likeness of Henry VIII as reinterpreted by William Scrots for the boy king, Edward VI. This is not the only innovative portrait of the Prince by Peake, for an even more startling one has recently come to light in Turin, where it must

42   have been sent as a gift to the Duke of Savoy.[74] Once again the Prince is set into one of Peake's naïve landscapes, this time with a moat and castle in the distance, perhaps an allusion to Richmond Palace. The pose, however, is a totally original one in English royal portraiture, the Prince being shown about to unsheath his sword in a defiant gesture, one foot being placed on a shield bearing his arms of the three feathers. The costume is close to the 1604 group and it must have been painted between that date and 1610. This time we can pinpoint the

43   source, for it is lifted direct from Hendrik Goltzius's engraving of Manlius Torquatus from his *The Roman Heroes* (*c.*1586). It is difficult not to think that the Prince deliberately chose this, thus casting himself into the role of one of the great heroes of Roman history. Payments for portraits by Peake of the Prince straddle the years 1608 to 1611–12, when he was finally paid £50 for 'twoe great Pictures of the Prince in Armes at length sent beyond seas'.[75] Peake was an artist directly in the Hilliardesque linear tradition, with its accent on pattern and decoration, its use of pastel shades, its seeming obliviousness of linear or aerial space and its total avoidance of any form of *chiaroscuro*. In a way the Prince's retention of him in his service is fully consonant with the ambiguities of his cultural policy which always looked consciously back to

and glorified the Elizabethan era that it was reviving but simultaneously overlaid it with the latest developments in the arts.

One portrait by Peake is so important that it must be discussed in
even greater detail: the astonishing life-size picture at Parham Park,
which has recently been cleaned.[76] The picture was entirely over-
painted and slightly reduced at the top in the late seventeenth century;
from beneath this Italianate overlay in the manner of Titian has
emerged virtually a new painting. The cleaning uncovered what must
rank as Peake's most ambitious portrayal of the Prince. British mon-   45
archs were traditionally represented on horseback on the reverse of
their seals and there are precedents for both James and Henry in popular engravings. But the source here must be French and the closest parallel is an equestrian portrait of Henri II attributed to Clouet. The   44
poses of both horse and sitter in this portrait are virtually identical to
those of Peake; also alike is the treatment of the foreground with its
grass and foliage on which the horse parades. In both, the background
consists of a wall, in the case of Henry inset with two plaques bearing
his triple plume and motto and his initials, HP.

What is added, however, is a quite unprecedented allegorical overlay, the figure of a nude old man with wings and a beard walking behind the horse, bearing in his hands the Prince's lance and helmet
while his forelock is drawn forward and tied to the favour extending
backwards from Henry's arm. There can be no doubt that what we are
looking at is the Prince seizing Opportunity by the forelock. The more
familiar Renaissance casting of *Occasio* was as feminine, due to her fusion with *Fortuna*, but here we have the original masculine figure of
Time as 'Kairos', that is that brief, decisive moment which marks a
turning point in the life of human beings or in the history of the universe.

On the bases, which he wears over his armour, and on the horse caparisons there is an *impresa* depicting a hand clutching an anchor arising out of the waters backed by a range of mountains with a sun rising
behind them. There is no motto but the allusions are clearly to a combination of the familiar emblem of the ascending sun, embodying future hopes, with a reworking of the Arthurian legend of the sword Ex-
calibur, which the chosen warrior receives. In this version the anchor
of hope has replaced the sword.

That the Prince was interested in revamping his portrait image there
can be no doubt for he sat for de' Servi in the summer of 1611 and
again in 1612.[77] Already, at the beginning of that year, we have evidence that he had begun a serious quest for a court painter and had
reached the conclusion that, as in the case of his architect and

engineer, such a person would have to be recruited from abroad. On 5 (15) February 1611 Sir Edward Conway, Governor of Brill, one of the cautionary towns held by the English, wrote to the Prince's secretary, Adam Newton, about the 'painter of Delft' whom the Prince had commissioned him to approach.[78] The painter's name is never actually given in the correspondence but it must have been Michiel Jansz van Mierevelt (1567–1641). Conway encloses a copy of a letter from the painter, together with a translation (neither survives), and writes: 'I beseech you, that I may hear from you, whether his Highness will command me any farther in it.' Some months later he returned to the topic:

I have spoken with the painter of Delft, who hath been wonderfully confounded with the variety of propositions, and trouble, that he hath not received answer of his letter from Sir Noel Caron (the Dutch ambassador in London); but now he is fully resolved to go into England, and to give himself wholly to his Highness's service, and depend upon his reward.[79]

He awaits not money but the Prince's pleasure. On 11 (21) June he sent through Conway a second letter, but Conway saw no point in the painter crossing into England then as the court would be on progress until the end of August.[80] He petitioned for instructions again in July and August,[81] but the matter was dropped until January 1612, when he reported that 'the painter of Delft is so fantastical, as I cannot get conditions'. Obviously negotiations had taken a turn for the worse.[82] The last reference appears in a letter of 14 (24) February, with the painter still apparently earnest in his desire to cross the channel.

But he loves himself and his acquaintance so well, as can hardly resolve how to value his time and his skill. This was the time he took to bring me his resolute demand, that I might receive your advice upon it. But yet he is not come, and I may in part excuse it.[83]

And there the matter rested.

Michiel Jansz van Mierevelt was born and died in Delft.[84] He is best known for his portraits of members of the House of Orange-Nassau, which is doubtless how the Prince came to know his work. For him also sat a number of the English who served in the wars. As court portraitist to the martial Prince of Wales he would have been ideally suitable. He specialized in aristocratic portraits, often only head and shoulders, in which his plasticity of modelling gave a brilliant three-dimensional likeness of his sitters, whose costume was rendered with minute precision as lace cascaded over black damask and silk. A glance at any of his portraits of Maurice of Nassau in comparison with the feeble work of Peake makes the point admirably. What was more, the studio production was far superior to anything in England at the time, being able to produce endless copies and variations of a single portrait without the dramatic loss in quality which was such a marked feature of the Jacobean workshops. Sandrart records that during his lifetime Mierevelt painted more than 10,000 portraits. It is significant that both the Princess Elizabeth and the Elector Palatine sat for him en route for Heidelberg in 1613. The project to bring over Mierevelt harmonizes also with the Prince's predilection for Netherlandish art, and it is interesting to add as a footnote that it was his pupil Daniel Mytens that was eventually recruited to introduce the new style of portraiture in, or a little before, 1618.

Prince Henry's portraiture is in one way a monument to frustration but its iconography reveals vividly his unfulfilled aspirations as much as it does his ambiguity. Spenserian knight and Roman imperator rolled into one in the same way that the Elizabethan iconic tradition continues to live side by side with these new up-to-date essays in a more international style. Two artists Henry never patronized; one was William Larkin, the exponent *par excellence* of the insular style, the other Marcus Gheeraerts, his mother's painter. The latter is more surprising for around 1610 his work certainly betrays the influence of the St James's circle. Two portraits of young men *à l'antique*, with looped togas around their shoulders, reveal familiarity with Oliver's image of the Prince and, probably, the antique costumes worn by Henry and his companions in both the *Barriers* and *Oberon*. So too must Larkin's portraits of Lord Herbert of Cherbury and Sir Thomas Lucy, both in the same manner painted in 1609–10.[85] These images form part of a group of works of art that reveal the earliest serious stirring of interest in the antique in the Jacobean period traceable simultaneously also in engraving, architecture and monumental sculpture.

Although Robert Peake was to remain the Prince's 'picturemaker' until his death, the problem of finding someone to supplant him as the purveyor of large-scale portraits was to be solved in a surprising way, for in the funeral cortège it was Isaac Oliver who was to walk as his 'Paynter' and a 'Mr Bilford' as his 'lymner'.[86] We know a little about Bilford for he is recorded as one of the 'principal gentlemen' in the entourage of Sir Henry Wotton. It was Wotton who had laid a wager that this man would 'draw or pourtray the Prince better than Isaack the French painter in Blackfriers'.[87] The bet was in terms of 'choice pictures' on the part of Wotton and horses by the Prince. No identifiable miniature has come to light which we can assign to Bilford, but his appearance as a member of the household in its last months indicates that whatever the result of the wager, Oliver had been moved over to large-scale portraiture and Bilford had been brought in to provide the miniatures. All this must have happened in the aftermath of the collapse of the negotiations in February 1612 with Mierevelt. Oliver, of course, was quite capable of painting on canvas and panel, although again we are faced with the fact that nothing has so far emerged. Three oil paintings by him descended to Theodore Russell, whose son, Anthony, was Vertue's informant about the artist. The subjects were a self-portrait, a Holy Family and a St John the Baptist.[88] For the moment, however, let us put this problem to one side and look instead at how this extraordinary artist reflected exactly the aesthetic preoccupations and ambitions of the St James's court.

Oliver, like de Caus, was a Huguenot, a fact that would certainly have recommended him to the Prince. As far as we disentangle his career, he must have travelled a great deal on the Continent before settling in London at the close of the 1580s. And, as in the case of de Caus and of Inigo Jones, he had travelled in Italy in the mid-1590s. In June 1605 he was appointed 'painter for the Art of Limning' at £40 p.a. to Anne of Denmark, a post into which we need not read any exclusion from the ability to paint in other forms. The early miniatures of Henry are surprisingly not by Oliver but by Hilliard or attributable to his pupil, Rowland Lockey. The Lockey miniature is dated 1607 and the year after Hilliard was paid for one given to the Landgrave of Hesse.[89] One in the Royal Collection by Hilliard dates from about the same period.[90] It is noticeable that from the moment that Henry developed his precocious aesthetic consciousness he switched his patronage to Oliver. All the miniatures of him as Prince of Wales stem back to two sittings. The first is a profile image *à l'antique*, of which three versions are known.[91] These depict him silhouetted against a classical shell niche wearing a cuirass in the antique manner with a crimson mantle looped around his shoulders secured by a jewel.

In view of the descriptions of his face, which at the close of 1611 evolved from boyishness into a lean angularity resembling his mother's, we can date these portraits to sometime during that year. They reflect exactly the image projected in the two major festival manifestations of the *Barriers* and *Oberon*. In the first he is described as 'like Mars ... in his armour clad'; in the second he actually appeared as a Roman emperor processing in triumph. In addition, the profile brought with it an allusion to his ancestor, the warrior Henry V, 'to whom in face you are / so like', as Jonson states in the *Barriers*. All the portraits of Henry V, familiar through repetitions for inclusion in the long gallery sets of kings and queens, show him in profile. The allusion at the time would have been an obvious one.

48

The second sitting must have been in 1612, and the prime original is without doubt Oliver's greatest royal portrait, the large miniature still **33** in the Royal Collection, in which the Prince stands before a crimson curtain wearing splendidly gilt armour with the Garter ribbon swagged across it and the Lesser George projecting out over the gold border, providing precisely that element of optical illusion and trickery admired by devotees of 'curious painting'.[92] The portrait is rendered with bravura brilliance in his tight manner, while the encampment behind, with its tents and warriors *à l'antique* in the manner of the School of Fontainebleau, and the gun in the foreground, are painted with loose flickering brushstrokes to produce the picture's dreamlike quality. A number of other versions exist of this portrait on a smaller scale but we can rarely tell whether they were painted before or after the Prince's death.[93]

So integral was Oliver to the provision of the princely image that it was he and not Peake who was called upon to make the drawings for the two major engraved portraits produced after Henry had been created Prince: those by Simon van de Passe and Cornelius Boel. These I shall discuss shortly. In addition, payments in the accounts to Oliver indicate that he was of use to Henry in other ways, mainly as an agent for the purchase of pictures for the collection.[94] His qualification for this would have been his remarkable knowledge of the work of the major artists of the sixteenth century through travels and work in Italy, France and the Low Countries. We can enlarge on this by considering the most tantalizing aspect of the artist's work, his drawings.

Isaac Oliver's drawings still constitute one of the enigmas of Elizabethan and Jacobean art.[95] The earliest is dated 1586 and it is likely that they were produced throughout his life, although there is no doubt that the evidence, or what little that we have, would suggest that the majority were executed in the Jacobean period. Jill Finsten wrote of them:

In their self-conscious virtuosity these drawings are the visual counterparts of the learned treatises commissioned for the most part by Prince Henry; in their technical achievement they give evidence of a kind and a degree of artistic vitality and ambitiousness not previously known to exist in England during this period.[96]

Finsten lists nearly fifty drawings that could be by Oliver, thirteen of which are or appear to be signed.[97] Many of the attributions are inevitably debatable and not helped by the artist's wide-ranging eclecticism. Within the certain signed ones he draws from sources as diverse as Wtewael and Bloemart through the School of Fontainebleau to the Caracci and Zuccari. Broadly, the result is what we would categorize as northern Mannerist. In addition, the references are to a taste which would have been thoroughly at home in the contents of the picture gallery at St James's.

I do not intend to embark on a detailed consideration of these drawings. What is significant is that they are the first drawings ever done in England as works of art in their own right, something which had happened in Italy as early as the *quattrocento*, and that a number of important ones appear in early catalogues of the Royal Collection. One of the inventories was made between 1662 and 1685 and the second in the reign of James II. The items are:

Charles II[98]
(i) 'A drawing of many figures with a glass over it'
(ii) 'A Baccanale. A small drawing in greenish & white Colo:^{rs}'
(iii) 'Many figures, wth a dog at one end. A drawing in black & white'

James II[99]
(iv) 'A drawing in black and white of the rape of the Sabines'
(v) 'A drawing in black and white of the journey of the children of Israel'
(vi) 'A drawing in black and white of satyrs and women sporting'.

51, 52   Numbers (ii) and (iv) are identical and the drawing is still in the Royal Collection, as is number (v). The others are lost or unidentifiable. Although it is conceivable that they entered the collection at a later date there is no reason to doubt that they went back to Charles I and the possibility that they were part of Prince Henry's collection cannot be eliminated.

This cannot be proved but the sudden emergence and appreciation of drawings as works of art can be linked to the Prince's circle. In 1612 Henry Peacham, a hanger-on of the St James's court and a popularizer of its ideals, published his *Graphice,* an updated edition of his *The Art of Drawing with the Pen* (1606), which is the earliest publication to make any plea at all that gentlemen should learn to draw.[100] The *Graphice* was also issued in the same year under another title, *The Gentleman's Exercise,* and this was one of his most widely read works. The 1612 editions were graced with the Prince's arms and there are major revisions in the content revealing that Peacham in the intervening years had seen pictures and other works of art that he had not known about six years earlier. Apart from the Prince, he lists Salisbury as 'the principall patrone of this art' and the Earls of Arundel, Worcester, Southampton, Pembroke, Suffolk and Northampton. The picture gallery at St James's must have been a contributing factor to this experience and, as a result, drawing in this publication emerges with an immensely enhanced status.

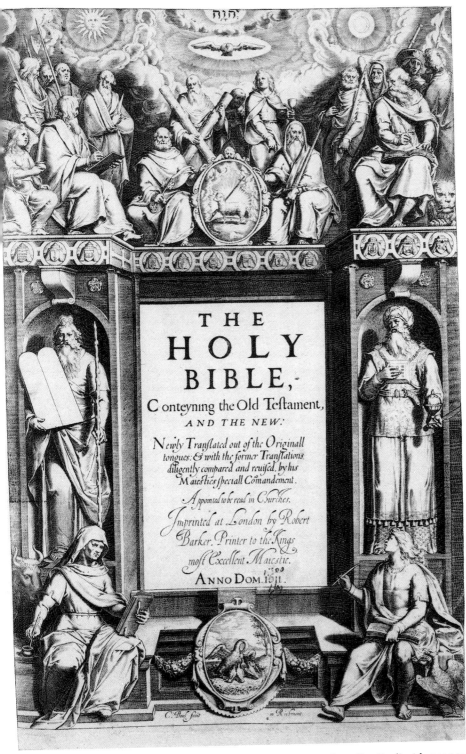

THE
HOLY
BIBLE,

Conteyning the Old Testament,
AND THE NEW:

Newly Translated out of the Originall
tongues: & with the former Translations
diligently compared and reuised, by his
Maiesties speciall Comandement.

Appointed to be read in Churches.

Imprinted at London by Robert
Barker, Printer to the Kings
most Excellent Maiestie.

ANNO DOM. 1611.

C. Boel fecit   in Richmont.

53 Cornelius Boel's title-page to
the Authorized Version of the Bible, 1611

William Hole, engraver to the Prince's circle

54 Inigo Jones's design probably for Merlin in the *Barriers*, 1610

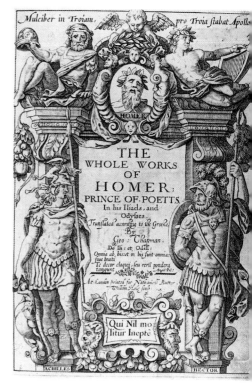

55 Hole's title-page to Chapman's *Homer, Prince of Poets*, 1610, perhaps after a design by Inigo Jones

Architectural innovation

56 Sir Charles Cavendish's Little Castle at Bolsover, 1612–14

57 Title-page to Pierre Matthieu's
L'Histoire de la France, 1605

58 Hole's title-page to Drayton's
Poly-Olbion, 1612, perhaps after a
design by Inigo Jones

59 The classical portico added to
Byfleet Lodge by Sir James Fullerton, Gentleman of the Bedchamber
and Keeper of the Privy Purse

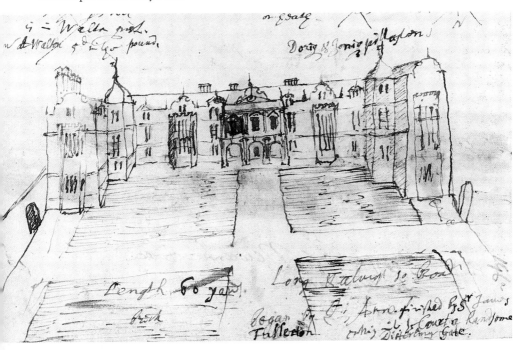

Heere lyeth one yᵗ
heauen sent to earth
doest no doubt her pu-
rer soule, conioynd
with immortall mindes, she
findes a death,
virtue so sprightly that sh
at first vesieged
of her mortall breath, and
of first adorned
of [?] Immortalitye.—
Borne with decaye growing
already proued
the first alternatiue.—

60 Design by Inigo Jones for the tomb of Sir Rowland Cotton's wife, 1608

61 The tomb as executed in St Chad's, Norton-in-Hales, Shropshire

Classical and Renaissance influences on sculpture

62 Michelangelo's Lorenzo de' Medici

63 Monument to a son of Sir John Holles, the Prince's Comptroller, by Nicholas Stone, perhaps after a design by Inigo Jones, *c.* 1622

The Prince's festivals I

The Barriers, *January 1610*
Designs by Inigo Jones

64   The main scene: St George's Portico: the revival of chivalry and the vanished glories of Ancient Britain

65   The opening scene: the fallen House of Chivalry: the classical world of Ancient Britain in decay

66   Polish knight

67   The first *intermezzo* in *Il Giudizio di Paride*, 1608

68   The tragic scene from Serlio

69   Design probably for the Prince's helmet

70   Design probably for the Prince's *impresa* shield with the figures of Minerva and Chivalry

fore

Chi non fa' servala bottica · Moo $\frac{w}{3}$

The Prince's festivals II

The Accession Day Tilt,
March 1610

71 Inigo Jones's elephant pageant
for Sir Richard Preston, the Prince's
instructor-in-arms

Indeed, the book was not only 'for all young Gentlemen' but more importantly for the mechanical classes: 'divers Trades-men and Artificers, as namly Painters, Ioyners, Free-masons, Cutters and Carvers, &c.' What was this due to? Certainly it must have owed a debt to someone whom Peacham refers to as one of his 'especiall and worthy friends': Inigo Jones. The latter was the first person in England to use drawing as a means of conveying to his patrons his ideas for buildings, costumes and scenery, even tombs. Jones's work, however, is awkward during this period when he was learning and he was not to become a really accomplished draughtsman until the 1630s. Oliver, however, was unique in producing drawings as works of art for the contemplation of connoisseurs and collectors. That Henry was taught perspective by de Caus implies that he must have been taught how to draw exactly as Peacham wanted, on the grounds of its usefulness to the upper classes in terms of travelling and the art of war. The indications are that drawing in the sense that it was used by the Renaissance artist was first understood and appreciated within the St James's court.

Oliver died in 1619 and was to continue after the Prince's death as limner to the Queen and Prince Charles. His work, however, sums up the incipient internationalism of Henry's circle. It, like the picture collection and the garden schemes, speaks of a process of assimilation in one gigantic stride of the whole of what the mainland of Europe had achieved in the preceding century. It cannot be coincidental that it is precisely during and just after this period that Oliver embarks on some of his most startling subject miniatures: the *Diana* (1615), the remarkable *Madonna and Child in Glory*, the *Head of Christ* and the *Entombment*.[101]

Painting is only one of the two-dimensional arts. Engraving is another. By 1610 there was no lack of engravers in England but they were still working in the hieratic iconic idiom of late Elizabethan England.[102] The introduction of line engraving in the 1540s came a century later than in the rest of Europe and engravings only began to be produced in any quantity with the influx of Netherlandish refugees in the late 1560s: Franciscus and Remigius Hogenberg, Marcus Gheeraerts the Elder, Theodore de Bry, Jodocus Hondius, Robert Boissard and the various members of the de Passe family. These brought with them the vigorous florid style of the mid-sixteenth-century Antwerp Mannerist school which was taken over by native practitioners such as William Rogers and Thomas Cockson, who reinterpreted it in terms of the archaisms of the Elizabethan aesthetic.

As in the case of a portrait painter, the Prince seems initially to have been satisfied with the work of a native engraver who must certainly have been closely related to his court, although no payments exist. William Hole (d. *c.* 1624) was active from 1607 and in 1618 was appointed 'Head Sculptor of the Iron for money in the Tower and elsewhere for life'.[103] Nothing else is known about him but his *oeuvre* reads like a roll-call of names of people either directly members of the Prince's household or of the close circle. It includes engravings for Sir John Hayward's *Sanctuarie of the Troubled Soul* (1616), Michael Drayton's *Polyolbion* (1612–22), dedicated to the Prince, Angelo Notari's *Prime Musiche Nuove* (1613), Joshua Sylvester's translation of Du Bartas's *Diuine Weekes and Workes* (1613), Thomas Coryate's *Crudities* (1611), dedicated to the Prince, Chapman's *Homer* (1610?) and its second version *The Iliads of Homer Prince of Poets* (1611), both dedicated to Henry, the record of the Prince's funeral hearse attached to the same poet's *Epicede or Funerall Song; on the death of Henry Prince of Wales* (1612 and 1613), Jonson's *Workes* (1616) and Raleigh's *History of the World* (1614). It is hardly surprising, therefore, to find him the engraver of one of the earliest maps of Virginia attached to *A True Relation of such occurences as hapned in Virginia* (1608), besides being connected with a number of items dedicated to or celebrating the Palatine couple.

Hole was also responsible for an engraving of the Prince which exists in several states separately but which was certainly used in Michael Drayton's *Poly-Olbion* published in 1612.[104] The original drawing was made for the engraving by Henry's limner, Isaac Oliver, and was later given to Charles I by Inigo Jones:

> Item a drawing in little of Prince
> Henry where he is playing with a lance
> beeing side faced in a black frame
> with a shiuer [i.e. a glass over it].

In another version of his catalogue van der Dort writes, 'at lengt don bij isak oliffers vor a patron to bi ingraffing bij bin in bot in blak and Wijt' (at length done by Isaac Oliver for a pattern to be engraved by him in both black and white). As in the case of several of Henry's other portraits the image is so original that it must have been in response to a programme. There is no iconographical precedent in royal portraiture and it deliberately projects the Prince in *à l'antique* profile as a man of war, skilled in arms, posed as he would have fought at the famous *Barriers* of 1610.

The connection between Hole and Inigo Jones and Isaac Oliver is important. It establishes that engravers worked from drawings and designs provided by other artists. Nicholas Hilliard certainly did this, and it is likely that we can detect his hand behind many of the portrait engravings of the royal family by Elstracke.[105] In the case of Hole we have another instance in his title page of Chapman's *Homer*, which can with some justification be ascribed to his close friend, Inigo Jones.[106] On either side Achilles and Apollo face each other in costumes that evoke designs for the masquers in *Oberon*. Above, there is an even more definite link, for the head of Homer is taken from Marcantonio Raimondi's engraving of Raphael's *Parnassus*. The figure of Homer that appears there was drawn on by Jones for a costume design probably for Merlin in the *Barriers* during exactly the same period.[107] It is conceivable that Jones could have been responsible for providing designs for other title pages engraved by Hole, who would have rendered what was a sophisticated original into his awkward provincial idiom. Two spring to mind. One is the famous title page to Ben Jonson's *Workes* (1616), which could have been based on an early post-Italian tour drawing by Jones,[108] and the second is Drayton's *Polyolbion*, which is adorned with figures that seem to have stepped straight out of the *Barriers*.[109] As regards the ambience of the Prince's court it is significant that the figure of Britannia is a reworking of the image from Roman coins as published by Camden in his *Britannia* in terms of the gigantic figure of Gallia adorning the frontispiece to Pierre Matthieu's *L'Histoire de la France ... durant sept années de paix* (1605). Matthieu was court historiographer to Henri IV, the Prince's 'second father'.

Henry cannot have been satisfied with Hole and should the original drawing of him by Oliver have survived we would have had more tangible evidence of the gulf in quality between the work of the draughtsman and the end product by a pedestrian craftsman. In the accounts there appears an enigmatic reference to 'A Duche graver sent for xiij^{li}'[110] but we are not on certain ground until 1611–12, when a payment for £10 occurs to 'A Frencheman that mad the Frontispiece of the Byble'.[111] This was Cornelius Boel (b. *c.* 1576), who actually resided and worked in Richmond Palace, as the inscription on his most important work, the title page to the Authorized Version of the Bible, records.[112] Boel's work was far in advance of anything being produced in England at the time. His background was Antwerp as it had developed under the new civilization that was being created around Albert and Isabella and which was to reach its apogee in the art of Rubens. Boel had in fact engraved one of the most famous of all emblem books, the *Amorum Emblemata* of Otto van Veen (Vaenius), published in 1608 and dedicated to William Herbert, 3rd Earl of Pembroke, and his brother, Philip, Earl of Montgomery. Vaenius was one of that generation of artists who had been to Italy and whose work presaged that of Rubens, whom he taught. It was Italianate and learned in its allusion, with a clearer and firmer grasp of the antique than the previous generation. Boel belonged to this milieu and combined exactly those qualities needed to be engraver to the Prince of Wales.

50 As well as his painted portraits there was the Prince's engraved image. Boel's portrait of Henry dates from late 1611, or more likely 1612, and is far more sophisticated than any other mass–produced likeness of the Prince. It is based on Oliver's face pattern of the great miniature. Verses below hail the new Greece that this young man, endowed with the fruits of Minerva and Nature, will inaugurate. In allegorical terms the portrait is a coherent statement of the ideals of the new court and the future reign. To the left, Minerva, the warrior goddess of wisdom, has above her a putto who writes in a book and holds the mirror of prudence. To the right, many-breasted Nature has above her a putto who clutches in his right hand mathematical instruments while with his left he measures the globe of the earth with a pair of dividers. It is a vision of a prince who through wisdom and learning will unlock, by means of science, the mysteries of nature. The iconographic programme must have been deliberately compiled at Richmond and its native sources are two engravings by William Rogers, both of Elizabe-
49 than chivalrous military heroes, one of Essex as commander of the
46 army in Ireland in 1599, and the second of the sailor Cumberland, issued in celebration of his prowess as a privateer against Spain (*c.*1598).[113] The frame which is closer to the Boel portrait is the one on the Essex, which is in turn derived from a border to a portrait of Martin de Vos by Gilles Sadeler. A continental source belonging to the same ideological context is the print distributed of the Prince's idol, Henri IV, after his consecration at Chartres. The King is depicted as the Gallic Hercules, the victor of battles, flanked by Gallia and Minerva.[114] Nor should we ignore its resemblance to Jones's design for what is likely to have been Henry's *impresa* shield in the *Barriers*, with
70 its supporting figures of Minerva and Lady Chivalry.

More important even than this, Boel executed actually in Richmond
53 Palace the title page to the Authorized Version of the Bible, which was published in 1611.[115] Nothing could more forcefully associate the Prince with this landmark in the history of the Church of England than this engraving. The design of the title page has its roots in the last edition of the Bishops' Bible (1602), but in symbolic and stylistic content it is far in advance. Stylistically it is international, not insular, and this surely was the intention. The figures of some of the Apostles, it has been suggested, could have been influenced by Rubens's series for the Duke of Lerma (1610–12). Rubens had been taught by van Veen, for whom Boel worked. Whether this is so or not, the choice of Boel reveals a desire that the work should not be entrusted to any of the in-

digenous old-fashioned engravers. Its programme was presumably drawn up by some of the translators but it is woven together with a skill and subtlety that are close in spirit to the title pages of Rubens and poles away from the piled-up hieroglyphs of Jacobean England. Moses, the prophet, and Aaron, the High Priest, stand within the niches of the mighty wall of the Old Testament, so the Four Evangelists are depicted borne up by or seated upon various parts of the wall. The radiance, of the Tetragrammaton outshines both sun and moon and the Trinity is completed by the dove of the Holy Ghost and the Agnus Dei, supported by St Peter and St Paul, behind whom the Apostles are ranked, each bearing his symbol. The appearance of Aaron the High Priest was an overt statement on the Anglican theological position, in which the priest alone has power to administer the sacraments.

Apart from portraits of the Princess Elizabeth and of the King and Queen[116] these are the only certain works by Boel in England. But one might ask whether others were intended? Engraving was a chief means of manifesting princely magnificence to the world in the form of the great flood of *fêtes* books that evoked the splendours of the *intermezzi* of the grand dukes or the state entries of the rulers of the Low Countries. We know Henry was interested in these publications. Could it have been his intention that Boel was to do such work? It is not inconceivable. On one of the designs for a knight in Polish costume by Inigo Jones appears the inscription: *The paterne for Paper for the Booke of the Barriers.*[117] This is the only scrap of evidence we have that there may have been an idea of publishing a commemorative volume, but it would have been entirely consistent with the Prince's policies to establish the prestige of the dynasty in international terms. Like other aspects of the Henrician renaissance Boel's engravings stand as reminders, as heralds of one part of the mosaic of a new court culture that was never to be.

Bacon wrote of the Prince: 'He was much devoted to the magnificence of buildings and works of all kinds, though in other aspects rather frugal; and was a lover both of antiquity and arts.'[118] In both the *Barriers* and *Oberon*, as we shall discover, his renaissance is seen in visual terms as a superimposition of the Ancient British classical style onto that of the intervening Gothic centuries, to both of which traditions Henry was heir. Sadly we have no building or design for a building, or even the modification of an existing one, which we can associate with him. All that survives is the groundplan and a detail for the Riding School and the evidence of the accounts for the appearance of his library. To round off this account of the visual arts I shall therefore look at other evidence to reinforce the view that St James's court was the true fount from which there descended to the Caroline period both a serious interest in the antique and a desire to come to terms with the achievements of Italian Renaissance architecture and sculpture.

We can start with a major piece of evidence, the translation of Serlio's *Architectura* entered in the Stationers' Register on 14 December 1611: 'London Printed for Robert Peake and are to be sold at his Shop neere Holborne conduit, next to the Sunne Taverne. Anno. Dom. 1611.' The book is dedicated to the Prince and lays emphasis on the importance of geometry:

The ignorance and want whereof in times past (in most parts of this Kingdome) hath left vs many lame Workes, with shame of many Workemen.[119]

The note to the reader explains that this is necessary because 'the common Workemen of our time hath little regarded or esteemed to Worke with right Simmetrie.' Peake's role was his 'great adventure in the charge', by which he means the printing and procuring the translation. The nearest we get to who did that translation occurs right at the very close: 'And this also is the end of the whole worke of Sebastian Serlius: Translated out of Italian into Dutch, and out of Dutch into English, at the charges of Robert Peake. Printed at London, by Simon Stafford. 1611. B. W.' The dedication to the Prince by his 'picturemaker' in the year that he was looking for another portrait painter speaks for itself, but who is the elusive B. W.? I can offer no solution, but the translation ranks among one of the major events in this country's architectural history and it is one firmly linked to the St James's court.

It is when it comes to identifying actual buildings erected during this period which embody these ideals that we run into problems. It is surprising, for instance, that Charlton House, Greenwich, built by the Prince's tutor, Adam Newton, shows no trace of any Italianate features. More interesting are the revisions, probably by Inigo Jones, to the south front of Hatfield House during its building. What has not been suggested is the possible influence of Salisbury's son, the Prince's friend, William Lord Cranborne, with his enthusiasm for the monuments of antiquity and the works of Palladio. The epitome, however, of this reform of architecture is not Hatfield but Sir Charles Cavendish's Bolsover Castle, begun a few days before the Prince's death on 2 November 1612.[120] Mark Girouard has already placed it into the perspective of the chivalrous tradition of the Accession Day tilts, but this is surely too simplistic an approach to this unique building which provides us still with the visual equivalent of the *Barriers* and *Oberon*. Sir Charles Cavendish (1552–1617) was sixty in 1612, old in terms of the period, when he embarked on this project. His links with the court of St James's, to whose ideal, on account of his skill both as a horseman and as a swordsman, he would have been sympathetic, were direct. His greatest friend was his brother-in-law, Gilbert Talbot, Earl of Shrewsbury, and his niece, Aletheia, was married to Thomas Howard, Earl of Arundel. Here is a building which matches exactly the scenario of the Prince's court, the superimposition onto the Gothic past of the new classicism as an expression of an historic British continuum. The work was carried out by John Smythson (d. 1634), son of the famous Robert, acting under the direction of his patron. The result is something closely resembling a medieval castle keep, with crenellations exactly in the vein of Jones's palace for Henry in Jonson's masque, *Oberon. The Fairy Prince*. Within the rooms the most remarkable feature is the series of chimney pieces derived from Books IV and VII of Serlio. Although these were all put in after Sir Charles's death in 1617, the basic type had been evolved by then and indeed one is dated 1616. William Cavendish, who succeeded, considered his father a 'good architect' and there is every reason to believe that these were part of the schema from the outset in 1612. That their appearance in a building started in the year of the publication of Serlio in English cannot be a coincidence. They represent exactly the type of Italianate detail which Jones embroidered onto Oberon's palace. Bolsover remains architecture's solitary but supreme monument to the lost Renaissance.

The others occur in the realm of monumental sculpture. Sir Rowland Cotton (born about 1577) is recorded as having been in one of the Prince's masques, possibly *Oberon*; he contributed a panegyric to Coryate's *Crudities* and memorial poems allude to Henry as being 'his master'. In 1608 his wife died and it was to Inigo Jones that Cotton turned for a design for her tomb which still stands in the remote Shropshire church of St Chad at Norton-in-Hales.[121] It is likely, as John Newman has demonstrated, that Jones worked from a symbolic programme drawn up by the great Hebrew scholar, Hugh Broughton (1544–1611), who lived in the house of Cotton's father in the 1580s and who returned from the Continent to die there in November 1611. Executed by a provincial sculptor in Burton-on-Trent, the result is at once closer to what must have been the iconographic programme and, at the same time, stylistically more awkward than Jones's design. Lady Cotton is shown propped up on a large pillow with her arms limply resting on her lap, a motif, it is suggested, derived from tomb figures at the end of J. A. du Cerceau's *Second Livre d'Architecture* (1561). The sarcophagus beneath, however, is quite unlike any other tomb in England at that period. It is of a classical type with harpies at the corners and if it strikes a

60

61

familiar note it is hardly surprising, for it is but a variant of Merlin's
65 tomb in the opening scene of the *Barriers*.

The Cotton tomb is unique and it is not until the arrival of Hubert le
Sueur in 1625 that a sculptor with a first-hand knowledge of all that
had been achieved in Renaissance Italy was to reach England. Until
then the Anglo-Flemish workshops were to retain their sway, although
there is one exception, the tombs of Francis (d. 1622) and Sir George
63 Holles (d. 1626), sons of the Earl of Clare, in Westminster Abbey.[122]
These are both by Nicholas Stone (1586–1647) and are quite unlike his
other work, for they are derived, however crudely, from the two seated
62 figures of the Medici on Michelangelo's tombs in the sacristy of San
Lorenzo. Although these take us a decade on beyond the Prince's
death they belong to the saga, for Clare, as Sir John Holles, was Comptroller of the Prince's household. And the earliest allusion to the Medici tombs appears in the sarcophagus placed to the left in the second
64 scene of the *Barriers*. Francis Holles was a soldier who served with dis-
tinction in the Netherlands, which would immediately make the choice
of formula apposite. It would also suggest that these two tombs, like
the one of Lady Cotton, go back to drawings provided by Jones.

These are indicative fragments in an area of activity so admirably
summed up by W. H.: 'He delighted much in Architecture and building, & had already made some beginning thereof at Richmond house;
And doubtless, if God had prolonged his dayes, he had caused build
many curious and sumptuous buildings.'[123]

There can be no doubt that the course of the visual arts would have
run in a different way had the St James's court not been dissolved at
the close of 1612. Whatever our estimation of de' Servi and de Caus, if
they had stayed and brought to completion their projects they could
not have failed to be major influences. At the least they would have accelerated a change in taste and style that now had to wait a decade to
be taken up again forcefully by the crown. De Caus's work was, to
some extent, picked up by his brother Isaac in the middle of the 1620s
but no Florentine was to succeed de' Servi. Indeed his departure effec-
tively broke the direct relationship and interchange of artistic ideas
with the Medici court. Henceforth Venice, with the ambassadorial
presence of Wotton, was to be the stronger influence.

Isaac Oliver reminds us of one very important fact, the interest in
French court art. It is perhaps misleading to overstress the Italianate
context at the expense of other preoccupations. In spite of the direct
contact with Venice and Florence on a scale unknown for almost a century, in the main France retained its role as a filter. The Prince and his

circle were francophile, with a passionate cult of Henri IV, and all Henry's friends travelled in France and attended its court. Not only was Isaac Oliver French but so was de Caus, reinterpreting Medicean Mannerism in terms of the School of Fontainebleau. Boel too was French, as the accounts state, even though he came to England via the Low Countries. The French element, as we have seen, may also account for Henry's choice of Jones as his Surveyor, which came soon after his visit to France in the summer of 1609. The headdresses for the ladies in the *Masque of Queens* are derived from engravings after Rosso, the revisions to the south front of Hatfield are French based, Lady Cotton's tomb draws on du Cerceau, as does in part the architecture of *Oberon*. Nor should we ignore the interest in Dutch art, for it was Mierevelt that the Prince pursued for his portrait painter. In other words we must regard the St James's court as international in cultural terms and perhaps the elusive figure of Oliver can act as a touchstone for that factor, for the references in his work range over the whole experience of Renaissance art, both south and north of the Alps, drawing on sources as varied as Michelangelo and Raphael, Primaticcio and Rosso to Wtewael and Bloemart. After 1613 the future of everything rested upon the shoulders of one man, Inigo Jones. This chapter only serves to heighten the extraordinary abilities of that person. At the age of forty he left England with the Arundels to voyage to Italy to make good in knowledge all that he now knew he lacked. What is breathtaking is his ability to rise to this supreme challenge and return to reign triumphantly as 'Vitruvius Britannicus', carrying to fruition so many of the ideas and visions first glimpsed during the brief flowering of the court of Henry, Prince of Wales.

The Prince's Festivals

On 3 August 1608 Ottavino Lotti, the Tuscan Resident in London, reported to the Grand Duke's secretary the impending visit of the Prince's closest friend, John Harington.[1] Prince Henry, who was just fourteen at the time, had sent Harington for a purpose: to witness and write an exact – 'relatione puntualissima' – report on the festivals that were shortly to be staged in celebration of the marriage of the Grand Duke's son, Cosimo, to the Archduchess Maria Maddelena. On 1 January 1609 Lotti was able to report to Florence that His Highness had received letters (they do not survive)[2] from Harington describing the marvels of these *fêtes*, which had spread over some three weeks of the previous November, and in which the art of festival at the Medici court reached new heights.[3] The events included a state entry into the city, a *calcio*, a *corso al Saracino*, banquets and religious processions, dominated by four spectacles that must have come as a revelation to anyone used to entertainments within the Elizabethan–Jacobean tradition. One was Francesco Cini's *Notte d'Amore*, a sequence of scenic wonders punctuating a court ball, taking its participants through a single night in allegorical terms. The account of the others would have been read even more avidly by the young Prince. One was a horse ballet, recreated from Classical antiquity; another was again a revival of an antique form, a *naumachia*, entitled the *Argonautica*, in which fantastically disguised barges bore knights in symbolic guise along the Arno. The last and the most spectacular of all these events might have seemed familiar from the work of Inigo Jones, although they must have made the English work seem awkward and provincial by comparison. These were the five *intermezzi* interspersed between the acts of the play, *Il Giudizio di Paride*, in which the architect Giulio Parigi staged a series of astounding transformation scenes, entailing brilliant feats of engineering, evoking emblematic tableaux celebrating the virtues of Medici rule. They were presented behind a proscenium arch like moving pictures in perspective, a format first developed at the Medici court in 1586.

Not long after Henry had received Harington's accounts of these events, on 2 February 1609, he attended Ben Jonson's *Masque of Queens*, which represented a significant step forward in the development of that form of entertainment in which the poet introduced for the first time an anti-masque of witches. The Prince understood such a spectacle in the spirit in which it was conceived, with a deep seriousness of purpose, and he asked Jonson to compile for him an annotated text.

This Jonson duly produced and presented to 'the Glorie of our crowne and greefe of other Nations....'

Where, though it hath prou'd a worke of some difficulty to mee to retriue the particular *authorities* (according to yor gracious command, and a desire borne out of iudgement) to those things wch I writt out of fullnesse, and memory of my former readings....[4]

By the beginning of the year 1609 the Prince was already deeply concerned with festivals, aware that they were essential adjuncts of princely magnificence, aware too that they required authors of erudition and that at the Florentine court this art form had reached a perfection as yet unknown to England. It would be interesting to be able to identify the source of his curiosity about Medici festivals. The main *fiorentini* in proximity to him were Sir Thomas Chaloner, Sir Edward Cecil and Inigo Jones. Someone must have been responsible for arousing the interest of a fourteen-year-old boy in the Florentine festival tradition, perhaps by way of some of the commemorative books and engravings issued to record the events. From January 1610 onwards the young Prince was to become the driving force behind a sequence of festivals that were designed explicitly to present himself and his policy to both court and public. If he had lived, the art of festival in Stuart England would have taken a very different course from that which ended in the sterility of the self-adulatory masques of the Caroline age.

Renaissance festivals[5] in the main embrace three forms: the state entry into a city, the exercise of arms, and forms of spectacle making use of acting, singing, music and dance that took place within a palace. For the Prince the most important of these was the exercise of arms. In 1610 the format remained the same as that evolved by Sir Henry Lee for the annual Accession Day Tilts in honour of Elizabeth I.[6] In these tournaments knights entered the tiltyard of Whitehall Palace in fancy dress of their own devising in tribute to the crown. Scenery was almost exclusively in the form of pageant cars and occasional rare uses of scattered permanent features, such as the Temple of the Vestal Virgins in 1590. The same system applied to the indoor barriers, in which knights fought across a barrier with sword and pike, although by the close of the reign the gentlemen from the Inns of Court framed their sport with an overall plot and dénouement. James I was to be a poor substitute for Gloriana as the hero of King's Day, 24 March, and the tournaments soon began to go into decline. The format remained unchanged from that of the previous reign, decidedly old-fashioned in European terms. It was in Italy, initially in Ferrara, and subsequently in Florence, that the tournament developed rapidly into a new form in the second half of the sixteenth century. The main development was the elaboration of the *tournoi à thème*, the event being framed by a sustained allegorical plot with a predetermined finale within which combatants were expected to take on relative roles.[7] This was accompanied by an increasing use of dramatic ingredients in terms of speech, song and action, aided by the introduction of scene changes and the eventual rearrangement of the tournament arena to meet the demands of artificial perspective. The tournaments held in Ferrara developed this format, beginning with *Il Castello di Gorgoferusa* (1561) and closing with *Il Mago rilucente* (1570), as did the two *sbarre* of 1579 and 1589 staged in the Palazzo Pitti in Florence. Prince Henry's *Barriers* belong to that line of descent as an attempt to bring exercises of arms at the Stuart court up to date in European terms.

This is similarly true of his court masques. The Stuart court masque in its Jonsonian phase is, owing to its literary content, perhaps the best studied field of all. In fact so great is the scholarly industry on the court masque that the result has been to distort the true balance of court *fêtes* in the years immediately after 1603.[8] The masques begin with the alliance of Jonson and Jones in 1605 in the famous *Masque of Blackness*, where for the first time a recondite scenario in homage to the monarchy was married to the machinery and perspective stage settings that we associate with the revolutionary Medici *intermezzi* of 1589. The pictorial content as well as the technology of these *intermezzi* was to be seminal for the development of Baroque court theatre and embodied an arrangement in terms of illusion totally unknown to the court of Elizabeth I, the subjection of an audience to a succession of scenic spectacles achieved by a mastery of engineering. Such scenery visibly evoked heaven and earth, or rather heaven come down to earth and earth exalted up to heaven, in homage to the Prince, in whose eyes the lines of the stage perspective met. From 1605 to 1610, under the patronage of Anne of Denmark, Jones attempted to stage the masques in this manner, but as no designs for scenery survive it is difficult to gauge his success. Jones's greatest technical leap in the evolution of his stage as a machine was in fact made for Prince Henry with the advent of the *scena ductalis*, the multiple use of sidewings and shutters to change the set, in *Oberon*.

Owing to the fact that Henry used the King's poet, Jonson, we have also for too long viewed the spectacles as one continuous evolving series since 1605. We have perhaps overlooked the fact that they were the products of the demands of quite different people with quite different preoccupations. The *Barriers, Oberon, Love Restored* and, to a degree, *Tethys' Festival* are expressions of the Prince's and Queen's courts: not only their thoughts but also their aspirations in terms of new ambitions in the arts as well as in politics. In both the Prince's and the

Queen's festivals there is a preoccupation with the visual arts, painting, garden design, sculpture and architecture. In the case of Henry there is a cult of British history: the mythology of the previous reign besides an aggressive militaristic message. All of these ingredients had to be reconciled and transformed into a homage to James, whose iconography centred on expositions of Divine Right, extolling, in sharp contrast to his son, the virtues of peace and mediation.

The *Barriers* performed on Twelfth Night 1610 inaugurate the Prince's public career.[9] Hawkins wrote that Henry conceived the event so 'that the World might know, what a brave Prince they were likely to enjoy'.[10] And, as with all his festivals, there were problems from the start with the King. 'He found', wrote Correr, the Venetian ambassador, 'some difficulty in obtaining the King's consent, but his Majesty did not wish to cross him.'[11] Why, and what were these difficulties? In the first place Correr writes that the Prince was planning a tournament, which could indicate that initially he wanted a public spectacle in the tiltyard. James was always suspicious and, by implication, jealous of his son's public appearances. When, however, the latter did happen the festival took the form of fighting at the barriers *inside*, a type of entertainment that the gentlemen of the Inns of Court had brought to Whitehall in the last years of the old queen's reign and which, from time to time, was revived for the Jacobean court. In one sense, by casting himself as the hero of tilts and tourneys Henry was taking upon himself even more forcefully the role played by Elizabeth's favourite, Robert Devereux, 2nd Earl of Essex, in the nineties: that of popular idol and hero of the Accession Day Tilts. But there were greater difficulties, because the *Barriers* presented the Prince as the exponent of a policy diametrically opposed to the royal one. We see the young Prince present the new court of St James's as the thinly veiled focus for a revival of the Elizabethan war party, fiercely Protestant and anti-Habsburg. James I, the British Solomon, must have viewed his son's début as a man-at-arms with very mixed feelings.

As was usual, the *Barriers* were prefaced by a challenge which was issued at Christmas when persons, 'strangely attired', proclaimed its contents in the Presence Chamber, accompanied by the din of both drums and trumpet. The challenge was delivered in the name of the Prince under the pseudonym of Meliadus, Lord of the Isles. William Drummond of Hawthorndon records that the Prince 'in the challenges of his Martial Sports & Mascarads, was wont to vse, *Moeliades Prince of the Isles* which in Anagramme maketh *Miles A DEO*'.[12] Such a pseudonym established the Prince at once as a Protestant Christian knight, a 'Soldier to

God'. The challenge rehearsed how, on his instruction, British knights had been despatched abroad to find out 'where true Virtue triumphed most'.[13] On returning, they reported that only in the island of Great Britain could such Virtue be found. It was this that inspired Meliadus to present the first fruits of his chivalry to its King. In his challenge Henry was aided by six assistants: the Duke of Lennox, the Earls of Southampton and Arundel, the Lord Hay, Sir Thomas Somerset and Sir Richard Preston.

The *Barriers* took place on 6 January in the Whitehall Banqueting House and for their realization in verbal and visual terms the Prince employed Ben Jonson and Inigo Jones. Both obviously worked under specific direction, for the scenario and themes could only have stemmed from the Prince himself. Jonson was not attracted to Arthurian themes and indeed this forms his only use of the material. For it he drew on *Les Prophecies du Merlin*, a late thirteenth-century work from which he extracted the characters of the Lady of the Lake, King Arthur, Merlin and the knight, Meliadus. From the romance he adapted the presentation by the Lady of the Lake of Meliadus, long preserved for this occasion, at the court of King Arthur. In this Jonson alters the original story, making Meliadus not the Lady of the Lake's lover but her foster child. Very little is known about the technical aspects of this production but it was undoubtedly innovatory in at least one respect: barriers were normally enacted against scenery scattered around an arena, but this one made use of perspective staging hitherto employed only for the masques. It opened with a curtain of some form falling to reveal a shutter depicting Classical ruins. The text describes these ruins as being ancient British, and the Lady of the Lake appears to prophesy a revival of chivalry which will coincide with the resurrection of the Empire of Great Britain back to its former unity. This *renovatio* she sees already accomplished, acknowledging it in the glittering British court and its monarch assembled before her, but

> Only the House of Chivalry (howe'er
> The inner parts and store be full, yet here
> In that which gentry should sustain) decayed
> Or rather ruined seems, her buildings laid
> Flat with the earth that were the pride of time,
> And did the barbarous Memphian heaps outclimb;
> Those obelisks and columns broke and down
> That struck the stars, and raised the British crown
> To be a constellation....[14]

Now, lamenting the vanished glories of chivalry, all she sees are rusty shields and swords and tarnished helmets. At this point the sky opens to disclose King Arthur, who tells her that the times are now propi-

65

142

tious, and that Merlin's prophecies are to be fulfilled in a young knight for whom the fates have fashioned a shield. And here follows the crucial line:

> Defensive arms th'offensive should forego.[15]

In this line the militaristic message of the *Barriers* makes its first appearance. From the outset, aggression is blunted, for it is a shield of defence and not a sword of offence with which the Prince is to be presented. One may well ask whether Jonson, who was *par excellence* the King's poet, was trying to please both parties simultaneously.

Merlin is raised from the grave and the whole front shutter parts to reveal Meliadus and his assistants in tableau before St George's Portico. The Lady conducts them in procession to a tent to one side of the hall while Merlin embarks on a mighty review of the British past as he reads the shield. Here the irreconcilable aim of pleasing both King and Prince collapses, for the speech falls into two scarcely complementary sequences of regal examples drawn from the pages of history and the result is curious and uneasy in the extreme. What we are presented with are two views of the Prince which might be said to be how the King wished him to be, contrasted with how he wished himself to be. It opens with the former. The adventures of knights of chivalrous literature are dismissed:

> His arts must be to govern and give laws
> To peace no less than arms.[16]

There then follows a list of warlike kings notable for their cultivation of the arts of peace: Edward I, who encouraged trade and agriculture; Edward III, who created the clothing industry; Henry VII, who amassed money, 'To be the strength and sinew of a war / When Mars should thunder or his peace but jar.'[17] Then follows Henry VIII, who built forts and encouraged military training, and Elizabeth who constructed 'a wall of shipping'. No battles or campaigns are referred to, and these kings of England are held up as neither more nor less than prototypes and justifications of James I's policy of inertia:

> That civil arts the martial must precede,
> That laws and trade bring honours in and gain,
> And arms defensive a safe peace maintain.[18]

In complete contradiction to this feeble parade, Jonson then embarks on a eulogy of the warlike kings of England. So different is it in content, one wonders whether the first half of the speech might not have been an afterthought added to appease the King. This part, in contrast, is fiercely patriotic and aggressive, opening with Richard Coeur de

Lion, '... armed with wroth and fire, / Ploughing whole armies up with zealous ire ...',[19] and continuing with Edward I, who 'lets no less rivers of blood', the Black Prince, 'Mars indeed' (Henry, when he appeared, was compared by Jonson to Mars) on the field of Crécy, Henry V, 'the other thunderbolt of war, ... to whom in face you are / So like ... lightened by your flame / That shall succeed him both in deeds and name.'[20] Finally, inevitably, the text goes on to mention the defeat of the mighty Spanish Armada by Gloriana's knights. In this speech Henry has placed himself within a continuum of mythological and historical figures, warriors of Greece and Rome, flowers of chivalry both from the chronicles and from romantic literature. Ancient Britain is seen as the native counterpart to the civilizations of Greece and Rome. Henry is the heir to both, as he is to the monarchs of medieval England. This is emphasized in the scenery where Classical and Gothic architecture, symbols of the two historic periods, stand side by side. But he is also casting himself as the heir of Tudor chivalry of the kind embodied in the warrior-prince, Henry VIII, and in the humanistic knights of Elizabeth's court. They, like the medieval knights in the Arthurian romances, had their literary counterparts in the knights of Edmund Spenser's *Faerie Queene* and Sir Philip Sidney's *Arcadia*. All of these were now to find their embodiment in Prince Henry.

The speech had somehow to reach its apogee in James I, but not even Jonson could be faithful to such a brief, except by floundering into a hymn of praise of James's union of the kingdom, a reference to the conquest of Ireland and the repair of Eliza's 'wall of shipping'. How could one possibly cast James in a convincing role at the climax of a series of martial rulers and call upon the Prince to emulate his father? (Jonson was in fact reworking the *Masque of Queens* of the previous year, and encountering the same problems. There Anne of Denmark headed twelve queens valiant in war to pay tribute to her husband cast meekly as Virtue.) Finally, the figure of Chivalry stirred from slumber in her cave to hail Prince Henry, the true climax of regal heroes, and the barriers followed. No fewer than fifty-six challengers came, each with his 'several showes and devices', and the entertainment lasted from ten at night until the dawn of the next day.

What those other shows and devices were it would be interesting to know, and they would certainly enlarge our comprehension of the spectacle as a whole. There is a design by Inigo Jones for what is surely the Prince's helmet, an elaborate confection topped by a sphinx, symbol of wisdom. An annotation on another costume design indicates that a series of drawings for Polish knights, based on engravings in Vecellio's costume book, were for the *Barriers*.[21] This would indicate

69

66

the homage of the knights of other nations. A design for what must be meant to be an ancient Briton holding an axe is likely also to relate to the *Barriers*, and so too is a figure copied from Raphael's Homer in the *Parnassus*, who must be the prophetic Merlin. The Prince, it is recorded, performed his part 'to the great Wonder of the Beholders', sustaining thirty pushes of the pike and 360 strokes of the sword, 'which is scarce credible in one so young in Years, enough to assure the World, that *Great Britain's* brave *Henry* aspired to Immortality.'

At any Elizabethan and Jacobean tournament each knight carried a pasteboard shield on which was painted his device or *impresa*, a combination of image and motto expressive of his aspirations. Jonson does not tell us what *impresa* the Prince used, although there is a drawing for a shield to bear one among Jones's designs which is likely to be that for the occasion. The cartouche is flanked by the figures of Minerva and what is likely to be Lady Chivalry supporting the victor's garland of laurel. Among the papers of the Prince's tutor, Adam Newton, there is a series of devices for the Prince by a 'Mr Guin' which could have been drawn up with the *Barriers* in mind.[22] They are undated. One *impresa* was 'A Hemisphere with bright starres' and the motto, *Interminatis fulget honoribus* (It glitters with honours unending); the second 'A rose invironned with sharp prickles' with *Vt potiar, patiar* (I will suffer that I may possess), and the third 'King Arthurs round table' and *Priscum instauro decus* (I revive the ancient glory). The compiler must be Matthew Gwinne (1558–1627), Professor of Music at Oxford, and subsequently first Professor of Physic at Gresham College, the fountainhead of the new London science.[23] In the 1580s Gwinne had been an associate of the group that centred on Sir Philip Sidney and he was also an acquaintance of Giordano Bruno, who refers to him in the second dialogue of his *La Cena della Ceneri* (1584). Gwinne encouraged Fulke Greville to write his life of Sidney, helped edit the 1590 edition of the *Arcadia* and was a friend of many of the men of letters of the day, above all of John Florio, who had taught the Prince Italian. In 1607 Gwinne had dedicated to the Prince his play *Vertumnus*, which had been performed before him two years previous at Oxford and which had been adorned with scenery by Inigo Jones. Gwinne and these *imprese* provide a direct link between the new circle of the Prince and that centring in the previous reign on Sir Philip Sidney. Gwinne gives us a clue to which I shall return later.

The *Barriers* were also indicative of the Prince's passion for history, which stemmed from a reading of chronicles of the type compiled by Holinshed and Stow. With others of his generation he was celebrated as an heir to an heroic tradition:

54

70

145

> His fate here draws
> An empire with it, and describes each state
> Preceding there that he should imitate.[24]

This, as we have seen, is a highly selective history from Richard I down to the present. That the writing of history was part of the Prince's programme we know from Sir John Holles's tragic letter recounting that Henry granted Dr John Hayward an annuity of £200 p.a. to write 'the universall historie of this kingdome' and that four days before he was taken ill Hayward had presented his account of the first three Norman kings along with one of the opening years of Elizabeth I's reign.

Sir John Hayward (1564–1627) was in some ways an odd choice as court chronicler. Taking a degree in Civil Law at Cambridge he had subsequently practised as a Pleader in the Ecclesiastical Courts.[25] His first appearance as an historian caused a stir. The publication, in 1599, of *The First Part of the Life and Raigne of King Henrie the IIII* was dedicated, under the influence of the publisher, to the Earl of Essex, in the most fulsome manner: 'dominus meus plurimum observandus' (my most esteemed lord). The work of a young man seeking patronage, it tells the story of the misgovernment of the country by a king and his advisers and the succession to the throne, by dint of popular force, of Henry of Lancaster. The book, which in its time was a kind of bestseller, could hardly have appeared at a more inopportune moment, for the Queen's ire knew no bounds and at the trial of Essex the book was referred to as a seditious pamphlet. Although protected by Francis Bacon from a charge of treason, Hayward went to prison, where he seems to have remained until after Essex's execution.

Under James I he rapidly re-established himself in favour by writing, firstly, a defence of the succession, followed by one in favour of the union of the kingdoms. So successful was he in gaining royal favour that in 1610 he, along with the far more distinguished William Camden, was appointed by the King to the short-lived Chelsea College, to which the Prince also lent his support. It was not, however, until the last year of the Prince's life that any direct contact seems to have been formed and that Hayward received a formal commission to undertake a history of Britain. Furthermore Hayward has provided us with a fascinating verbatim account of his conversation with him on the subject of history. This must have taken place during the spring or summer of 1612 and is recorded in the dedication to Henry's brother, Charles, of his *The Lives of the iiii Normans, Kings of England* (1613).

The Prince, he relates, had sent for him (it was their second encounter) and the conversation had begun with Henry holding in his hand

Hayward's notorious account of the rise of Henry IV, for which he had been imprisoned and for which he had only narrowly missed a charge of treason, a fact which Henry must have known. One cannot help but speculate as to Henry's interest in a book detailing the misgovernment of the realm by a decadent king under the influence of favourites. Hayward was a prime exponent of the Tudor belief in the exemplarist value of history, 'both for private directions and affairs of state'.

According to Hayward, Prince Henry began by complaining during their meeting 'much of our Histories of England; and that the English nation, which is inferiour to none in honourable actions, should be surpassed by all, in leauing the memorie of them to posteritie.' The Prince seems to be condemning the standard histories from Hall to Stow, and also taking a conservative standpoint that history is to be studied for moral example, above all in the deeds of great rulers and men. This attitude is corroborated by W. H., who records: 'It being the custome of his Highnes and the young Noblemen about him to tell every one an History by turne, all of them delivering some observation upon the Historie told ...'.[26] As the *Barriers* scenario demonstrates, history was an essential aspect, too, of the cult of the dynasty. The Prince's interest, therefore, belongs to the mainstream of the Tudor cult of history for political and propaganda ends. May McKisack, in her study of the Tudor attitude to the Middle Ages, sums this up very well:

A long and glorious past was an indispensable asset to any nation desirous of making its influence felt in Europe; and, though it was none too easy to declare with conviction that the long centuries of the Middle Ages were centuries of barbarism and superstition, and in the same breath to claim for Britain a glorious history, the difficulty did not prove insurmountable ... medieval history ceased to be dangerous and became a valuable asset to the enthusiastic nationalist.[27]

In the same conversation, according to Hayward, Henry went on to berate the quality of the historians: 'We make choise of the most skilfull workemen to draw or carue the portraiture of our faces, and shall euery artlesse pensell delineate the disposition of our minds?'

The Prince then went further:

... he desired nothing more than to know the actions of his auncestors; because hee did so farre esteeme his descent from them, as he approached heere them in honourable endeauours. Hereupon, beautifying his face with a sober smile, he desired mee, that against his returne from the progresse then at hand, I would perfect somewhat of both sorts [i.e. earlier medieval and near-contemporary history] for him, which he promised amply to requite; and was well knowen to be one who esteemed his word aboue ordinary respects. This stirred in mee, not onely a will, but power to perfourme; so as engaging my duety farre aboue the measure either of my leisure or of my strength, I finished 'The liues of these three Kings of Norman race,' and 'Certaine Yeares of Queene Elizabeth's Reigne'....

On his return to St James's, in September 1612, Hayward presented both these texts to the Prince, and the latter desired that the lives of the kings be published.

The Prince was moved to commission Hayward to put right the work of 'artlesse pensells'. But to whom did this refer? Was it the Tudor chroniclers, or was it also as contemporary an eminence as William Camden? Camden was the greatest historian of his age, with an international reputation since the publication of the first edition of his *Britannia* in 1586, which had brought English historical writing and scholarship into the European mainstream. Although it is difficult to conceive that Henry would have applied the term 'artlesse pensell' to Camden and his work, it is curious all the same that he should have commissioned Hayward to write an account of the reign of Elizabeth I when everyone knew that Camden had been working, since 1608, on his *Annales*. As in the *Barriers*, is this an indication of the intellectual polarity between the King's and the Prince's courts? Camden, like Jonson, was very much a King's man and belonged to that international group of historical scholars who, in the aftermath of the wars of religion, hoped for an end of all war and a new ecumenical tide.[28] His view of Elizabeth's role is essentially that of 'politique', a role which descended to Henri IV, the moderate Huguenot who had placed country before faith, and the scholar-king, James I, whose peace-making with Spain heralded new hopes that a *via media* could be found. Henry and his party had no sympathy with this view. Was Hayward now being cast by Henry as *his* historian viewing history through the eyes of the Elizabethan war-party?

The onlookers at the *Barriers* would have been struck also by what they heard and what they saw. In this aspect the *Barriers* represented a kind of manifesto as to Henry's intentions for architecture. At the beginning of the performance, as we have seen, the Lady of the Lake embarks on a lamentation about the state of the House of Chivalry:

> More truth of architecture there was blazed
> Than lived in all the ignorant Goths have raised.
> There porticos were built, and seats for knights
> That watched for all adventures, days and nights;
> The niches filled with statues to invite
> Young valours forth by their own forms to fight,
> With arcs triumphal for their actions done....[29]

The speeches equate Henry's revival of Ancient British chivalry with a revival of Ancient British architecture seen not as the type built by the 'Goths', but in the Classical style, with porticoes, heroic statuary and triumphal arches. It is King Arthur who introduces the Prince as the man who will restore architecture to a state of pristine purity:

> ... that by the might
> And magic of his arm he may restore
> These ruined seats of virtue, and build more.[30]

Significantly, the Prince and his fellows were revealed to the court, not in a grove or bower or in a ship, but seated, framed by architecture. This must have been at the Prince's direction.

The designs for the *Barriers* remain the earliest complete set of drawings we have by Inigo Jones for a court spectacle, and the first which record his use of scientific perspective. No earlier entertainment by Jonson contains any specific allusion to architecture as a major theme. We are looking at one of the major statements which the Prince was never able to bring to fulfilment because of his death: the introduction of Renaissance classical architecture to England. Inigo Jones always saw its introduction as a revival of Ancient British architecture. Later he was to argue that Stonehenge had been built by the Romans in order to instruct the Ancient British in the laws of harmonious architecture built according to what became Renaissance architectural principles.[31] What is interesting is how Inigo Jones visualizes Ancient British architecture. In the first scene we are presented with a jumble of Roman ruins derived from engravings, together with identifiable monuments: the pyramid of Cestus, the Temple of Antoninus and Faustina and the arch of Titus. The scene is a phantasmagoria depicting the Empire of Great Britain in decay in terms of a *Nova Roma*. The main set elaborates the point by adding examples of the architecture of the 'Goths' of the intervening centuries: a castle, a crenellated tower and Romanesque arcading. But these stand alongside Classical 'British' architecture, including Trajan's column, a triumphal arch and, more oddly, one of Michelangelo's Medici tombs. More interestingly, the Prince and his companions were housed in the untouched St George's portico, which is a deliberate mingling of the Classical and Gothic styles, thus matching exactly the text, which presents Henry as the heir of both eras of the island kingdom's history.

The set is in the Renaissance tradition of the synoptic view whereby various famous architectural features of a place are combined.[32] This was an established format, for example, in settings for plays at the Medici court, where a view of Pisa would incorporate the major buildings. There was, however, no precedent in England, nor was there one for staging a tournament before a perspective stage set presumably framed by a proscenium arch. (One is not referred to, but it was a feature of the masques both before and after it, and the scenic action presupposes it). More remarkable is the fact that this arrangement was even in advance of Italy, for the Teatro Mediceo in Florence was not to be used in this manner until 1613.

We can only speculate as to what prompted this remarkable arrangement. The masques which preceded it, which had been designed by Jones, generally started with a front shutter or curtain that parted to reveal the main setting, which, in turn, generally incorporated a scene by means of a revolving machine or *machina versatilis. Hymen* (1606), the *Haddington Masque* (1608) and *Queens* (1609) had all used this device. The *Barriers* are, in contrast, much more static, making little or no use of major machinery. The point of departure for the main set was probably Serlio's *scena tragica*, with its strong lines of perspective leading back to a central opening with the sides flanked by buildings. This is repeated in Jones's drawing where the paper is scored to the vanishing point in the central arch where the Prince must have stood. But is there another allusion? Henry, we know, had heard all about the 1608 Florentine *fêtes* from his friend Harington. The opening *intermezzo* was on the subject of the Palace of Fame.[33] In that, the audience saw *'edifici magnifici, e superbi, Teatri, Tempi, Logge, Palagi, Archi'*, some of them in good repair, others ruined. In the centre of the stage arose a palace of mirror glass with an arcade at its base and a tower ascending from it. Celebrated ancestors of the bride and groom appeared and eventually entered the Palace which sank beneath the stage again. It is as though Jones had been told of this, although he had clearly not seen the engraving by Cantagallina; it has, however, been argued that it is a source also for the Palace of Fame in *Queens*, the previous year. The *Barriers* is much closer. There, on either side, are noble buildings in ruins receding backwards and in the centre there is a pavilion. The disposition and idea are the same, although the execution is awkward, almost crude, which would explain the Prince's search for a replacement. Are we looking at the earliest direct attempt to copy the effect of a Medici *intermezzo*?

The *Barriers*, as all court *fêtes*, was a *pièce d'occasion*. All through the winter of 1609–10 the political atmosphere at court was dominated by the Julich-Cleves succession problem, which, as we have seen, Henry followed closely, and which was leading up to a European conflict. The diplomatic correspondence encapsulates the atmosphere very succinctly. As Sir Ralph Winwood wrote from Brussels to Salisbury on 7 October 1609:

For the Question being (if I rightly understand the State of it) *not of the Succession of* Cleves *and* Juliers (two inland Countries and petty Principallities) *but whether the House of* Austria *and the Church of* Rome (both now in the Wane) *shall recover their Lustre and Greatnes in these Parts of* Europe.... [34]

Henri IV was about to align himself publicly with the Protestant Union, 'a deeper Mistery then every Man's Capacity can conceive', observed Winwood. James, as always, continued to drift, in the hopes that the problem would resolve itself without England being committed in any way to conflict. At the close of December 1609 La Boderie, the French ambassador, was sent to London by Henri IV to persuade James to join the alliance, stressing the religious side, and to tell him, if pressed, that an alliance with Savoy in February would reopen the Italian wars with an attack on the Spanish-held Milanese.

This is the background against which we must place the *Barriers*, that of a Europe dividing itself into two camps as Henri IV was preparing to launch a crusade that would destroy once and for all the Habsburg domination of Europe. No wonder that the timorous James, the epitome of appeasement at almost any price, was so reluctant for the heir to the throne to present himself to the world as the leader of British Protestant chivalry revived.

The *Barriers'* prime context is the Europe of 1609–10. The theme is war, not peace, and it is aggressive and not passive. It overtly casts the Prince into a revival of Elizabethan chivalry that in its wildest fantasies could see England at the head of a pan-Protestant, European, anti-Catholic and anti-Spanish crusade. Twenty years after his death a Latin panegyric of Henri IV by Claude-Bartholémy Morisot of Dijon was published in Leiden. In it there lies embedded an early version of the Grand Design, what was believed to be Henri IV's plan for the reshaping of Europe in the aftermath of Habsburg defeat. In this Spain was to be confined to her peninsula, the Milanese conquered and Italy freed. The French king's armies were to be led by the Prince of Anhalt and the Margrave of Brandenburg and, he adds, it had been Prince Henry's wish to make his début fighting at the side of Henri IV in the great war to liberate Europe from Habsburg and Catholic Counter-Reformation domination. [35] Poetic fiction this may be, but atmospherically it is right, in terms of the young Prince's aspirations. And this was the message of the *Barriers* of 1610.

The investiture or creation of Henry as Prince of Wales in June 1610, for which the *Barriers* had acted as a prologue, was prefaced by one other event, the customary tilt on King's Day. A week after the *Barriers*, Chamberlain had written that 'Yf the charge do not hinder yt he wold faine undertake another triumphe or shew against the Kings day in March.'[36] Throughout the intervening period there was much tiltyard activity by the Prince, principally to impress the visiting Duke of Württemberg and his cousin, the Prince of Brunswick, who was present at the Accession Day Tilt. Participation in the latter was, however, denied Prince Henry, one would suspect by his father, although the tournament turned out to be a vivid expression of the revival of chivalry. Now the Prince's co-challengers from the *Barriers* were to dazzle the populace in the tiltyard with spectacle evoking memories of the vanished days of yore.[37] The Duke of Lennox 'exceeded all in feathers' but it was the Prince's instructor in arms, Sir Richard Preston, now Lord Dingwall, who eclipsed them all with a pageant designed by Inigo Jones. A huge elephant with a palanquin on its back ambled its way across the tiltyard and this lord's *impresa* carried a motto, in Italian, contrasting knightly service with that of mere commerce. Although Inigo Jones may have had the elephants in the frescoes of the gallery at Fontainebleau in mind when he came to design this pageant, elephants, as we know, were part of the Elizabethan Accession Day Tilt mythology.[38]

The investiture of Henry with the principality of Wales was for the King initially a financial move to solve the problem of crown finances by conceding old feudal dues for a guaranteed income in the form of the Great Contract; the background to the *fêtes* of June is therefore domestic as opposed to international. The assassination of Henri IV on 4 May had thrown both the Prince and the court and kingdom into mourning. Four weeks after the event, no one could know as yet precisely what would happen, but the anti-Habsburg European crusade, which had been the background to the winter months and to the *Barriers*, had vanished. For the Prince this was a crushing disappointment. For his father it was a relief, as France with a child king went into a long period of regency. The spectacles of the Creation therefore belong to the narrative of James's domestic troubles, the Parliament of 1610 and the efforts by Salisbury to solve the crown's financial difficulties by means of the Great Contract.[39] In all this, Henry's role was a peripheral one, but both the King and the Treasurer were well aware of the powerful emotional impact of a young Prince upon a people who had not known the security of a male heir to the kingdom for sixty years, and who had been nurtured on the disasters of the Wars of the Roses. The problem of providing for the new Prince of Wales, therefore, became a recurring one, and the association of Parliament with his financial dilemma was emphasized by his investiture before the two Houses, a ceremony that owed much to the antiquarian labours of the heralds. Early

71

on in the session James had already, in an act of deliberate stage-ma-
nagement, shown the Prince to the assembled members and said that
without adequate funds provided by them he could not advance his
son to the nation's service. For James it must have been a distasteful dilemma to have had to rely on the mounting popularity of his heir to
solve his own financial problems.

As in the case of the *Barriers*, there were tensions between father and
son. Carleton wrote to Edmondes after the event that it had all been
done as privately as possible to save money, 'whereas otherwise there
was to have been a solemn entry and passage through the City of London'.[40] Correr, the Venetian, provides a somewhat different gloss, stating outright the Prince's desire to go to Parliament in procession, 'but
the King was not content and has ordered him to go and return by water'.[41] The difference did not end there, because the Prince objected to
his father's choice of those to be made Knights of the Bath and he
crossed out several names on the list, 'because they were not to his
taste'.[42] Wilson, always the hostile but perceptive chronicler of the Jacobean scene, writing of this period explains how the Prince

... put forth himself in a more *Heroick* manner than was usual with *Princes* of his Time, by
Tiltings, Barriers, and other exercises on horseback, the Martial Discipline of gentle
Peace, which caught the peoples *eyes*, and made their *tongues* the Messengers of their
Hearts, in daily extolling his hopeful and gallant towardliness to admiration.[43]

To begin with, Wilson continues, the King found nothing wrong with
his son's youthful preoccupation, but gradually he 'saw him (as he
thought) too high mounted in the peoples love, and of an alluring
spirit'. And this was the truth of it. From now on every source points
to the Prince's perpetual frustration in any attempt to present himself
alone as the focus of public spectacle.

The Creation ceremonies began on Thursday 31 May, when the
Prince entered London by water from Richmond.[44] It was not until six
days before that the City was actually told that this was to happen.
Even more pointed was the amazing instruction that they were to welcome him 'in such sort as is vsed when the Lord Maior goeth to Westminster to take his oath'.[45] In other words, he was in no way to be received as Prince, and the delay in imparting this information prevented
any elaboration by the City of their reception. Both decisions must
have come from James, whose instructions were duly met. Henry was
greeted on the River Thames by a flotilla of company barges covered
with banners and flags. There was only a slight entertainment rushed
together by the author of the Lord Mayors' pageants, Anthony Mun-
day, the river *fête* of a Lord Mayor's Show in diminished form. The
theme was Ancient Britain revived in her Prince, and it was articulated

by Corinea, Queen of Cornwall, and Amphion, both astride dolphins. The published account does not conceal the City Fathers' frustration in 'their zealous forwardnes, which else would have appeared in more flowing and aboundant manner'.[46] The King had achieved his objective. There had been no state entry on horseback with triumphal arches and street pageants as in 1604 and 1606, when the City had paid tribute to King James on his accession and had welcomed his brother-in-law, Christian IV of Denmark. Henry was received on the steps of Whitehall where, on Sunday 3 June, the King created twenty-four Knights of the Bath.[47] Characteristically, the Prince had refused to associate himself with the sale of honours so typical of his father, and 'when one of these had, by the ordinary means, secured the entry of his name on the list, the Prince complained that his blood was inferior to that of the others and caused the note to be cancelled'.[48] On Monday, 4 June, followed the investiture. By that date, relations with Parliament were decidedly cooler than they had been in March. At the end of April James increased his demand for an annual income by means of the Great Contract from £100 to £200,000 p.a., which was greeted with stupefaction, and, on 21 May, he had subjected the members to a second speech exalting the royal prerogative, which again was ill-received. It was therefore this deteriorating relationship with Parliament that the investiture was designed to ameliorate.

The ceremony was of a type which still has vigour in Britain to this day, when the hierarchy of state is made manifest by dress and symbolic gesture.[49] In the early seventeenth century its potency would have been even greater. The magnificence of dress was such that a Wiltshire MP wrote: 'I thought myself to be like a crow in the middes of a great many golden feathered doves.' It opened with the peers and members assembling in the Court of Requests to await the arrival of King and Prince by water from Whitehall. It was noted that the King should have preceded his son so that he should be enthroned to receive him. Instead he chose to travel the short distance by water with him both ways, thus eliminating any possible solitary exhibition of the heir apparent to the London populace. The ceremony itself was processional in form, the Prince preceded by heralds, Knights of the Bath and great lords of the realm bearing the robes and insignia. Henry himself was supported by Nottingham and Northampton. After Salisbury had read the Letters Patent of Creation, James invested Henry. The King, it was noted, made public signs of affection, 'now playfully patting his cheek and giving him other tokens of love'. The Prince, however, on his return to Whitehall, dined alone in state with 'music of forty several parts'.

That night the Queen's masque, in the planning since December of the previous year, attempted to restage the investiture in allegorical form.[50] No use was made of Jonson and instead the task was assigned to Samuel Daniel, who had been responsible for the very first of Anne's masques in 1604. The result was far from satisfactory although it reflects an effort to find a poet other than the King's who could write masques. In it Henry retained his mythological *persona* of the *Barriers* as Meliadus, Lord of the Isles. It began with a star-spangled cloud giving way to a scene of a haven dominated by 'the figure of a castle commanding a fortified town', with a harbour full of ships. For the audience this was an allusion to the Prince's interest both in maritime power and the art of fortification. It was the more topical in that it was only a few weeks later that the entire royal family was to go to Chatham for the launching of the *Prince Royal*. It must also have looked like one of the Prince's Dutch sea pieces that he had recently acquired for his gallery brought to life. And it was ordered, Daniel writes, 'according to perspective'.

The view of the port, however, whose topographical location is not referred to by Inigo Jones in his description of the scenery and costumes inserted into Daniel's text, is revealed in the speech by Triton on behalf of Zephyrus:

> All these within the goodly gracious bay
> Of manifold inharbouring Mulford meet,
> The happy port of union, which gave way
> To that great hero Henry and his fleet
> To make the blessed conjunction that begat
> A greater and more glorious far than that.[50]

Henry VII, the founder of the Tudor dynasty, had landed at Milford Haven in 1485 prior to the battle of Bosworth Field. As in the *Barriers*, six months earlier, the onlooking audience found themselves yet again asked to see the Prince in the perspective of British history, this time as the future Henry IX. A triton emerged to warn both King and Prince that Tethys, Queen of the Ocean and wife to Neptune, was shortly to appear in tribute to the investiture attended by the nymphs of the rivers of Great Britain. These were headed by the Lady Elizabeth as the Thames. The Triton was spokesman also for the Duke of York as Zephyrus, surrounded by a bevy of aristocratic girls attired as naiads. Two presentations then followed. The first to the King, as Oceanus, of a trident, 'ensign of her [i.e. Tethys's] love and of your right', the second of a scarf and sword to the Prince, as Meliadus.[52] The sword, which was so significantly denied the Prince in January, was here bestowed but with a gloss that cast it into one of its customary symbolic roles, that of Iusti-

74

tia, 'Which she unto Astraea sacred found, / And not to be unsheathed but on just ground'.[53] Astraea, or the Maiden Justice, was one of the most familiar of all the 'severall loues' whereby poets expressed their adulation of Elizabeth I.[54] And here the masque entered into a series of somewhat disconnected allusions to the old Elizabethan mythology. First, Henry received Astraea's sword: a symbolic enactment, in one sense, of the neo-Elizabethan revival. And what followed confirms this interpretation.

As in the *Barriers* the martial element was blunted, for not only was the sword cast as Iustitia, but also the Prince was reminded to keep within the confines of his watery empire. This was the symbolic message of the scarf:

> ... the zone of love and amity,
> T'ingird the same, wherein he may survey
> Infigured all the spacious empery
> That he is born unto another day.
> Which, tell him, all be world enough to yield
> All works of glory ever can be wrought.[55]

Treasure, the Prince is told, lies not in actions of arms beyond the Pillars of Hercules, symbols of the boundary of the ancient world, but in the plentiful gold to be made from the fishing industry! The mundane message could hardly have been a welcome one.

The *machina versatilis* (whose movement was masked by revolving lights) then turned to reveal Inigo Jones's amazing grotto, of a type that his colleague Salomon de Caus was at that very moment constructing at Greenwich, Somerset House and Richmond. In this glittering watery cavern the Queen and her ladies sat in tableau, subsequently descending and making their way across the arena in imitation of winding waterways, towards 'the Tree of Victory, which was a bay erected at the right side of the state, upon a little mound there raised'.[56] There they each laid in tribute a vase of flowers. A bay tree on a mount appears on a medal of Elizabeth I in which it arises out of a stormy monster-infested sea as a symbol of the inviolability of the island kingdom, together with the motto: NON ALTER CIRCVLVS ORBE DITIOR IN TOTO, NON IPSA PERICVLA TANGVNT (no richer crown in the whole world, not even dangers affect it) [57] The medal had been struck to celebrate the defeat of the might of Spain on the seas, and the masque was about sea power, a revival of Elizabethan sea imperialism epitomized in port, fortress, ships and rivers. The theme of rivers paying tribute recalls yet another image of Gloriana, the Ditchley Portrait, in which she stands on her island kingdom, on which the rivers are delineated, amidst the encircling ocean, with a sonnet nearby that speaks of 'Rivers of thanckes still to that oc[ean pour], Where grace is grace aboue, power po[wer]'.[58] But the mount is also a celebration of the creation of the Empire of Great Britain and an expression of the new imperial myth of Ancient Britain revived.

The masque had a third scene. Anne of Denmark and her ladies returned to their grotto and 'suddenly vanish', presumably the machine revolving back again. Mercury descended and summoned the Duke of York, dressed as Zephyrus, and six young noblemen. The *machina versatilis* revolved for a last time, revealing the masquers 'in their forms' seated in 'a most pleasant and artificial grove'. Technically *Tethys' Festival* is no advance on *Queens* of two years previous, apart from the addition of this extra scene 'to avoid the confusion which usually attendeth the desolve of these shows'.[59]

Although John Finnett described the masque as 'glorious' and the dancing of the little girls as 'to the Amazement of all Beholders', it was far from satisfactory. The presentation of the sword sat very awkwardly in the action and once again it proved irreconcilable to pay tribute simultaneously to father and son. Daniel was aware that all was not well and wrote, at the end of the published text, that it was printed to 'expose it to the censure of those who make it their best show to seem to know'.[60]

Daniel's most likely contemporary source for his masque's subject matter was Michael Drayton (1563–1631), who was one of the Prince's poets with a salary of £10 p.a.[61] That in itself was important, for Henry was deliberately employing an author who was disliked by his father. A prolific writer, it would have been his historical and patriotic poems that would initially have appealed to Henry, poems such as The *Barrons Wars* (1603) and the *Ballad of Agincourt*, which appeared in the 1605 edition of his *Poemes*. Drayton was also to associate himself with the Prince's colonial endeavours in the ode *To the Virginian Voyage*. But the most important of all was the appearance in 1612 of the first eighteen songs of his *Poly-Olbion. A Chorographical Description of all the Tracts, Riuers, Mountains, Forests and other Parts of this Renowned Isle of GREAT BRITAIN*. Fully in tune with the celebration of Stuart imperialism (although he had in fact begun it in the 1590s), Drayton's poem was accompanied by a learned commentary by John Selden. The dedication to the Prince is to him as 'the hopeful Heir': 'The influence of so glorious and fortunate a Star may also reflect upon me: which hath power to give me new life, or leave me to die more willingly and contented.' The title page, engraved by William Hole, sums up in one composite image the whole imperial vision:

> Through a *Trimphant Arch*, see *Albion* plac'd,
> In *Happy* site, in *Neptune's* arms embrac'd,
> In *Power* and *Plenty*, on her *Cleefy* Throne
> Circled with *Neptune's Garland*, being alone
> Styled *th'Ocean's Island* ...

The image evoked is close to that of her as Empress of the Isles in Peacham's *Minerva Britanna* of the same year. Drayton also prefaces his work with a famous engraved portrait of the Prince as hero and future *imperator Britanniae* in proud imperial profile:

> BRITAIN, *behold here portray'd to thy sight*
> Henry, *thy best hope, and the world's delight;*
> *Ordain'd to make thy eight Henries nine:*
> *Who, by that virtue of the treble Trine,*
> *To his own goodness (in his being) brings*
> *These several Glories of th'eight English Kings:*
> Deep knowledge, Greatness, Long Life, Policy,
> Courage, Zeal, Fortune, Awful Majesty.
> *He like great* Neptune *on three Seas shall rove*
> *And rule three Realms, with triple power, like* Jove.
> *Thus in soft peace, this in tempestuous wars,*
> *Till from his feet his fame shall strike the stars.*

Poly-Olbion was written for Henry as the first Prince who, from birth, was destined to rule over the whole island as the descendant of the Trojan, Brutus and King Arthur. This geographical celebration by Drayton of the Empire of Great Britain in 1610, in which the rivers are personified, must have been completed at precisely the same time as Daniel was constructing his masque conceived in identical mythological terms.

On the following day, 5 June, came the tilt.[62] Fourteen lords and gentlemen headed by the Duke of Lennox paid their separate tributes to the Prince. The occasion was noted for the splendour of the horse caparisons, which were 'wondrously imbroydered with pearls, gould, and siluer, the like rich habilaments for horses were never seene before'. Pembroke exceeded all by arriving in 'two Caparisons of Peach-coullored Velvet embroidered all ouer with orientall Pearls'. One of Jones's designs from this period is for a horse caparison adorned with antique masks, swags and tassels. There are two costume drawings, one previously associated with *Oberon*, which repeat these motifs exactly, so that the two should relate to the entry of the same knight.[63] What was really of interest was their 'ingenious devices and trophies'. A Scottish nobleman, likely to have been Lord Hay, came in a raincloud from which erupted thunder and lightning and which opened before the King dis-

75
78

closing elaborately dressed women and children. The most spectacular of all was staged by Lord Compton who, an onlooker reports,

... buylded himself as it were a bowre oppon the topp of the walle which is next to St James Parke, it was made in the maner of a sheepcote and there he sate in a graye russet cloke as long as a gowne, and he had a sheepe crooke in one hand with a bottell hanging theron and a dogg in chayne in th'other hand, as thoughe he had bine a sheephearde, and thorowe the topp of the bowre there stoode up as it were the mast of a ship gilded rounde about with goulde and uppon the topp thereof there was fastned a panne with fyre burninge in it, and as some thought there was a pitche in it and an iron to marke sheepe withall.... 76

From here Lord Compton sent a squire who delivered a speech to the King, the knight himself subsequently descending to make the customary processional entry on horseback across the tiltyard, his men 'everie one wearing a hat of strawe, and haveinge theyer faces paynted as blacke as the devill'.

William Compton, Lord Compton, later Earl of Northampton, (d. 1630), had been a central figure at every Accession Day Tilt since 1589. In 1590 he and his entourage appeared all in virgin white and in 1599 he entered 'like a Fisherman, with 6 men clad in Motley, his Caparie-sons all of Nett, having caught a Frogge'. In 1610 his father-in-law died leaving a vast fortune, of which he 'did within lesse than 8 weekes spende 72,000 *l.*, mostly in great horses, rich saddlery and playe'.[64]

Hitherto unidentified, Inigo Jones's design for this extraordinary décor survives in part. The drawing for a mount with a winding path running up it, a mast atop, with ladders and a blazing cauldron at its summit, must be what the observer saw.[65] Our Shepherd Knight inhabited a cave whose entrance was hung with *impresa* shields. His disguise, however, was pure Elizabethan revivalism, for the pastoral theme was embedded in the mythology of the Accession Day Tilts from a very early date.[66] It was a legend epitomized by Sir Philip Sidney in his guise as Philisides, the Shepherd Knight, who records his appearance in the tiltyard in this manner in the *Arcadia*, his squires bearing lances disguised as sheephooks and his *impresa* a sheep marked with pitch with the motto *Spotted to be known*. What could be more apposite for Prince Henry than this revival of Elizabethan arcady? For in him there had been found the true heir of 'that great shepherd, good Philisides'. The day was rounded off, at the expense of the City, with a sea battle and firework display on the Thames in which a Turkish ship and fort were vanquished.[67]

So the festivals for Henry's investiture drew to their close. What is striking, apart from their varied success, is their number, for they stretched over almost a week. They included a river triumph, the creation of knights, a formal investiture, a masque, a tournament, a firework display and an aquatic battle. No comparable series of *fêtes* had ever been staged before by the Jacobean court. What prompted the belief that major dynastic events should be marked in this way must have been Prince Henry's knowledge of Medici festivals, which likewise consisted of several types of entertainment arranged over a period of days. They, in their turn, owed much to the sets of *magnificences* staged at the Valois court, under the aegis of Catherine de' Medici, in the late sixteenth century. Their aim was always both national and international prestige for the ruling house. In this the festivals for Henry's investiture probably succeeded, although in terms of immediate political advantage for the King they were a failure. Relations with Parliament, far from improving, went steadily downhill through the autumn and mounting royal rage led to its dissolution early in 1611.[68] The Great Contract ended in breakdown in November. And, in spite of the King's efforts, the festivals had established a rival star in the firmament with a rival court in the making but had not solved the problem of the royal finances. At the end of June, Correr summed up the results of the whole operation with characteristic perceptiveness:

He [the Prince] has not yet received his revenues; this is being put off till October next, and possibly further; nor has the King been pleased to allow him to increase his household as he desired. It seems that the King has some reasonable jealousy of the rising sun; and indeed the vivacity of the Prince grows apace, and every day he gives proof of wisdom and lofty thoughts far in advance of his years.[69]

Jonson was first and foremost the King's poet and we have already sensed his ambivalence in working for the Prince in the *Barriers*. The fact that Anne turned to Samuel Daniel in the summer of that year probably indicates a quest for a masque writer other than Jonson. *Tethys' Festival* was clearly unsuccessful and Daniel was not used again, which must account for the reversion to Jonson for the Prince's and the Queen's masques in 1611.

Oberon. The Fairy Prince is one of the most studied of all Jonson's masques.[70] It reflects accurately the radically different political climate which marked the months subsequent to the assassination of Henri IV. One is immediately struck by its obvious insularity. As in the case of *Tethys' Festival* there is no European context and it reinvests the Prince with the mythology of the Elizabethan age. The masque opened with a curtain painted with a map of the kingdom, an appropriate compliment to both King and heir at the beginning of the year which saw the publication of John Speed's mighty *Theatre of the Empire of Great Britain*.

72 Bay tree on the inviolate island
of England. Reverse of a medal of
Elizabeth I

73 Elizabeth I. The Ditchley Portrait. The Queen arises above the
rivers of England.

74 Inigo Jones's design for a river
nymph

The Prince's festivals III

*The creation of Henry as Prince
of Wales, June 1610
The Queen's masque,*
Tethys' Festival

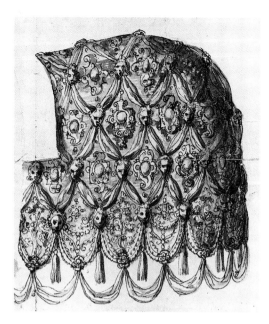

The Prince's festivals IV

The creation of Henry as Prince of Wales, June 1610
The tilt: designs by Inigo Jones

75 Horse caparison

76 Mount and beacon for Lord Compton as a Shepherd Knight

77 Lancebearer

78 Henry as Oberon, The Fairy Prince *(see over)*

A.

The Prince's festivals V

Oberon. The Fairy Prince,
January 1611
Designs by Inigo Jones

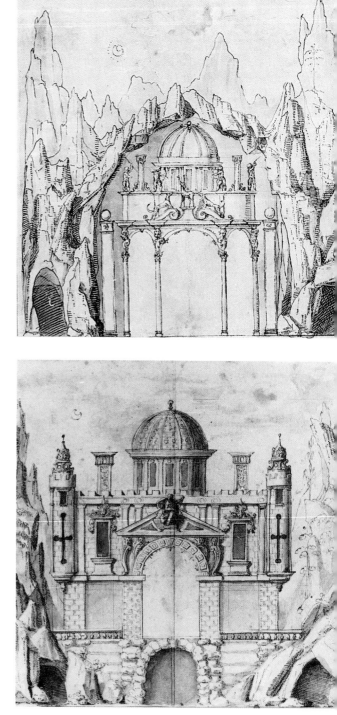

81   Project for *Oberon*

82   Exterior of Oberon's Palace

79   Attendant in Ancient British dress

80   Costume design for a fairy

83   Design for the Queen's
masque, 1611: *Love Freed from Ignorance and Folly*

Music

84 *(left)* Angelo Notari, the Venetian composer in the Prince's service

85 *(left, below)* Title-page to Notari's *Musiche Nuove*, 1613, perhaps after a design by Constantino de' Servi

Science

86 *(below)* Perpetuum mobile machine by Cornelius Drebbel

The Prince's collections I

Antique gems and cameos

87 *(opposite)* Abraham Gorlaeus and his collection

88, 89 *(opposite, below)* Engraved gems set into rings in the Gorlaeus collection

Aetatis Suae 5 ... m... 1603

Bassein fe.

| AN . FER . GEM . SARD INCISA. IVL . CAESAR. | AN . FER . GEM . SARD INCISA. HERCVL . ROMANVS |

| AN . FERR . GEM . ACHTES . INCISA . AEQVITAS | AN . FERR . GEM . ACHATES . INCISA . MV . SCAEVOLA |

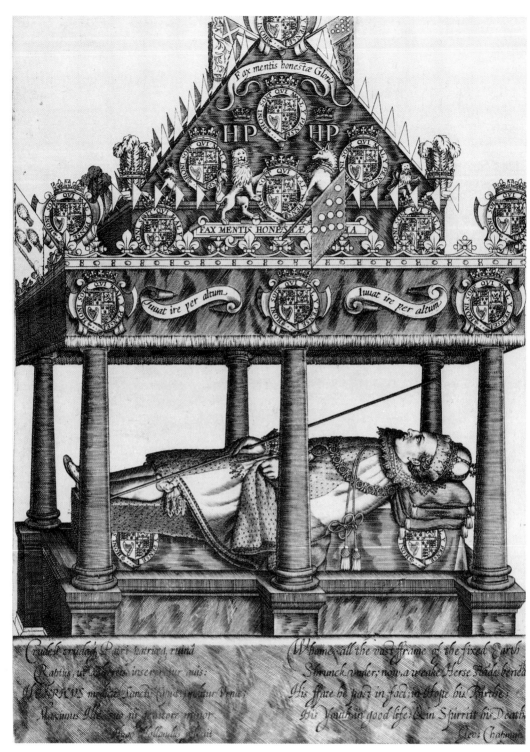

90 William Hole's engraving of the
Prince's hearse, 1612

This curtain fell to reveal a vast range of mountains bathed in moon-light and inhabited by satyrs. Silenus presides over them and proceeds 'to explain to his creatures the values of order and constancy, the social and moral virtues the Prince represents'.[71] Under his tutelage they re-nounce their old way of life:

> Grandsire, we shall leave to play
> With Lyaeus now: and serve
> Only Ob'ron?[72]

This progression to a new virtuous order was also achieved visually as the front shutter of rocks parted to expose the façade of Oberon's palace; the gates and walls of the palace were transparent, and within could be seen the Prince and his companions arranged in tableau.

82

As in the case of the *Barriers*, the Prince chose to associate himself with a reform of architecture, of the same kind as that of the previous year, a mingling of Ancient British Classical with Gothic elements, re-stating to the court Henry's role as heir to both eras of the country's his-tory. An eyewitness, William Trumbull, described the effect of this ap-parition, how the audience saw through the exterior of the palace 'a great throne with countless lights and colours, all shifting, a lovely thing to see'. Jonson's texts rarely provide us with any detailed infor-mation of a masque's visual appearance, thus depriving us of knowl-edge of what must have been an extensive contribution by Jones in the form of scenic effects and stage movement amplifying Jonson's bald textual statements. The report we have describes the masquers making their entry on foot, but Jonson records something much more com-plex:

There the whole palace opened, and the nation of fays were discovered, some with in-struments, some bearing lights, others singing; and within, afar off in perspective, the knights masquers sitting in their several sieges. At the further end of all, Oberon, in a chariot, which to a loud triumphant music began to move forward, drawn by two white bears, and on either side guarded by three sylvans, with one going in front.[73]

Whether this was in fact what happened or not, Jonson states that the Prince was placed at the meeting point of a perspective arrangement.

In the light of the *Barriers*, we ought to pause and consider the exact nature of that perspectival arrangement. The *Barriers* and *Oberon* are the earliest examples of perspective being used to focus the eye on the central masquer, the Prince. There is no evidence in any of the earlier masques that perspective had ever been used in this way. Instead, the perspective element was more concerned with the King, from whose onlooking eyes the visual triangle radiated. The extension of this to ar-rangements on stage was logical. It reinforces the view that the initial use of perspective was always in symbolic terms rather than as a fundamental premise for the total reordering of pictorial space, and that these new moves concerning perspective must have stemmed from the Prince himself. Henry, in fact, worked from knowledge, for, as we know, he had been taught perspective by Salomon de Caus, who was to dedicate to him in 1612 his *La Perspective avec la raison des ombres et mirroirs*.[74] In the preface, de Caus states that he had been instructing the Prince in perspective for two or three years, which would take us to 1607–8 and would certainly account for the new developments in its use in his festivals.

81   Jones's designs for *Oberon* are confusing for they include two sets, both incomplete and both making use of different machinery. The first series utilizes a *machina versatilis* and its imagery includes *putti* aiming arrows at a stag. In addition there is a design for the palace interior, which is strongly in terms of perspective and directly related to the arrangement of St George's portico in the *Barriers*. The Venetian ambassador records that Henry had wanted 'a masque on horseback' but his father refused to allow it.[75] The designs which were finally used strike one above all by their extreme flatness, with no use of perspective, confirming that this must have been confined to the tableaux in the palace, for which the design does not survive, and whose purpose was solely emblematic. In European terms, they show the limitation of Jones's knowledge at this point.

As the stage scenery unfolded to reveal the Prince and his companions we have also been witnessing a revolution in Jones's stage technique: the first extensive use of the *scena ductalis,* that is the use of side wings and backshutters running in grooves, that enabled him to achieve a multiplicity of scene changes effortlessly, a system which he was to adopt as his standard practice for the rest of his career. It has been overlooked that this major development was achieved in a masque for Prince Henry. Although Jones makes use of front shutters in earlier masques, *Oberon* is the great step forward, enabling him to match exactly the demands of the poet's text in which order, exemplified in heroic architecture, triumphs over the rude world of untamed nature. Did Jones reach this decision himself, or does it reflect the Prince's knowledge, through Harington, of the *intermezzi* of 1608? *Oberon* is the first occasion on which the *scena ductalis* was adopted as a fundamental of every change of scene.

80   The costume designs are no less interesting. Oberon and his attendants are all attired *à l'antique* and, whether they entered on foot or in a chariot, from stage to hall, there can be no doubt that the effect aimed at was akin to a Roman imperial triumph. Trumbull, who has provided

us with our eyewitness report of the performance, states that they appeared 'as Roman emperors are represented'. Where they were not *à l'antique* they were dressed in what Jones used as Ancient British costume, vaguely Tudor with slashing and flat bonnets. As in the case of the *Barriers* there was a visual emphasis on the historical continuum, marrying antiquity and the intervening Gothic centuries.[76]

The *Barriers* was both in text and design a statement of the Prince's desire to reform architecture. There is nothing, however, about architecture in Jonson's poetry for *Oberon,* although the fact that Henry must have decreed that he be revealed in a magnificent palace was clearly part of the brief from the outset, as Jones's designs for the masque in all its successive versions retain the palace as the dominant scenic feature. Although it has been argued that these designs represent an effort by Jones to create a 'Great British' style, the successive drawings for this edifice can hardly be ranked amongst the architect's finest concepts.[77] They remain awkward, are highly derivative and fall far short, for instance, of the sophistication of the work by his colleague Salomon de Caus. The synthesis of references used by Jones ranges over the French Renaissance, late Tudor neo-medieval and borrowings from Serlio. In the main, the allusions are to French architecture, which Jones would have studied during his visit to that country in 1609 and in du Cerceau's *Les Plus Excellents Bastiments de France.* From these sources he would have been familiar with *châteaux* which arose from rocky hillsides progressing upwards into ordered architecture adorned with Italianate detail and medieval turrets. In Jones's final design for Oberon's palace, Serlio is the main source for the overall concept, as well as for details such as the windows, and the drum and dome of the cupola, derived from Bramante's *Tempietto.* But the end result is oddly provincial and English, not so far from the neo-medievalism of John Smythson. Indeed the castle skyline may well have been designed to evoke the Prince's palace of Richmond. There is, however, a ladder of symbolic ascent, matching the progression of the masque text, that moves upwards from rocks to Tuscan rustic to Doric and thence to that ultimate neo-Platonic symbol of perfection, a dome.

In the masque, the Prince is presented as the heir to the Elizabethan world of fairy. But, as in the case of the *Barriers,* Jonson found it awkward having to serve two masters, King and Prince. *Oberon,* from this point of view, makes an unhappy document. The poet kept running into difficulties whenever he reached the crucial moment at which he had to subsume the mythological apotheosis of the Prince into the greater one of the monarch. In the case of Henry and James the mythologies contradicted each other, heavily in the case of the *Barriers,* just awkwardly in that of *Oberon.* In the latter the Prince is the heir of the 'nation of fayes', the son of King Arthur:

> Whilst we in tunes to Arthur's chair
>   Bear Oberon's desire,
>   Than which there nothing can be higher,
> Save James, to whom it flies:
> But he the wonder is of tongues, of ears, of eyes.[78]

Henry would, of course, have fitted the bill admirably as the new Arthur, the role advanced for him in the *Barriers,* the warrior king, hero of romance and battles. But the convention of the masque required him to be cast as Arthur's son, and James in the unlikely role of the Ancient British warrior king. The King sat in his 'chair', but Jonson fails to take the parallel any further, and here the structure of the masque collapses. Instead he embarks on a feeble eulogy of James, stemming from an exposition of the Divine Right theory: 'He is a god, o'er kings.' In this way *Oberon* draws to an unsatisfactory close.

A final aspect of *Oberon* which cannot be divined from the printed text is its extraordinary importance in the evolution of music in the court masques. At the time, this would have struck the onlooker as the one element that formed a major contrast to the *Barriers* of the previous year, which had consisted only of spoken dialogue and a scene change. *Oberon* was quite different. Jonson's references are cursory: 'At which the satyrs fell suddenly into this catch,' 'The song ended...', 'The SONG, by two fays', '... again excited by a song' and 'they were invited home by one of the sylvans with this song'.[79] Our observer, William Trumbull, however, provides a very different picture, strongly evoking the impact of the musical effects: 'Before passing into the hall ten musicians appeared each with a lute and two boys who sang very well some sonnets in praise of the Prince and his father;' or 'With vocal and instrumental music the masqueraders approached to the throne...'.

The musicologist John Cutts has demonstrated that *Oberon* as a masque was musically enormously inventive compared with its predecessors. The whole of it, except for the dialogue of the satyrs and that of Silenus and the first satyr, was either sung or danced.[80] For the first time in this masque, Jonson abandoned the traditional madrigal format for the songs in favour of sung dialogue. This was undoubtedly a step in the direction of opera and it was one, like other aspects of the arts as they were developed by the Prince, which he anticipated, not to be taken up again until 1617 in Jonson's *Vision of Delight,* when *stile recitativo* along the Italian lines was introduced. In yet another aspect, the festivals of the Prince are revealed to be quite different from those of either his father or mother or any of his predecessors.

The composer of nearly all the music for *Oberon* was Robert Johnson (d. 1626), musician to the King from 1603 to 1633 but also to Prince Henry. He composed the music except for two songs by Alfonso Ferrabosco (d. 1628). The latter had taught the Prince music and dedicated his *Ayres* to him in 1609. Hawkins refers to Henry's devotion to martial music, and W. H. is specific when he writes: 'He loved Musicke, and namely good consorts of Instruments and voices ioyned together.'[81] He certainly had distinguished musicians in his service, among them Walter Quinn, John Bull, Robert Johnson, Thomas Lupo, Thomas Cutting and Thomas Ford.[82] His death attracted a steady stream of musical laments parallel to the literary outpouring and including Giovanni Coperario's *Songs of Mourning* (1613). A close member of his circle was Sir Henry Fanshawe, who was 'a great lover of music', particularly Italian.[83] The Prince's financial accounts too contain material which would indicate a degree of commitment. These include payments for an organ from Dort, i.e. Dordrecht (probably that described by a visitor from Hesse as inlaid with the Prince's arms in mother-of-pearl), and others to French musicians; payments for conveying instruments to and from Woodstock, and 'for songe Booke(s) and prickling of songs with a guilded Coffer to keepe them in'.[84] More important, however, are two other references, one in the correspondence of the Tuscan Resident, Lotti, reporting the arrival of the latest music by Jacopo Peri, author of *Euridice,* from Florence[85] and the second Henry's employment of Angelo Notari (1566–1663/4).[86] The latter, if his birthdate is correct, died at the enormous age of ninety-seven, three years after the Restoration. These two facts do reveal a commitment to the more advanced Italian styles coming out of the Medici court. Notari was to publish, in 1613, his *Prime musiche nuove,* which was engraved by the artist closely connected with the St James's court, William Hole, and which the composer must have been compiling during his period in Henry's service. It is difficult not to believe that the title page and portrait of Notari stem from designs by de' Servi, who belonged to the same circle.

All the evidence indicates that a great amount of creative energy involving all the arts went into the production of *Oberon,* and the startling novelties it included must owe their impulse to the Prince himself. It is regrettable that we do not know who danced in this masque, apart from Southampton, because that too would probably emphasize its innovatory nature. The heir apparent is presented as the future *Imperator Britanniae* in a visual and musical spectacle of the most advanced type, combining new developments in scenic engineering and optics used in the theatre with instrumental and vocal music designed not to be occasional and interjectory but to be part of a sustained scenario. Although

84

85

this could not be foreseen, *Oberon* was to be the apogee of Henry's contribution to the art of festival.

83   The Queen's masque which followed a month later, *Love Freed from Ignorance and Folly*, had been composed for 1610, but had been put off for a year.[87] What is interesting is how much more easily the homage of the Queen was able to fit into her husband's passive and pacificatory mythology. In this masque Anne and her ladies come as the 'Eleven daughters of the morn'. As Jonson explains: '... these ladies, being the perfect issue of beauty and all worldly grace, were carried by Love to celebrate the majesty and wisdom of the King, figured in the sun...'.[88] A 'Monster sphinx' had cast these ladies into the Prison of Night until a riddle had been answered. Love, aided by the wise Muses, deciphers the riddle, and vanquishes Ignorance and her attendant Follies, thus releasing the Daughters to pay homage to the King. Scenically the masque repeated exactly the arrangement of the *Masque of Queens* of 1609. Below, there was the Prison of Night, a Gothic castle, with doors through which the masquers could enter; above, a fixed celestial vision in which the masquers were revealed seated on three *machinae versatiles*. What is striking here is the total absence of any element of perspective.

Love Freed shows how the Prince's festivals were far more advanced and innovatory than his mother's. It is possible that her masque had made use of scenery made a year earlier, but it is old-fashioned compared with either the *Barriers* or *Oberon*. Both these were concerned with developing new stage techniques which would allow a multiplicity of scene changes and also with exploring the use of perspective. These developments allowed the masque form to be a vehicle of many more complex ideas. What we do not know from the existing evidence is what the reaction was to Jones's work of the Prince's circle. Did he really give Henry what he wanted, or was the Prince simply making do with someone who could not match up to all the mechanical wonders which had been reported to him from Florence in 1608? One important fact would suggest that Henry was not satisfied with Jones. In September 1610, when he must have been beginning to think about *Oberon*, he opened up negotiations for an architect–engineer from the Medici court.

After the glories of *Oberon*, the momentous year of 1612 was ushered in by a masque reflecting the reality of crown finances: *Oberon* had cost the enormous sum of £1087; its successor, *Love Restored* (also by Jonson), produced to grace Twelfth Night, cost just £280. The Prince himself did not appear in it and the event is referred to in the Revels Accounts as a 'princes Mask performed by Gentelmen of his High(ness)', who appeared as the ten Ornaments of the Court: Honour, Courtesy,

Valour, Urbanity, Confidence, Alacrity, Promptness, Industry, Hability and Reality. They escorted a triumphal chariot bearing the god Cupid and there is nothing in the text to indicate any other scenery. The designer is unknown but it should logically have been Constantino de' Servi, in which case it would have been like one of the *carri trionfali* familiar to the Medici court, with its tradition from Vasari through Buontalenti to Parigi. The theme of the masque was the old one of the conflict between love and riches, the defeat of the latter ushering in an allegorical vision of the virtues of the King and court. As it was a 'prince's mask', what we see is a parade of the attributes cultivated, by implication, by members of Henry's household. Apart from the antimasque, *Love Restored* is far from Jonson's best.[89]

The masque, however, had a message. Its presenters were Masquerado, Robin Goodfellow and Plutus, god of riches, the latter in the guise of Cupid, a deception which is unmasked leading to some tart words on the subject of equating marriage and money:

'Tis that impostor, Plutus, the god of money, who has stol'n Love's ensigns and in his belied figure reigns i'the world, making friendships, contracts, marriages, and almost religion; begetting, breeding and holding the nearest respects of mankind, and usurping all those offices in this age of gold, which Love himself performed in the Golden Age.

No one in the audience, least of all the King, to whom it was primarily addressed, would have escaped the reference to the marriage negotiations. Furious at the collapse of the offer of a Spanish infanta, James had made serious overtures for the hand of the Infanta Caterina, sister of the Grand Duke Cosimo II, a match for which the King aimed at extracting a sum equal to that the Tuscans had bestowed on Marie de' Medici on her marriage to Henri IV. Later in 1612 also was to come the revival of a Savoy match for Henry and once again the obsession with money.

Over the fate of his daughter, James had already made up his mind, for she was to be married to Frederick V, Elector Palatine, the match for which the Prince of Wales's party had striven so hard. And this was to be marked by the most splendid series of spectacles, expressly designed to establish the Stuart court in the eyes of Europe as the fount of revived Protestant chivalry. The unperformed and half-conceived *fêtes* for the Palatine wedding would have formed the climax of Henry's festival policy as it had evolved since 1610.

On 16 October the young Count Palatine landed at Gravesend and was met by the Duke of Lennox accompanied by a large train of gentlemen.[90] There he rested for two days before setting out by river for London. John Finnett in a letter describes the bridegroom thus: 'He is *straight* and *well-shaped* for his growing Years: His Complexion is brown, with a *Countenance pleasing*, and a promising *Wit, Courage* and *Judgment.*'[91] The entry by water was one long triumph. Accompanied by 150 boats, the river was crowded with vessels decorated with flags and pennons. The guns from the Tower shattered the air with a salute and the atmosphere was laden with smoke; the ears were deafened by the blast of trumpet fanfares, the beating of drums and the cheering of the crowds. At Whitehall Stairs stood the young Duke of York attended by the Earls of Shrewsbury, Sussex, Southampton, and a vast concourse of lords. It was they who escorted the Count Palatine to the Banqueting House, in which the royal family and the court were arranged in a brilliant tableau.

The Palatine cavalcade, together with that of Count Henry of Nassau, swept into the Hall. James embraced his future son-in-law, who responded, it was noted, with suitable humility. He then saluted Anne (who despised the match) who 'entertained him with a fixed countenance' and coldly extended a hand to be kissed. Then came the moment everyone had waited for. The Palatine turned his attention to the Princess Elizabeth, 'who was not noted till then to turn so much as a corner of an eye towards him'. He made to stoop to kiss the hem of her robe, at which point she descended into a deep curtsey and presented him with her cheek to kiss; this he did, at which she was noted to blush.

In the days that followed, the Palatine was lodged at Essex House and spent his time playing the ardent wooer. Chamberlain reported: 'he seems to take delight in nothing but her companie and conversation'.[92] Henry of Nassau meanwhile was with the Prince. So the days were to pass until interrupted by the terrible event of 6 November. Elizabeth and Frederick were eventually married on St Valentine's Day 1613, an occasion marked by a great series of *fêtes*, but between November and February the world had changed. What we have lost sight of are the festivals for this marriage as they were initially conceived, for the alliance was the foundation of Henry's future policy. They are its climax. If they had been staged or their texts had survived intact we would have had a marvellous key as to how this marriage was viewed and publicly presented by the Prince and his circle.

From the very first, Henry is mentioned as the prime mover in organizing the *fêtes*. Hawkins explains how he left Richmond Palace 'to give order for everything, and to dispatch all Affairs both of his own, and concerning the following intended Triumphs, for his Highness the Palsgrave's better Welcome'.[93] Shortly after he had landed, Finnett wrote to Trumbull in Brussels that 'we talk of *Masks, Tilts,* and *Barriers,* but they are yet under Invention, not in Resolution'.[94] And Correr wrote on 9 November (30 October, old style) that the Princess was preparing a sumptuous masque of sixteen maids, of which she was to be one. He also spoke of a barriers, tournament and jousts and mentioned that the marriage was to be at Easter. A week later he reported that the four Inns of Court were preparing sumptuous *fêtes* 'in obedience to the Prince's orders'.[95]

Doubtless there were to have been two sets of festivals, the usual Christmas and Twelfth Night revels, followed by those for the actual marriage. When the latter eventually took place there were three masques, Thomas Campion's *Lords Masque,* which was a double one of lords and ladies, George Chapman's *Memorable Masque* for the Middle Temple and Lincoln's Inn, and Francis Beaumont's Inner Temple and Gray's Inn Masque. From this we can deduce that a masque presumably for Twelfth Night, in which the Princess was to have danced, was abandoned, as were all the martial sports of tilt, tourney and barriers, apart from a running at the ring. This means that the plans must have changed in relation to both the form and content of the marriage *fêtes*. Certainly none of them celebrates the match in quite the way that it was seen by the Prince's party, as a militant pan-Protestant European alliance to curb Habsburg power. As in the aftermath of the assassination of Henri IV the emphasis is on conciliation and reconciliation.

One little entertainment and one only did take place and it is a clue in reconstructing what the rest might have been. Sometime during the weeks before the Prince succumbed to illness, a hack poet, William Fennor, declaimed before the King and Queen, Prince Henry and the Princess Elizabeth 'A description of the Palsgraues Countrey'.[96] It is stoutly Protestant in content and casts the future in terms of five noble reformist princes:

> Five Princes in this iron age suruiue,
>> which makes it seeme the siluer worlde againe:
> To match them hardly shall we finde out fiue
>> yet weell forbeare to speake of *France* or *Spaine,*
> Fiue heires, fiue youths, fiue kinsmen, and fiue Princes,
>> Of one Religion, though in fiue Prouinces.

The five are the Prince of Hesse, the Prince of Brunswick, the Prince of Brandenburg, the Count Palatine and Prince Henry:

> Each of these are their Countries ioyfull hope,
>> friends to the Gospell, foes to th'Diuell and Pope.

And these are matched by three virgin princesses headed by '*Englands* faire *Phoenix*'. Despite its crudeness the mood is what we would expect: reformist and missionary in a European sense.

This minor entertainment surely gives us a clue as to the theme of the festivals as they were to have been and, moreover, it enables us to examine those that took place with a new eye as to what was salvaged and recast. One of the events that immediately springs to mind is George Chapman's *Memorable Masque*.[97] The Inns of Court masques were commanded by the Prince himself, and Chapman, who was part of his circle and that of Raleigh, would have been a natural choice for author. The subject matter, moreover, is British imperial expansion into the Americas. At the heart of the masque is a statement endorsing a policy of colonial expansion which was specifically anti-Spanish, Protestant and anti-Catholic. The masquers were Knights of Virginia, sun-worshippers, attended by musicians as Priests of the Sun and torch-bearers as Indians. They were revealed seated in a mine of gold, enshrined as it were in the fabled wealth of the New World that animated every voyage. The dénouement is one of religious conversion. Just as the pagan cults were enlightened by the Christian revelation, so, in the context of the Renaissance hermetic tradition, the sun-worshipping Virginians were in some senses acknowledging only One God. The Orphic Sun could become the Christian Sun and the priests sang what in parts was a paraphrase of the Orphic hymn to the Sun, giving the masque powerful overtones of Renaissance neo-platonic magic – so saturated is it with solar attributes. The climax came when Honour summoned the Virginians to undergo an act of conversion from the worship of their One God, the Sun, to a discovery of the true One Christian God by acknowledging his earthly representative, the Sun King, James I:

> Virginian Princes, you must now renounce
> Your superstitious worship of these suns,
> Subject to cloudy dark'nings and descents;
> And of your fit devotions turn the events
> To this our Briton Phoebus, whose bright sky
> (Enlightened with a Christian piety)
> Is never subject to black Error's night,
> And hath already offered heaven's true light
> To your dark region....[98]

This could only ever refer to the Virginia plantation with which Prince Henry had been intimately associated since the age of twelve as a major patron of the revival of Elizabethan colonialism. As we have seen, the re-establishment of Virginia was conceived not only in political but also in religious terms as extension beyond the seas of the Church of England. Chapman's masque, therefore, is still moving *au fond* in the ethos of October 1612, with its predictions of a consolidated anti-Habsburg Protestant alliance combined with a reformist zeal to convert the globe.

William Crashaw, who had preached the sermon at court launching
the Virginia enterprise casting it as a Protestant crusade, was precisely
the type of minister whose ideas had currency at the Inns of Court, for
he was in fact preacher to the Inner Temple, which, together with
Gray's Inn, presented the other masque at the Prince's command.[99] In
the production of this, several sources designate Francis Bacon as its
'chief contriver' and the river triumph which preceded it was organized by the Prince's friend Phineas Pett. Although it is a far less taut or
elegant entertainment, Beaumont's masque shares with it a strongly religious aura. This time the masquers were revealed as Olympian
Knights, who were also priests, arranged in a tableau before tents festooned with armour and military trophies 'as if it had been a camp'. The
scene depicted is reminiscent of the background view in Isaac Oliver's
miniature of the Prince. The priestly nature of these knights was heavily
emphasized.

... the Knights appeared first, as consecrated persons, all in veils, like to copes, of silver
tiffiny....In the midst between both the tents, upon the very top of the hill ... was placed
Jupiter's altar, gilt ... and Jupiter's Priests in white robes about it.[100]

What we are seeing is a vision of Protestant Henrician chivalry, reforming missionary knights and zealous clergy presented in allegorical
terms.

> Behold, Jove's altar, and his blessed priests
> Moving about it! – Come, you holy men,
> And with your voices draw these youths along....[101]

And they descend and dance a reconstituted Olympic Games presaging
the glorious future awaiting both bride and groom.

Both the entertainments from the Inns of Court, which were under
the auspices of the Prince, were notable for another fact, and that was
that Ben Jonson, the King's poet, was not used. Although for part of
1613 he was certainly abroad, overtures for poets must have been made
in the autumn of the previous year and the use of Chapman and Beaumont indicates a renewed quest by the Prince for a masque-writer sympathetic to the ideas and ideals of his own court. Even Jonson admitted
in 1619 to Drummond of Hawthornden that 'next himself, only
Fletcher and Chapman could make a mask'.

Francis Beaumont (*c.* 1584–1616) was a natural choice for the Gray's
Inn and Inner Temple masque, for he had been a student at the latter
and contributed to their revels at an earlier date, when he penned what
was described as 'the most ploddenly plotted shew of Lady Amity'.[102]
He had, in addition, it seems, close links with the Prince. In an undated letter he refers to Henry as 'his most excellent lord and good

maister' and writes in a jovial way how he has pressed a dozen men-at-arms 'out of your armie of Cockes' for his service. They are only as yet 'young and inexperienced' soldiers who have never looked 'their aduersaries in the face', so he has sent them out on a mock sally to test the enemy's strength, 'that so I may be better prepared when I shall bring on your whole armie of twenty cockes, to perfourme your challenge for a hundred pound against all England'.[103] The most likely context of this letter is the period leading up to the marriage festivals, indicating that what ended up as a masque may have begun as a device for a combat at the barriers, more in keeping with the Prince's tastes and also with what the Inns had taken to court at an earlier date. Indeed, Beaumont's highly militaristic masque of Olympian Knights would make far more sense with fighting at the barriers for the Olympic Games than a tame round of choreographed dances.

The masque by George Chapman (*c.* 1560–1634) was for the other two Inns. As a poet and playwright, Chapman also enjoyed a close relationship with the Prince.[104] It is stated that from the beginning of the reign he occupied a lowly place in his household as a sewer-in-ordinary and that it was at the Prince's request that he undertook the translation of Homer. He should be identical with the 'Mr Chapman' who received cloth for the Prince's funeral in the capacity of one of the 'Gentlemen extraordinarie servauntes to the Prince'.[105] The first instalment of the Homer appeared in 1598, dedicated to Essex, and it was in the *Corallarium ad Principem* at the close of his *Euthymiae raptus; or the tears of peace: with interlocutions* (1609), dedicated to Henry, that he reveals that the Prince acknowledged 'his Homer after the publication of the *Twelve Bookes* and commanded him to proceed with the rest of the translation'. The complete translation appeared in 1611, dedicated again to the Prince of Wales, so that out of all the poets with connections with the St James's court, Chapman by 1612 was beginning to emerge as the most important. According to the poet, Henry ordered a life-pension for him on his deathbed, so that it is hardly surprising that Chapman regarded his demise as a personal disaster: 'The most unualuable and dismaifull loss of my deare and Heroicall Patrone, Prince HENRY'. Had the Prince lived it is likely that Chapman's career as a masque-writer might well have unfolded. He was ideally suited to take up that position for, like Jonson, he was closely connected with Inigo Jones who, as we have seen, is likely to have been the designer of the title page to his Homer, who certainly worked with him on the masque, to whom Chapman dedicated his *Musaeus* in 1616, and who, almost twenty years later, designed his tomb in St-Giles-in-the-Fields.

There is a complication to the story of the Gray's Inn and Inner

Temple masque. In 1613 in Heidelberg an account was published in French of the festivities for the marriage.[106] The author, D. Jocquet, clearly had access to some of the masque texts, for he translates a considerable amount of Chapman's. In contrast, in the case of Campion's he writes only a paragraph which gives an inaccurate account of it. More surprising is the fact that Beaumont's masque does not appear at all. Instead the gentlemen of the two Inns of Court stage a completely different and far more interesting masque. Jocquet had its text before him as he wrote, for he translates some of its poetry. Claude Ménéstrier, the seventeenth-century French authority on festivals, also includes an account of it in his *Des Ballets Anciens et Modernes* (1682), where he states that it had been written by 'les ministres protestants'.[107] As a masque it is an amazing document, overtly political with tremendous messianic overtones. Certainly no other source provides us with such a penetrating insight as to how the Palatine match was viewed by the Prince and the pan-Protestant league. The death of Henry would most definitely have rendered the staging of such a masque out of the question.

The masque was to have been performed in the Whitehall Banqueting House, and its setting focused on a semi-reclining figure of Truth holding, in one hand, a globe and, in the other, a Bible, while on each side of her were the arms of England and of the Palatinate. The argument was as follows:

That Religion had united the world with England, for although the poets say, *divisus ab orbe Britannus*; yet the marriage, made in heaven, and consummated on earth, of the only daughter of this wise King of Great Britain with the Serene Prince Frederick V, Elector Palatine ... had given occasion to contradict the poet, and to believe, that one day, if it pleased God, the world (quitting its errors) would come to give recognition to Truth which resides solely in England and the Palatinate. That is what has made Atlas, in order to discharge his terrestrial globe into the hands of Alithie, that is to say Truth, choose his habitation in this island. From the globe come the three corners of the known world, Europe, Asia and Africa, being summoned by the trumpets of Truth, who are the divine Muses, and by her lieutenant, Atlas, to come to apprehend Alithie, and by means of her protector, the King of this fortunate isle, the true path of salvation, by way of which each ought to consecrate his soul to the glory of Almighty God.

The text then goes on to describe the action. The nine Muses enter attending upon Atlas, who tells the onlookers how Truth has found her refuge in this island and how all nations wish to come and pay her homage. This signalled a series of anti-masques of the three continents, each led in by a queen and each attended by a train attired in national dress. This led to a grand ballet after which the Muses sang, exhorting the three continents to follow Truth:

Imitez ce ROY débonnaire,
Qui a tiré en Angleterre
Le pure service divin.
   Bruslez dans le feu de son zèle
Ceste réligion nouvelle
De Mahomet & de Iupin.

Vous Empires & Républiques,
Amenez tous vos hérétiques
Aux pieds de ceste VERITE.
   Affin qu'ayant sa cognoissance
Ilz soynt touchez de Repentence,
Et recherchent la Pureté.

CHOR

Vous Affrique, Europe, & Asie
Délaissez vostre Idolatrie
Pour recognoistre l'Eternel.
   Il nous concède ceste grace,
Qu'il a choysay en ceste place
Son sacré temple & son Autel.

The continents then prostrated themselves before Truth. Atlas thanked her for accepting his burden, and the scene changed to a starlit paradise from which descended an angel who presented a sword to Truth. There then followed 'un grand Concert de musique' by angels and cherubim, and so ended 'ce fameux ballet'. Famous it most certainly would have been if it had ever been performed! It was the aims and ideals of the pan-European Protestant party in courtly masquing guise, acting in something not so far removed from a post-Reformation mystery play. The marriage was cast into terms of universal religious reform stemming from England.

This was not as fanciful as it might seem in the context of the yearnings of the age. During the opening decade of the century the expansion of the Church of England into an international institution was in the air. The accession of James I brought not only the Union of the Kingdoms in 1603 but, in the eyes of mythographers of the *Ecclesia Anglicana,* the recreation of the Ancient British Church as it had existed in the island when Christianity had first been brought by St Joseph of Arimathea. As we have seen in 1606 it was widely hoped that Venice would go over to some form of Anglicanism and thus reform gain a foothold in Italy, a dream forever cherished by Sir Henry Wotton. And all the colonial endeavours, which were central to Henry's maritime policy, were cast in terms of the *Ecclesia Anglicana* conquering the New World and halting the spread of Catholicism. The marriage of Elizabeth and Frederick epitomized above all an alliance of reformist churches throughout northern Europe under the auspices of the theologian king and prime disputant of papal claims, King James. In the longer term it would mean a holy war against the might of the Catholic Habsburg powers, with Henry IX, having succeeded his father, occupying a Messianic role similar to that of Henri IV in the events of 1610.

These Inns of Court contributions form a sharp contrast to the court's *Lords' Masque* by Thomas Campion – a writer not associated with Henry – which made use of the Prometheus myth in order to evoke star lords and statue ladies.[108] Only in a Latin prognostication by a sibyl 'to the future mother...of kings, of emperors' do we catch a modulated form of the ethos of the unperformed masque: 'Let the British strength be added to the German: can anything equal it? One mind, one faith, will join two peoples, and one religion, and simple love. Both will have the same enemy, the same ally, the same prayer for those in danger, and the same strength. Peace will favour them, and the fortune of war will favour them; always God the helper will be at their side.'[109] Flickers of the dead Prince of Wales's vision perhaps survive in the naval battle of the Thames organized by de' Servi on the basis of Florentine examples, and in which the English navy vanquished a Turkish fleet and stormed and took a fort.[110] The festivals as they were finally staged in February 1613 must have been very different from the way Henry had conceived them in the early autumn of 1612. What was missing was the feats of chivalry which had been such an essential feature of court entertainments in the previous three years, the exercise of tilt, tourney and barriers. Nothing was to be done to remind anyone too much of the brilliant youth whose prowess in arms had excited the populace so much in the tiltyard. For no doubt these festivals would have found their focal point in some martial spectacle focusing on Prince Henry. Devised as a counterstatement to the festival which dazzled Europe in the spring of 1612 – the three-day carousel in the Place Royale to mark the double marriages of France and Spain – the *fêtes* of February 1613 celebrated the Protestant riposte: the marriage of Elizabeth and Frederick.[111]

The Prince's Collections

In the second half of the sixteenth century princes all over Europe collected works of art, except, that is, in England.[1] Visitors to the palaces of Elizabeth Tudor, to Whitehall, Hampton Court, Nonsuch and Windsor record splendid interiors replete with tapestries, portraits, furniture and the occasional curiosity, such as a glass lute, the picture of an eskimo or a unicorn's horn, but what they saw had almost without exception been collected by Henry VIII. Elizabeth I had no passion for works of art. For seventy years, therefore, the Royal Collection stood still. When, in 1610, Henry Prince of Wales began to create his court, there was no collection of pictures purchased as works of art, no paintings by the great masters of the Italian Renaissance, no gallery of Classical antiquities, no cabinets of antique coins and medals, no library, no bronzes, no museum of natural curiosities or natural history. A whole movement that was close to the essence of the Mannerist era, the development of the palace, its architecture, interior décor, gardens and environs as a *mundus symbolicus* had yet to happen. Such collections were profound expressions of the yearnings of the age. They spoke of a desire to re-establish a new universalism in the face of the break-up of established order, of the old cosmology by the Copernican theory, of the geographical confines of Europe by the colonizing of the New World and the voyages of discovery, and in view of the collapse of the universal church with the Reformation and the ensuing decades of religious conflict. Such vast visual encyclopaedias within and without the palace walls expressed Mannerist man's obsession with knowledge of the physical universe and a quest for its underlying principles.

It was the Florentine court under the Medici grand dukes which was to set the fashion in collecting in the Mannerist age.[2] Cosimo I reconstituted the Medici collections, adding to them, in particular, Etruscan antiquities, the result of excavations, and commissioning a complete set of copies of the portraits of famous men assembled by Paolo Giovio in his museum at Como. Under Francesco I, the collections were systematically arranged by Bernardo Buontalenti in the upper galleries of the Uffizi, with the *tribuna,* built according to his design, as its focal point. There he assembled the most precious items of the picture collection, works by Raphael, Andrea de Sarto, Pontormo and Piero di Cosimo. By 1600 the collections were indeed gigantic and were organized in sections: antique and Renaissance sculpture, the historical portrait museum of Medici ancestors and of famous men, the *tribuna* with its celebrated paintings, and Greek and Roman coins and medals, a room filled with 'precious objects from nature and art', an attic floor containing antique and modern armour, instruments for mathematics, physics, geometry and astronomy, a treasury of objects in silver, gold, cut glass and porphyry, as well as cameos, antique intaglios, gems and enamels and a cabinet devoted to natural history, for the Medici were no less forward in the sciences than the arts.

Collections of this kind were formed all over Europe as the sixteenth century drew to its close. François I had imported Italian works of art and Classical antiquities to Fontainebleau. The formation of collections of *antiquailles* by the aristocracy became an established feature, as was the *cabinet de curiositez*. Portrait collections, under the influence of Renaissance man's preoccupation with the human psyche, became huge. Catherine de' Medici had 400 portraits and 551 crayon drawings. In Germany, the Bavarian court, first under Duke William IV and subsequently under Albert V, amassed enormous collections of paintings, engravings, coins, ivories, armour and glass, all of which were displayed within a specially constructed gallery as part of an overall Mannerist décor. The first of the Habsburgs to accumulate in this way was the Archduke Ferdinand of Tyrol, whose castle at Ambras, near Innsbruck, became a veritable shrine to Mannerism with its art gallery, treasury, cabinet devoted to natural curiosities, armoury and natural history museum.

In 1610 the zenith of the phenomenon was represented by the Emperor Rudolf II, whose vast collections in the Hradčany Palace in Prague were on a scale unmatched outside Medicean Florence.[3] He indeed encapsulates the mood that motivated such collections as the old century gave place to the new. R. J. W. Evans sums this up as follows:

For him the assembling of many and various items reflected the essential variety in the world, which could nevertheless be converted into unity by a mind which brought them together and divided their internal relations with another. Once again we see the analogy from microcosm to macrocosm and the search for a 'key' to the harmony of the created universe; in other words we see an aspect of the pansophic striving.

The collections expressed a desire to present an encyclopaedia of the visible world and constantly to recall to the onlooker the parallelism of art and nature. Those of Rudolf were the *primus inter pares* in the Europe of the time, but they remind us also that such collections did not only exist within the walls of the palace but spread out beyond it in the form of gardens, stables and menageries filled with animate objects, plants and animals, which, like the inanimate ones indoors, also had their virtues and equally reflected the intellectual quest to unravel divine cosmological mysteries.

The Prince had direct knowledge of these collections. The *fiorentini* in his circle would have described to him the wonders of Medicean Florence, in addition to which he was, in 1611, to have an architect who had not only been in the service of the grand dukes but who had also worked for the Emperor Rudolf in Prague. There were to be two other direct links with Prague, Abraham van der Doort, who was appointed Keeper of the Prince's collections in 1612, and the magus Cornelius Crebbel, whose chief patron was the Prince. So that in the spring of 1610 when he began to form his own household and to collect, build, decorate and lay out the gardens of his two palaces at Richmond and St James's, the Prince was inaugurating a new era, in which he was deliberately placing himself and his surroundings in direct association with the aims and ideals that had motivated the Medici grand dukes and the Emperor Rudolf. In order to achieve this he had not only to form collections where none existed before, but also to attract to his court painters, architects, designers, hydraulic engineers, engravers, scholars and antiquarians who would be capable of carrying out his ideas. In his three brief years as Prince of Wales the story is one of achievement and frustration, as the young Prince's revolutionary artistic policies, perpetually dogged by lack of money, began to come to fitful fruition. The result was a potentially brilliant *mise-en-scene* with far wider intellectual and aesthetic implications than were ever to be inherited by his brother, Charles.

The old Tudor Royal Collection was largely the creation of Henry VIII, consisting almost entirely of portraits, sets of kings and queens glorifying the legitimacy of the dynasty, those of prospective brides and foreign rulers, a handful of anti-papal allegories, together with a few spectacular set pieces depicting the King and his family, or the great events of his reign, the Battle of the Spurs or the Field of Cloth of Gold.[4] In the main, these were housed in the Privy Gallery of Whitehall Palace, although pictures were also at Hampton Court and Nonsuch. There are no inventories for the second half of the century but Elizabeth I did not add to the collection and, although she admired the art of Nicholas Hilliard, the idea of a painting as an expression of human genius probably never crossed her mind. Nor did it cross that of her Stuart successor. The notion, too, of the systematic accumulation and display of works of art as an essential adjunct of monarchical splendour, already well established in the European courts, had little place in the Elizabethan idea of kingship.

James I had no interest in the visual arts and loathed even sitting for his portrait. Apart from bringing the collection of ancestral portraits south, he is not known to have purchased a single work of art. The new queen, in sharp contrast, was possessed of a high degree of visual awareness which she shared with her brother Christian IV, during whose reign Copenhagen developed into a kind of Northern equivalent of Rudolfine Prague.[5] Anne of Denmark expressed her taste in her patronage of the new wave portraitists, Isaac Oliver and Marcus Gheeraerts, in her introduction of the revolutionary stage settings for the court masques designed by Inigo Jones, in buildings as varied as the remodelled Somerset House and the initial Queen's House at Greenwich, and in gardening projects in the Mannerist style by Salomon de Caus. Her son, Henry, inherited these inclinations and preoccupations to an even higher and considerably more precocious degree. And, as we shall see, Henry's tastes were far more deliberate and advanced for his time.

Under the influence of the Queen, the Royal Collection began once more to expand.[6] All her residences contained large collections of pictures. Somerset House, her London residence, and her palaces at Greenwich and Oatlands not only contained considerable numbers of portraits of ancestors, family and friends in the old Elizabethan tradition, but went on to include, for the first time in England, subject pictures on some scale. Somerset House had still-lifes, mythological and religious pictures and topographical views. Oatlands had religious pictures in the Gallery, a number of devotional pictures in the Oratory, and in the Garden Stone Gallery a tantalizing number of important subject pictures, including *Diana and her Nymphs,* the *Entry into the Ark, Lucretia* and *The Angel Appearing to the Shepherds.* No artists' names are recorded in the lists and this makes the significance of the collection difficult to determine; some items at least came to her from Prince Henry after his death. How much of her collection was in existence in 1610 is open to conjecture, but there can be no doubt that Anne must have been one of the most potent influences on her son's decision in the spring of that year to form his own gallery.

Twelve years before, Richard Haydocke, in the preface to his translation of Lomazzo's *Trattato*, had actually referred to the formation of collections of paintings as works of art, alluding to the

... diligent observation of the excellency of Ancient workes; indevouring by all meanes to purchase them, and refusing no coste, when they may bee had. In which point some of our Nobility, and diverse private Gentlemen, have very well acquited themselves; as may appeare, by their Galleries carefully furnished, with the excellent monuments of sundry famous ancient Masters, both Italian and German.[7]

What these collections were and who formed them we do not know and one is more than sceptical as to their significance. None, anyway, would have been on the scale about to be embarked upon by the Prince.

The earliest reference that we have to his interest in painting comes in March 1610. In a letter to Salisbury, David Murray, Groom of the Stole, tells him to come before 10 o'clock with his pictures but that if he was hindered from doing so 'you may send my Lord of Arundel as deputy to set forth the praise of your pictures'.[8] Robert Cecil was already a collector and had been busy purchasing for his house at Hatfield, then under construction.[9] The 1629 inventory of Hatfield lists, among other works, a *Diana Enthroned* by Frans Floris, *Leda and the Swan, Mercury, Argus and Io, Petrarch's Laura, Adam and Eve,* a perspective interior of a church in Antwerp by Peter Neefs the Elder and the *Departure of Abraham* by Jacopo(?) Bassano. Such pictures indicate that Cecil was collecting subject pictures, both biblical and mythological, of the Netherlandish Mannerist and the Venetian Schools. In the case of the latter, Sir Henry Wotton was the key figure in disseminating the taste for Venetian painting, and we know that he was busy acquiring pictures for both Cecil and his heir. The idea of forming a gallery of subject pictures by famous artists, however, was totally new in 1610.

The allusion in David Murray's letter to Arundel perhaps provides us with the vital clue in explaining the sudden and dramatic impulse by the Prince, for the letter clearly takes it for granted that the earl would be the right person to pronounce on the aesthetic merits of paintings. Arundel was an intimate member of the Prince's household (the Earl never felt in quite the same way about Charles I). We do not know how he acquired his knowledge of and passion for works of art, which were already in evidence in 1610. He would have been familiar with his great uncle Lord Lumley's collection, but none of it was bequeathed to him when Lumley died in 1609. There is no certain evidence for a trip abroad in or around 1612, although we know that he was one of those aristocrats who had toured Italy, like Lord Roos, in the calmer politico-religious climate of the late 1590s.

The earliest reference that we have to the Prince acquiring a picture is that of 30 January 1610, when Arundel's man was paid £2 for delivering 'a great picture to his highness'.[10] The Earl is likely, therefore, to have been a strong influence on the decision of the Prince in the spring of 1610 to emulate the courts of Europe, regarding a collection of works of art as an essential attribute of princely magnificence.

During that year it became widely known that gifts of paintings would be highly acceptable to the Prince. The Countess of Cumberland, Thomas Edmondes, the Earl of Exeter, Sir Edward Cecil and Sir Noel Caron, the Dutch ambassador, were swift to respond.[11] Substantial purchases were also made. In January 1611 Sir Walter Cope wrote to Carleton in The Hague that the purchase of old paintings at a reasonable rate would be more than welcome news both to the Prince and to Salisbury.[12] Large payments occur throughout the next two years to various people, almost all Dutch, for paintings.[13] Three names in particular figure as major dealers and agents: Philip Jacob, the miniaturist Isaac Oliver and Philip Burlamachi. The payments to Oliver have in the past been mistakenly read as payments for pictures *by* him, but by far the largest sum, over £480, went to Burlamachi for a huge shipment from Venice. There is also the interesting payment to a Dutchman, 'Vandellivell', for a set of seven pictures of emperors.

Two transactions are of such importance that they must be treated separately. The first was the gift by the Prince's godparents, the States General, in 1610. Antonio Correr records the event in a dispatch of 2 June, written just eight days before the Prince's creation:

The Dutch Ambassadors, before leaving, presented to the Prince some very finished paintings on canvas. They were painted on purpose to adorn one wall of his gallery.[14]

This gift was one of a series that the States General had authorized should be given to influential English persons who might further Dutch interests in the aftermath of the Twelve Years Truce.[15] As a result of the truce the new republic became officially recognized as an independent state, and a suitably magnificent embassy arrived in England on 23 April. The King was to be thanked for his mediation in the matter of the truce, his help was to be enlisted over the Julich-Cleves succession, and efforts were to be made to obtain the annulment of James's decree that forbade all fishing along the coasts of the United Kingdom.

Already on 10 April, the States General had inspected 'A certain painting made at Haarlem by Master Vroom of the Sea Battle before Gibraltar under the command of Van Heemskerck of pious memory, against the Spanish galleons' which, it was thought, might be suitable for the Prince. Two days later, news arrived from Noel Caron that His Highness would appreciate a present of 'Some paintings by the best masters in the country'. So the States General had clearly been correct in their initial move and the subject matter, both naval and anti-Spanish, was especially appropriate. A second picture of 'a storm at sea', also by Vroom, was definitely acquired and we know that the ambassadors were formally received at St James's on 28 April. The Prince's accounts refer to 'divers pictures', so it is possible that there were more.

97   Hendrick Vroom's *Battle off Gibraltar fought against the Spaniards*

(25 April 1607) passed to Charles I and is recorded by van der Doort with the annotation: *Don bij de ault from* [i. e. Old Vroom] / *Was giffen bij der stats tu prinz henri*. This is now unidentifiable, although it is believed that what may be a workshop version of it dated 1619 is in the National Maritime Museum, Greenwich. As regards the *'zeestorm'* that was also purchased from Vroom in 1610 for the Prince, van Gelder believes that in fact it was a picture painted by Jan Porcellis (d. 1632) while he was in Vroom's studio, which was later listed two entries before the battle piece in van der Doort's catalogue. It was a large *'se storm'* on canvas and is no longer traceable.[16]

The second transaction is even stranger. At the close of March 1610 Ottaviano Lotti, the Grand Duke of Tuscany's representative, was taken by Sir Thomas Chaloner, the Prince's Chamberlain, to view the nucleus of the picture collection at St James's.[17] The tour included the new library, then under construction, and closed with a lengthy eulogy of the Prince by Chaloner, interlarded with references to the imminent Dutch gift, leading up to a request for books and pictures from Florence. This was in response to an offer of such a gift of works of art made by Vincenzo Salviati, the Florentine ambassador, the year before. He told Lotti that the Prince wanted the Michelangelo that was in the centre of the ceiling of the Medici palace in Siena and also the series of *uomini illustri* that were such a feature of the grandducal collections, and which today are hung as a frieze in the gallery that encircles the Uffizi. This collection had been initiated by Cosimo I, who had sent Cristoforo dell'Altissimo to copy Giovio's celebrated series in his museum at Como.[18] The Museum Giovianum was, for a long period, the established repository for the iconography of celebrated personages. Its contents were published at Florence (1551), at Paris (1552) and at Basle (1557). Like Cosimo I, the Archduke Ferdinand of Tyrol sent artists to copy the paintings. The reference to the Michelangelo is more puzzling. One can only guess that Henry might be referring to the series of scenes from Roman history by Domenico Beccafumi on the ceiling of the Palazzo Pubblico in Siena. That this could be so is perhaps borne out by what ensued.

A year passed until, at the end of June 1611, Constantino de' Servi, the Medicean painter and architect in the Prince's service, wrote to the Florentine Secretary of State that the pictures had arrived and that he would present them to the Prince himself.[19] In doing so, he writes, he would apologize for the uneven quality of the portraits of the *uomini illustri,* explaining that as they had to be executed in a hurry they had been farmed out to several artists. The consignment lacked the two pictures from the ceiling of the Sala del Consiglio which, however, he

97

98

states, are like the picture that has been sent by Domenico Beccafumi. The next day Lotti gives us this remarkable account of delivering the pictures to the Prince at Richmond Palace:

His Highness spent more than an hour looking at them one by one, some [portraits] he admired that seemed to be of more famous men than others, as Castruccio [Castracane] among the soldiers, Pico della Mirandola among men of letters, Macchiavelli among the politicians and so on with the others. Over the popes, cardinals and saints, he made neither comment or indication, except about a certain type of face, joking in a witty manner, making those around him laugh....Most of all he loved the picture by Mercarino [i.e. Beccafumi] which he wanted to place in a particular room so that it could be seen to better effect....And His Highness asked me several times about the decoration of their Highnesses galleries and if there were subject pictures and what kind of statues, and he confirmed his intention of using the aforesaid pictures for his new gallery.[20]

93, 94

In this letter Lotti paints a vivid portrait of the young connoisseur Prince whose discernment was such that he took the choicest picture into a separate room in order to study it. Henry, however, was not alone in England at the time in wanting detailed information on the actual arrangement and contents of the grandducal collections. In October of the previous year an agent of the Earl of Shrewsbury's wrote to Lady Shrewsbury a long account of the Capella dei Principi and the gallery with its paintings and sculpture, material he was clearly commissioned to report upon in detail.[21] The old redbrick Tudor palaces of St James's and Richmond were to be transformed to rival the splendours of the Medici *palazzi*. Strangely enough none of these pictures is ever referred to again.

The pictures were hung in the old Tudor long gallery at St James's, which in 1609–10 was wainscotted, with entablature and pilasters at ten-foot intervals to receive them.[22] For an account of the contents of the St James's gallery we have two descriptions by visitors, one by the Duke of Saxe-Weimar, in 1613, and the second by the Sieur de Mandelso, in 1640.[23] Both must be highly selective, as neither refers to more than about sixteen to seventeen items, nor do we know what was left at Richmond. There were three religious pictures, all life-size: *Cain and Abel, The History of Holofernes* and *The Sacrifice of Isaac*. The last is certainly recorded by van der Doort and was by the Venetian painter Leonardo Corona 'da Murano' (1561–1605), a mediocre artist working within the tradition of Tintoretto but adulterated by Palma Giovane, and also by the Bassani.[24] The second could be identical with 'A Judith with Holofernes head copied after Bronzino', listed at St James's by van der Doort.[25] There were only two portraits, ones of personal heroes, full-lengths of Henri IV and Maurice of Nassau. Conceivably these are the ones later in the Bear Gallery at Whitehall, as by Bonnel and Miereveldt respectively.[26] Henry would not have concentrated on portraits of ancestors and princely contemporaries, anyway, for these would have come when he succeeded to the throne. There was a group of pictures whose interest lay in their demonstration of the new art of single-point perspective: two architectural perspectives of palaces and 'A vaulted house, wherein several are wrestling with each other; perspectively rather than artistically painted upon a small table.' These are likely to have been pictures by Hans Vredeman de Vries (1527–after 1604), whose perspective handbooks were famous, or by his pupil Hendrick van Steenwijk the Elder (*c.* 1550–1603) or indeed his son Hendrick the Younger (*c.* 1580–before 1649). There was also a series of typically Netherlandish paintings within the still-life tradition: a kitchen, a table covered in sweetmeats with glasses of wine and one of a manuscript book with a half-turned page. The last is the only picture specifically described by the gentleman in the train of the Landgrave of Hesse: 'In the gallery exceedingly fine and splendid paintings which we much marvelled at, amongst them a book like a Psalter in monks' script on a board as if it hung there.'[27] The second was Nonsuch in 1639: 'a peece of fruits and Grapes and glasses with wine & a partridge in a dish' and measured 11 ft 9 in. by 2 ft 11 in. (358 by 89 cm) and was then hung as an overdoor.[28] The lists are rounded out by references to either one or three life-sized pictures (it is unclear which) of Venus, Bacchus and Ceres, a Tower of Babel, three royal genealogies and a painting of the Battle of Ravenna, the fatal encounter on 11 April 1512 between the French and Spanish troops in which Gaston de Foix, Duke of Nemours, perished.[29] The latter is still in the Royal Collection

92 and bears the brandmark *HP.* A *Venus, Bacchus and Ceres* was in Charles I's collection with an attribution to Francesco Albani[30] and a *Prometheus*

103 by Palma Giovane is also still in the Royal Collection.[31] It is possible that the small picture of 'the Tower of Babilon wth manie very litle and curious figures' by Valckenborch was that presented to Charles I by Henry's Groom of the Stole, Sir David Murray.[32]

Turning to van der Doort's listing of the contents of the St James's gallery in Charles I's reign, although later additions from Mantua are clearly in evidence, it is worthy of consideration as still containing a nucleus of Prince Henry's pictures which had not been moved.[33] *Prometheus* by Palma Giovane was still there, so was the *Judith and Holofernes,*

99 and the reference to 'A Battaile' could be the *Battle of Ravenna.* There are also two perspectives, one 'A Perspective Peece of Stenwick being in it a large Church' and a second by Valckenborch, 'A Perspective Peece of Balles Priests'. More interesting, if they had indeed been there in 1612, are the pictures by Tintoretto and Bassano, which would certainly square with the shipment from Venice. This could mean that

masterpieces such as Tintoretto's *Susanna Bathing*, now in the Louvre, was once Prince Henry's.

Three paintings were described hung together as a set piece. They were:

98   Three long tables of shipping. On the first how some are wrecked in a great storm; on the second, how ships sail in a fair wind; on the third, how some vessels fire at each other by night. They are particularly fine pieces.

Two of these three panels are still in the Royal Collections and bear the HP brandmark. They are attributed either to Hendrik Vroom or to Jan Porcellis, whose career was destined to transform the Dutch seascape tradition from a lively anecdotal one into one which was to become the aesthetic rival of landscape and still-life.[34] Norgate was later to write of Porcellis in his *Miniatura* (written 1648–50) that he 'very naturally describes the beauties and terrors of that Element in Calmes and tempests, soe lively exprest, as would make you at once in Love with, and forsweare the sea for ever'. In the first, on a turbulent sea scattered with wreckage, a battered ship is driven towards a rocky coast, while nearby a monstrous fish spouts and rolls its eye. This is a mixture of traditional motifs from the Vroom and Willaerts tradition with progressive elements which reach their fulfilment in the *Sea Battle at Night*, which is the only known picture of a battle by night in the history of Dutch art. The moonlight is so dim that it is difficult to decipher the scene. In the foreground, three small ships engage in the peaceful occupation of fishing by lantern light, while in the distance the flash of cannon-fire illumines three warships in conflict. Nothing could be further from the heroic commemorative canvas of Vroom's *Battle off Gibraltar*. They are pictures whose subjects characteristically epitomize the Mannerist mind, a combination of a detailed observation of the moods of one of the elements, together with a moralistic message within the emblematic tradition, of the ship of the human soul tossed through the sea of life (an emblem later to be used to symbolize the sufferings of Charles I in the *Eikon Basilike*).

Van der Doort in fact lists only five pictures as specifically belonging to Prince Henry. The one picture which has not as yet been referred to is a portrait by Tintoretto of a Venetian lady in yellow satin seated in a chair.[35] We can enlarge the list a little by those pictures which have since come to light carrying the Prince's brandmark on the reverse. Apart from the *Battle of Ravenna* there are six of them: the first is *A Boy looking through a Casement*, recorded among his mother's pictures at Oat-   96
lands as 'a Buffone looking out of a glasse window'; the second, *Christ in the House of Mary and Martha*, is a dated (1566) picture by Hans   100

101   Vredeman de Vries; the third is *The Parable of the Tares,* attributed to
       Abraham Bloemart;[36] the fourth, a recently discovered picture of a Clas-
102   sical figure on horseback by Holbein;[37] the fifth, an allegorical female
91   figure, possibly *Pictura*, by Hendrik Goltzius;[38] and the sixth, an anony-
95   mous *Old Woman Blowing Charcoal.* These confirm the Netherlandish
       bias of the collection, and the Holbein picture is by far the most distin-
       guished and intriguing item to come to light so far. It may have been
       painted in Antwerp, as the panel is part of the same wood upon which
       he depicted Erasmus. Together with the *Pictura* it shares a rare picture
       shape, the lozenge. The attribution to Holbein seems generally ac-
       cepted although its subject matter and use remain to be unravelled in
       detail.

   The picture collection, as far as we are able to reconstruct it, is very
different from anything that had gone before in England. It was concerned overtly with requests for works by the 'best masters' and we
know that it certainly included Tintoretto, Beccafumi, Holbein,
Vroom, Goltzius, possibly Porcellis and lesser Netherlandish painters
and probably works by Francesco Albani and Palama Giovane. As we
have seen, the Prince had also wanted and asked for a Michelangelo.
The range and subject matter is typical of that sought after by the late
sixteenth-century Mannerist courts, the new observation of nature epitomized in the still-life, the preoccupation with optical effects, such as
perspective and *trompe l'oeil,* and fascination with the physiognomy of
the great that resulted in vast portrait collections, endless books of engraved portraits and the strange works of della Porta. Nor was Henry's
reformist zeal of a kind that excluded religious subject matter, although none was of the post-Tridentine variety. When he died, in
1612, we must remember that it was still only a collection in the making.

At a meeting subsequent to Chaloner's request for paintings, the
Prince asked Lotti for a further gift of works of art.[39] The Tuscan agent
duly conveyed this to Belisario Vinta on 29 April 1610:

And in addition he would like some little stucco statues, about a braccia high, that one
finds there by worthy men, such as Giovanni Bologna and others, and amongst them he
would like to have in the same size, the Rape of the Sabines that is in the great Piazza in
Florence.[40]

Nothing follows this astounding request, which betrays knowledge not
only of the little bronzes produced in the workshop of Giovanni Bologna (1529–1608), but also of that master's most famous group. That
Henry had ever seen a Renaissance bronze is unlikely and he mistakenly refers to them as being made of stucco. A long silence ensues,

punctuated early in March 1611 when a merchant told Chaloner that the statuettes were at that very moment in the making in Florence. This was in fact not true, and nothing indeed was done about them until December, when the Florentine match was heavily under threat from the proposals by Savoy. At that moment, Vincenzo Giugni, *Provveditore* of the grandducal *Gardaroba*, asked the cousin of the former Florentine ambassador, the Marchesa Salviati, to lend seven bronzes from her own collection, all by Giovanni Bologna, to Pietro Tacca, his successor as Medici court sculptor. By then the gift had been elevated to one from the Grand Duke himself and was seen to be a significant gesture towards furthering the interests of the marriage.

In the amazingly short period of three months, Pietro Tacca, assisted by Antonio Susini, apparently cast the bronzes, fifteen in all. Ten were by Giovanni Bologna. The seven from the Marchesa's collection were *La Fortuna (Venus Marina)*, a kneeling woman, *Astronomia, Nessus and Deianeira, Hercules and the Centaur*, a large horse and a bull of the same size. Three more came from a second unspecified source: a *Bathing Venus, Hercules with his Club* and a *Birdcatcher*. To these were added five smaller bronzes, all probably by Tacca: *Diana, Pomona*, a *Shepherd with Bagpipes*, a *Shepherd with a Drinking Bottle* and a little horse.[41] Versions of all these survive in collections today. Although we are unable to identify which actually belonged to the Prince we can reconstitute fairly closely what this collection must have looked like.

The collection arrived in England in the middle of May 1612, and Andrea Cioli, temporarily replacing Lotti, who was on a mission to Florence, had them brought to his lodgings on Saturday 26 June. Sir Edward Cecil was so consumed with curiosity that he brought three of his friends to see them. On the Monday, Cioli and Cecil travelled in separate coaches to Richmond Palace, while the bronzes were conveyed simultaneously by barge. Cioli was welcomed by a member of the Prince's household who spoke Italian and was led through a secret garden up a spiral staircase into a gallery, where he found Chaloner; a discussion of the Savoy match ensued. On the arrival of the bronzes there followed a scene as vivid as the one that occurred the previous year over the Prince's reception of the paintings. Henry came in attended by Cecil, Sir David Murray and a third courtier. So delighted was the Prince with the statues that he seized the first and kissed it. He picked up and handled each one repeatedly, admiring, studying and praising every detail of their workmanship. At one point Edward Cecil took hold of the little horse and said, 'This will be good for the Duke of York', to which the Prince sharply replied, 'No, no, I want everything myself.' The *Birdcatcher* greatly intrigued him, and Cioli explained

105, 104, 109
110, 112, 111

108

107, 106

that Constantino de' Servi could easily make equipment of the kind the figure was holding. Subsequently Cioli accepted an invitation to dinner, after which Chaloner told him how the Prince had carried the bronzes to one of his cabinets and arranged them in person. On the return journey, Cecil confided to Cioli that the Prince wanted more bronzes, but this time he would pay. A fortnight later Cioli wrote to Florence stating that the Prince had asked in particular for a reduction of Michelangelo's *David*.[42] Nothing more is heard of this commission, which presumably died with the Prince.

To these statues Henry managed to add three more; eighteen bronzes, in all, are recorded in van der Doort's catalogue as having passed to Charles I from 'Prince Henry of famous memory'. The additional pieces were 'one of the biggest horses in brasse, and the other fellow horse of the same bignes, and a large Centaur of brasse', all 1 ft 7 in. (48 cm) in height.[43] Of their status as objects dear to the heart and mind of the Prince nothing could be more telling than the pathetic annotation to the entry for the little horse: 'being one of the no: of 18[en] w[ch] your Ma[ty] did send-for to Richmond in the last sickness time and there yo[r] Majesty gave it wth your owne hands to the Prince'.[44] Edward Cecil's jocular reference to the *cavallino* as being a suitable plaything for the young Duke of York must have had some truth in reality, for it was this bronze that the twelve-year-old child pressed into the hands of his dying brother.

As far as we know, these are the first Renaissance bronzes ever to reach England, the first contacts the country had had with Italian sculpture since the break with Rome. In Jacobean England sculpture was still the province of tombmakers. The idea of it as an expression of art for art's sake had yet to come. That Henry knew about Giovanni Bologna, however, is less surprising than it might at first seem. His work must have been familiar to everyone who had travelled to Florence within the Prince's circle, above all to Arundel, Chaloner, Cecil, the young Harington or Inigo Jones, who had already placed on stage, both in the *Barriers* and in *Oberon*, a considerable amount of sculpture in the Renaissance manner. Jonson's text in the *Barriers* postulates sculpture as part of the programme envisaged by the Prince for this revival of chivalry:

> The niches filled with statues to invite
> Young valours forth by their old forms to fight....[45]

In July 1609 William Cecil, Lord Burghley, the Earl of Exeter's heir, had written from Florence to Gilbert Talbot, Earl of Shrewsbury, telling him of the latest developments in the arts. In this letter he writes:

'there is a litle ould man caled John Bollogna ... who is not inferior much to Miccel Angelo ... for John Bollogna I count him the rarest man that was of any profession for his profession' *[sic]*.[46] Shrewsbury had been to Florence several times and Burghley once before in 1599. Every visitor would have been struck at least by the marvellous equestrian statue of Duke Cosimo I, which was unveiled in 1595. Fynes Moryson, the traveller, had seen it the year before when it was still incomplete:

In the house of John Bolena a Flemming, and an excellent engraver, I did see yet unperfected a horsemans Statua of brasse, fifteen els high, the belly of the horse being capable of 24 men, whereof foure meight lie in the throat; and this horse was made as going in the high way, putting forward the meere foot before, & the farre foote behind, & standing upon the other two, which statua was to be erected to Duke Cosimo, being valued at 18. thousand crownes.[47]

It is worth observing that in England the idea of public sculpture celebrating the monarchy did not exist.

England was half a century behind in responding to an artist whose fame was international, one whose skill was at the service of Medici diplomacy.[48] Such gifts of bronzes to European rulers went back as far as 1565, when a figure of *Mercury*, among others, was presented to the Emperor Maximilian II as an inducement for the marriage of Joanna of Austria to Francesco de' Medici. By the close of the century there were substantial collections of his bronzes in most German courts and an enormous group in Prague, where his work was passionately admired by the Emperor Rudolf.

On 12 August 1689 John Evelyn, diarist and author of *Numismata*, wrote to Samuel Pepys, on the question of the portrait galleries and of the coins and medal collections, praising, on the one hand, the noble example of Lord Clarendon, whose portrait gallery was the most extensive in Restoration England, and, on the other, lamenting the dispersal of Prince Henry's legendary collections at St James's:

For thus has a Cabinet of ten thousand Medals, not inferior to most abroad, & far superior to any at home, which were collected by that hopefull cherisher of greate and noble things Prince Henry, been imbezild and carried away during our late barbarous Rebellion, by whom & whither none can or is likely to discouer. What that collection was, not onely of Bookes and Medals, but of Statues & other elegant furniture, let the learned Library-keeper Patritius Junius tell you in his notes ad Epist. Sᵗⁱ Clementis ad Corinthos: *quem locum,* [speaking of St James's] *si vicinam pinacothecam Bibliothecae celeberrimae conjunctam, si Numismata Antiqua Graeca ac Romana, si statuas & signa ex aera et marmore concideres, non im'erito Thesaurum Antiquitates et Ταμιεῖον instructissimum nominare potes, &c.*[49]

What of this celebrated collection of antique Greek and Roman coins, medals and seals? In the list drawn up after the Prince's death of his income, debts and assets, the following entry occurs: 'certen Meddals of gould and straunge coyne, which cost his High: 2200li'.[50] Over £2000 was a very large sum of money in Jacobean terms; as Chamberlain recorded, the total value of the collections was only rumoured to be a little in excess of £3000, an amount inclusive of 'his medals and ancient coyns of gold'.[51]

The history of this once remarkable collection is fragmentary and inconclusive, as it became subject to endless disputes in the aftermath of the Prince's death and caused much distress to poor Abraham van der Doort (*c.*1575/80–1640), who is best known as the compiler of the catalogue of Charles I's collections.[52] His career began, however, under Prince Henry. Van der Doort was, it is thought, the son of the engraver Peter van Doort, and brother of the painter Jacob van Doort. He was one of a family of craftsmen who worked for the courts of the Mannerist princes. In 1625 he was to state that he had sixteen years' experience as the designer of the coinage, which would date his arrival in England to 1609. He is traceable in the Prince's accounts, however, only after July 1612, when he appears with the award of a salary of £50 p.a.[53] His early life is puzzling and could indicate that he had worked at the court of Rudolf II, and that he had moved to England after the Emperor's death on 20 January 1612. This would be a more logical account of his movements than that suggested by the somewhat cryptic entry he writes on an embossed polychrome wax which he had presented to the Prince:

Item an Imboast in cullord wax Soe bigg as the life upon a black ebbone laied in with Silver & gould pedistall was made for the Emperour Radulphus who did write diverse times for it to be brought to him....[54]

This may be so, but it would be a better explanation that van der Doort surfaced in England as a result of the dispersal of the Rudolfine Court. The wax is likely to relate to a payment in 1611–12 for 'A Case for the waxehead'.[55] In thè catalogue entry he goes on to say that as a result of this wax Prince Henry had offered him the Keepership of his Cabinet Room at an annual salary, but that the Prince had died before the room was completed.

The acquisition of the collection was in two phases. One is recorded in a payment to a certain 'Abraham van hutton' 'for antiquities of medals and coins bought of him'. The sum was enormous, £2200, and was paid in instalments between 10 May and 10 August 1611.[56] The second major acquisition is recorded in April 1612 when a docquet was issued for 'the custom and subsidy of a cabinet of antiquities brought into the realm by Hans van Dirbige and sold to the Prince'.[57] This cabinet was a famous one belonging to Abraham Gorlaeus (1549–1609) of Delft, who made a particular study of antique rings, engraved gems, coins and medals. The collection was published in 1601 in Leiden, under the title: *Dactyliotheca seu annulorum sigillorumque e ferro aere, argento atque auro promptuarium.* So important was the collection that a heavily annotated edition of the book was reissued in 1695, long after it ceased to exist. In this purchase we see the earliest major assembly of Classical antiquities enter the country. The Earl of Arundel was not to begin his collection of antiquities until his Italian tour of 1613–15 and the only person to precede him was William Cecil, Lord Roos (1590–1618), son of Thomas Cecil, 2nd Earl of Exeter. He was given a licence to travel for a period of three years in 1605 and was certainly in Italy in 1612 when the Prince died. The evidence that he formed a collection of antique statues is to be found in a letter where van der Doort describes how, in 1616, he 'gave the Earle of Arundell the statues he brought out of Italie at one clap'.[58]

Nothing more is heard of this cabinet until van der Doort was in the process of compiling his catalogue of Charles I's collection about 1640. The actual cabinet was a black ebony table inlaid with ivory, beneath which the coins and medals were kept in a series of round ivory tables.[59] Van der Doort provides a confused series of entries in the phonetic English into which he lapsed in moments of desperation.[60] As far as we can tell, it was in the Prince's lifetime that the cabinet and its contents came under the aegis of Sir David Murray and his deputy, one Flemming. After Henry's death it seems that access was had for valuing by the Earl of Arundel, Sir Henry Fanshawe, Sir Thomas Chaloner and Inigo Jones, and, reading between the lines, the likelihood is that they helped themselves. The keys then probably passed into the hands of one Thomas Carey, who refused to hand them over to van der Doort. When the King ordered the cabinet to be transported to Whitehall, Carey made off with the contents and apparently sold off a great deal for the value of the metal. All the same, some at least of the medals seem to have reached Charles I, as yet another anecdotal entry reveals. Going with Charles I one day into the Chair Room, van der Doort was shown twenty-seven golden medals in black turned hoops lying on the table. 'How comes these here?' the King asked van der Doort. 'I see by this that there is more keys than which your majesty hath given me', the Keeper replied, to which the King answered, 'Yes, I have one,' and proceeded to give into van der Doort's charge the twenty-seven gold medals, together with thirty-eight silver ones. A marginal note states that they had been the late Prince's, and they seem to have been mainly of Roman Emperors. It is unlikely that the collection was ever as large as John Evelyn indicates in his *Numismata,* but clearly only a trickle descended to Charles I, whose interest in Classical antiquities was never particularly marked.

On 22 October 1609 the following payment had been made: 'to Mr Holcock for wreating a Catalogue of the librarie whiche his highnes hade of my lord Lumley'.[61] In this way there is recorded Prince Henry's acquisition of by far the largest part of the second greatest library of the Elizabethan age, that belonging to John, Lord Lumley (?1534–1609).[62] The occasion was its removal from Nonsuch Palace, where Lumley had lived, to St James's, a move which was to precipitate substantial building work.

In order to place Prince Henry's collections into a line of descent we need to remember that another of his tutors had been Lumley, whose library he purchased. Lumley was described by Camden in his *Britannia* as 'a person of entire virtue, integrity and innocence, and now in his old age a complete pattern of nobility'.[63] On account of his Catholicism and his complicity in the Ridolfi Plot against Elizabeth I he had been denied public office. Instead, he concentrated on the genealogy of his family, built up the largest picture collection in Elizabethan England, was a founder member of the Society of Antiquaries and founded, in 1583, the Lumleian Lectures on anatomy at the Royal College of Physicians. In addition he had visited Italy, and in particular Florence, in the 1560s, and this without doubt must have been a major influence. The Medici portrait collection of *uomini illustri* seems to have been the source of inspiration for his own vast collection of them and at Nonsuch Palace, which he inherited from his father-in-law, he was to plant the first Italianate garden.

Prince Henry was the ideological 'heir' to Lumley. He owned his library, he was to emulate him in Italianate garden schemes, and he was to assemble a collection of pictures which had an iconographic emphasis in terms of physiognomy and scientific information as well as reflecting virtuoso skill. Even the idea of marking the collection could have come from Lumley, who had had a little paper *cartellino* painted on items in his possession.[64] Henry had his branded on the reverse with HP and, above, a crown. What was different about the Prince's collection was the overlay of contemporary preoccupations unknown to Lumley's era; the passion for what we now categorize as 'old masters.' In this, the Prince was a child of his own generation, reflecting the interest in what was referred to as 'curious painting', the ingredients of which included a mastery of scientific perspective and the use of light and shade, *chiaroscuro.*

92

The Prince's collections II

Pictures

91 *Pictura* by Hendrik Goltzius

92 Brandmark HP used on the reverse of panel pictures in the collection

The Prince's collections III

Pictures

93, 94 *Castruccio Castracane* and *Zanobi di Strada* from the Medici collection of *uomini illustri*, copies of which were given to the Prince by Cosimo II in 1611

97 *The Battle off Gibraltar fought against the Spaniards, 1607* from the studio of Hendrik Vroom. A version of this was presented to the Prince by the States General of Holland in 1610.

98 *A Storm at Sea*, attributed to Hendrik Vroom or Jan Porcellis. Presented to the States General in 1610.

95 *Old Woman Blowing Charcoal* by an unknown artist

96 *Boy looking through a casement* by an unknown artist

99 *The Battle of Ravenna* by an unknown artist

The Prince's collections IV
Pictures

100 *Christ in the House of Mary and Martha* by Hans Vredeman de Vries

101 *The Parable of the Tares* attributed to Abraham Bloemart

102 *Allegorical Figure on Horseback* by Hans Holbein

103 *Prometheus* by Palma Giovane

104   *Astronomia*

105   *La Fortuna*

The Prince's collections V

The collection of bronzes after
Giovanni da Bologna (104, 105 and 108–112)
and by Pietro Tacca (106–107)
presented by Cosimo II in 1611

106   *Shepherd with Bagpipes*

107   *Hercules with his Club*

108   *Nessus and Deianeira*

109   *Hercules and the Centaur*

The Prince's
collections VI

Bronzes (Cont.)

The lack of a suitable library for the heir apparent had been a matter of concern to the Archbishop of Canterbury, Richard Bancroft, who had launched a campaign for the Prince to be given one. Lumley's gift seems to have been in response to this, although it came subsequent to his death on 11 April 1609. The oldest nucleus was the theological books collected by Archbishop Cranmer, including a large collection of manuscripts that came through the Dissolution. These, on Cranmer's fall, were confiscated by the crown and passed to Mary I's Lord High Steward, Henry FitzAlan, Earl of Arundel, who had also acquired Nonsuch. Arundel's own library ran to some three hundred volumes and when his daughter, Jane, married John, Lord Lumley, he passed on the bulk of the Cranmer items. Lumley himself had a large library in his castle in the north which he moved south and placed in the charge of the antiquarian Humphrey Lloyd, who was physician to the household and later Lumley's brother-in-law. When, in 1579, Arundel died, 1000 printed books and 150 manuscripts passed to Lumley. Even then, by the time Lumley died, thirty years later, he had multiplied the library by three. It was a vast collection. Arundel, Lumley and Lloyd were all members of the Elizabethan Society of Antiquaries. As a result the antiquarian and historical section of the collection ran into some six hundred volumes in four languages. Genealogy was heavily represented. There was a similarly large array of books on philosophy and art, but the greatest concentration on any subject was science.

In 1596 the contents of the library had been organized under seven sub-headings: theology, history, arts and philosophy, medicine, cosmography and geography, law (both canon and civil) and music, totalling 3000 works in 2800 volumes. This great collection of books was exceeded only by the 4000 works in the library of the celebrated Elizabethan magus, Dr John Dee. Dee's library was his own creation and in it works of theological debate had no place, because it epitomized, as Frances Yates has written, 'the Renaissance as interpreted by Ficino and Pico della Mirandola, with its slant towards philosophy, science and magic, rather than towards purely grammarian humanist studies'.[65] In contrast there were theological works in the Lumley Library, but, in the main, they were inherited; the thrust of its expansion under Prince Henry was essentially in the direction John Dee had developed.

When the library came to Henry it was reduced in size. Duplicates were discarded and eighty manuscripts, and, more interestingly, virtually the complete medical and legal sections, were dropped. The task of organizing the library was assigned to Patrick Young (1584–1652), fifth son of Sir Peter Young, tutor to James VI, who came south in

1603. Young was to acquire a reputation as one of the great Greek scholars of the age and it was through the intervention of Dr Richard Montague, Bishop of Bath and Wells, that he was appointed librarian to the Prince.

The reorganization and expansion of the book collection necessitated the building, in 1609–10, of a library at St James's to accommodate the books.[66] Its position is recorded in a survey and plan made by Sir Christopher Wren, dated 1706, which indicates that it was on an upper floor of the palace at the extreme southeast corner. The room was 25 ft by 35 ft (7.6 by 10.6 m), divided lengthways by a fitting which seems to have had a double stack of shelves or boxes. That the interior was not purely utilitarian we know from the payments to the King's Master Sculptor, Maximilian Colt. There was an elaborate fireplace and 'four greate arches over the passages in the library with architrave round aboute them and the Princes armes in the spandrils'. The decoration also included both Ionic and Corinthian capitals, pyramids, pendants and satyrs.

The contents of this library can still largely be identified among the books from the old Royal Library presented by George III to the British Museum in the eighteenth century. It would be a formidable and wearisome task to identify all these volumes, but it is a perfectly possible one which perhaps a bibliophile might one day attempt. Some of these are in their original bindings, but the majority were rebound in the last century. What became the standard royal binding was, in fact, initiated by Prince Henry: a large block of the Prince's arms in the centre of the covers and four large heraldic blocks used in the corners.[67] This formula was applied only to folios; on octavos one of the corner ornaments was blocked in the centre of the covers. The quartos, in the main, have a different and smaller oval stamp of the arms within the Garter surmounted by a coronet. Sometimes this is elaborated with small heraldic ornaments at the angles. The evidence indicates that a large part of the library was rebound in 1610 by a number of binders who made use of a central pool of finishing tools.

The library continued to grow. The accounts are full of entries recording the presentation and purchase of books, both single and in quantity. On 21 February 1610 a servant of Robert Dallington, Gentleman of the Privy Chamber, was rewarded for delivering 'a fyne Cabinett full of bookes', and a month later, on 11 March, Richard Montague, Bishop of Bath and Wells, sent by a servant 'bookes to his highnes'.[68] In 1611–12, £21.16 s. was paid for 'Bookes and a Case to keepe Bookes',[69] and an undated payment records £122.15 s. to 'Edwarde Blounte stacyoner for certen bookes'.[70] Even in 1610 the Prince was making overtures to the Tuscan Resident, Lotti, for Italian books and Lotti consulted Sir Thomas Chaloner as to what was needed.[71]

Placed in perspective, the creation of this library was a significant event. It was Henry VII who had founded the first Royal Library at the close of the fifteenth century, but by the middle of the following one the impetus appears to have evaporated. There is no evidence of any activity under Elizabeth. Indeed, apart from a reference by the visitor from Hesse that James I had given it to his son there is little evidence of its continued existence.[72] That gift must have heightened the Prince's awareness of the library's stagnation. What we are witnessing under Prince Henry is the virtual refoundation of a Royal Library.

As the collections of art, antiquities and books stood on the Prince's death they were, to a degree, a distorting glass, for the balance was heavily tilted in favour of the visual arts. This, however, would be a misreading both of the range of the Prince's interests and of the actual nature of the art collections, for they embodied not only *exempla*, whether in the form of likenesses of the great and famous on canvas or in metal, but also revelations of truth in the form of biblical scenes or mythological compositions. More even than that, they were also scientific in that the pictures he collected were not only a celebration of man's virtuosity in paint, but a mine of information, recording in the minutest detail the world of nature in its diversity, besides providing demonstrations of optical principles in the form of perspective and *trompe l'oeil*. Lotti relates that the Prince not only asked for the *uomini illustri* and the Michelangelo, but went on to ask for plans of the latter's staircase in the Laurenziana Library, a magnet that had been invented on Elba, the latest book by Galileo, a recipe for the cement that joined terracotta piping so that it could carry water up hill and down dale, besides a horse that could caper.[73] So, although on the face of it, the cabinet of curiosities and natural history museum might seem to be missing from the programme, by implication they are not. The accounts give evidence of some activity in this direction. On 15 October 1609, a Gideon de Laune, apothecary to the Queen, was paid £16.13 s. 'for a fyne Cabinett full of singulare waters and oyles'. In January this was followed by a second payment to de Laune for 'a litle Cabinett full of glasses for his highnes vse'. These were presumably magnifying glasses. Later, in 1611–12 comes 'A Frenchman with Balownes and other thinges' and a 'Cabonett of Ebony curiously wrought'.[74] Even more interesting is the unique description of the Prince's menagerie at St James's supplied by the gentleman in the train of the Landgrave of Hesse:

We have seen the Prince's winter house, nearby a fine and spacious deer park, many beautiful birds, e.g. two ostriches, a male and a female one, Indian [i.e. American] chickens in white and black in great numbers, pheasants of various colours, also a rare Indian bird called an emu that can devour burning coals, rabbits of several colours, turtle doves and also very big doves, a large eagle-owl [Buhu], a very fine white parrot with a yellow crest and two other small ones.[75]

This was fully in the late Renaissance tradition of the palace as encyclopaedia as typified by Medici Florence and Rudolfine Prague. In other words, there is every reason to believe that Henry had the intent to construct the many rooms of the mansion of a late Renaissance encyclopaedia. But by his death he had achieved the furnishing of only a few.

It was Christopher Hill who first pointed out in 1963 how many members of the Prince's household and court were also participants and advocates of the ferment of scientific inquiry and experimentation that characterized the late Elizabethan and early Jacobean periods.[76] He also observed that the death of Prince Henry in 1612 could be taken almost as a terminal point of that particular renaissance. After that date there was a tremendous decline, and royal and aristocratic patronage of the sciences was notable for its absence. Centred on London and Gresham College, he argued, there was an important movement, radical Protestant in its theological bias, to popularize to the classes of society defined as 'a meaner sort of men' every aspect of the applied sciences. This was to be the work of merchants and craftsmen and not of dons cloistered away in the colleges of Oxford and Cambridge. It was to be written in the vernacular and aimed at everyday use by artisans. The men who clustered round Prince Henry were either at the heart or on the fringes of this revolutionary development: Raleigh and his friend Sir Arthur Gorges; the Prince's librarian, the navigator Edward Wright; the Prince's chronographer and cosmographer Thomas Lydiat;[77] another tutor and chaplain, William Barlow, expert too on navigation; Francis Bacon, who dedicated to the Prince the 1612 edition of his *Essays*; William Gilbert, author of *De Magnete*, 'the first physical treatise ... based entirely on experiment', who sometime before his death in 1603 dedicated his *Philosophia Nova* to the Prince; Matthew Gwinne, Gresham Professor of Physic, who also dedicated his play, *Vertumnus*, to the Prince in 1607. The Prince's friend Phineas Pett was a practical mathematician and also belonged to the tradition. Even the dedication to the young Prince in 1605 by Thomas James of the catalogue of the new Bodleian Library reflected an attitude that the interests of the heir to the throne would also be both anti-Catholic and pro-scientific. Of the former we have no doubt but what of the latter? Up until now we have approached the Prince's renaissance too much in the conventional terms of a proto-Caroline one. The anguish and grief that followed his death were on a scale never to be repeated. They mirrored a public awareness that some tremendous force had gone from within the royal circle that was irreplaceable.

Throughout this book I have tried to stress the need to see what might be categorized as the art side of his activities also in a scientific light. We now need to pick up that thread, for what I wish finally to argue is that the ideological framework of the lost renaissance is John Dee's revolutionary manifesto, his preface to Sir Henry Billingsley's translation of Euclid published in 1570. Since Hill's intuitively correct placing of the St James's court, the thought context has become far more complex than a simple link between the development within the applied sciences and Puritanism. We now have to add the important work of Frances Yates and Peter French in placing these developments within the mainstream of the Renaissance hermetic tradition.

It is impossible to embark here on anything other than the briefest summary, based on their pioneering work, of what that tradition was.[78] Renaissance hermeticism sprang out of the translation by Marsiglio Ficino of the *Corpus Hermeticum*, a collection of treatises believed to have been written by an ancient Egyptian priest, Hermes Trismegistus, a contemporary of Moses. The texts, which had a wide circulation during the Renaissance, fall into two parts. One, covering astrology, magic, alchemy and the occult sciences, embodied what has been labelled 'popular hermeticism', offering a view of these subjects quite different from Aristotelian science and Greek rationality. The second group, dealing with philosophy and theology, moved from the position that man was able to discover the divine within himself through mystical rapport with the world and mankind. The texts were saturated with piety and cast man as magus into a new and terrific role. By virtue of his divine intellect the magus is equated with God. Peter French usefully sums up in the following way:

It was out of the Hermetic texts, then, that the Renaissance magus developed his philosophy. The original and magical core of Hermeticism underwent many transformations after being introduced to the Renaissance by Ficino, whose own magic was inspired by the *Asclepius*. It was enriched and emboldened at the hands of magi like Pico, Agrippa, Bruno and Dee. Eventually, a philosophy evolved in which Pythagorean numerology, mystical geometry, music, astrology, the cabala, the theory of the four elements, the microcosm-macrocosm relationship and the Lullian art were inextricably tied together with the original Hermetic revelations. The universe was seen as a complex web of interacting forces that man was capable not only of understanding (as had always been the case with Aristotelian science) but of manipulating, even to the point of using God's angels for his own advancement. The belief in the manipulatory ability of man is all-important. The revival of Hermeticism marks the dawn of the scientific age because it unleashed the driving

213

spirit that inspired man to compel natural forces to serve him to an extent never dreamed of before.[79]

The result of this was that hermetic science was practical, unlike Aristotelian science, and that the desire of the Renaissance magus to control nature led to an interest in technology.

Dee's preface to Euclid outlines the whole state of science as it was then known, progressing from a Pythagoro-Platonic discussion of number and its mystical implications. He then lists the sciences dealing with number, arithmetic, algebra and geometry, and goes on to discuss those sciences dependent on number: the science of tactics for military art; law which depends on fair distribution; measuring which rests on geometry. Amongst the geometrical arts Dee lists geodesy or surveying, geography or the study of the earth, hydrography or the study of the ocean, 'stratarithmetrie' or the disposal of armies in geometrical figures, in addition to perspective, astronomy, music, astrology and 'statlike', which demonstrates causes of the lightness and heaviness of things.

Dee then moves on to a discussion of mathematics in relation to man, number, weight and measure as applied to man as microcosm. This leads on to the fine arts, 'Zographie' or painting, sculpture and architecture, with references to both Vitruvius and Alberti on man as the circle and square and to Agrippa, where the concept is cast in its astrological and magical light. He moves on to 'Trochlike', the properties of circular motion, of use in making wheels, mills and in mining; 'Helicosophie' concerning spirals, cylinders and cones; 'Pneumatithmie' or pneumatics, the study of mechanical devices using air or water, with reference to Hero of Alexandria; 'Menadrie', the science of moving weights by means of pulleys and cranes as well as engines of war; 'Hypogesiodie', which deals with underground measurements and surveys; 'Hydragogie' or the knowledge of how to conduct water from springs and rivers; and 'Horometrie', the art of measuring time by clocks and dials. He then returns to give a substantial section on architecture, with translations from Vitruvius and Alberti, followed by navigation, 'Navimaturgicke', the construction of mechanical marvels and finally 'Archmaistrie', in which all the 'arts mathematicall' are somehow embraced. What we are working through in terms of the vernacular is a huge programme for the exploration of every aspect of applied mathematics of use to builders, surveyors, mechanics, navigators, painters and makers of scientific instruments. It was a manifesto which was quickly to place England in the forefront of proto-scientific development in Europe in terms of the arts of navigation, map-making and ship-building as well as in those of experimental science. By 1603, when James I came to the throne, a whole generation had already responded to this, both in practical and theoretical terms.

As we read through this list we seem to find our feet firmly planted in the court of St James's. Dee's enumeration of what can be described as the Vitruvian disciplines – for the architect as the purveyor of these in terms of building was expected to be cognisant of them all – cover what we have identified already as the main concerns of the Prince. Henry emerges as a focal point for this movement which indeed he was seen directly to personify. W. H. tells us this when he writes: 'He admired great and rare Spirits, yea even those of mechanicall and meane persons, retaining divers of that sort, and went sometimes to see them work in their trades.'[80] To him were dedicated major books in the vernacular on precisely these kinds of subject: Peacham's *Graphice* (1612) with its mission to spread the art of drawing, the translation of Serlio (1611) designed to make artisans give their work 'right Simmetrie' or Edward Wright's *Certaine Errours in Navigation detected* (1610) for the use of mariners. Going down the Dee list, we know of Henry's certain interest in, or knowledge of, geodesy, geography, hydrography, 'stratarithmetrie', 'Zographie', music, perspective, 'Pneumatithmie', 'Menadrie' and 'Hydragogie'; unlike his father, Henry emerges as the Prince *par excellence* of Renaissance hermetic science in England.

Sir John Holles, in his letter to Lord Grey lamenting the Prince's death, refers to 'the Academy, to which he had given his stables, and other helps the better to "address" our youth'. That establishment, Holles records, perished in the aftermath of November 1612. It is unlikely that it ever advanced much beyond making accessible the facilities of the Riding School as a centre for training in the art of the new horsemanship. The Prince, however, was deeply committed to the establishment of an Academy Royal, a revival of an idea first mooted in the reign of Elizabeth by Sir Humphrey Gilbert, with the aim that its pupils should 'study matters of accion meet for present practize, both of peace and warre'.[81] The more immediate inspiration, however, was French: Antoine de Pluvinel's riding academy, which, though first and foremost a military and equestrian one, seems also to have taught the principles of honour besides some music, dancing, mathematics and drawing.[82] The Prince's Academy Royal significantly had as its objective first and foremost 'the learning of the Mathematiques, and Language; and for all kinds of noble exercises, as well arms as other'.[83] The project foundered on account of both the Prince's death and the perennial lack of funds, but if it had proceeded it would have radically affected, with its mathematical bias, the intellectual make-up of the governing classes. In a sense it would have been the equivalent of Gresham College for the aristocracy and gentry.

Most of the subjects of the 'arts mathematicall' we have covered, but what we would regard as the more strictly scientific and mathematical ones remain. Central to Henry's preoccupations in this sphere is a famous lost figure of the Jacobean age, Cornelius Drebbel (1572–1634).[84] He was born in Alkmaar and began his life executing etchings after works by Karel van Mander and Hendrik Goltzius, in whose house he lived and whose sister he married. But early on he was attracted to the invention of machines and automata and found service sometime about 1604 with James I, who took a great interest in his experiments. In 1607 we have a description by a Bohemian visitor of the King, witnessing a demonstration by Drebbel of two *perpetuum mobile* machines which he had constructed. One of these was described and illustrated in 1612 by Thomas Tymme, in his *A Dialogue Philosophicall, where in Nature's secret closet is opened, &c. together with the wittie invention of an artificial perpetuall motion*.... These machines were in fact a kind of air-barometer, whose motions derived from changes in atmospheric pressure but which had some kind of clock mechanism attached. Drebbel built them in addition as a defence of the old Ptolemaic system as against the Copernican. In the words of Philadelphus, in Tymme's dialogue:

86

> This wonderfull demonstration of Artificiall motion, imitating the motion celestiall, about the fixed earth, doth more prevaile with me to approve your reasons before aleadged concerning the moving of the Heavens, and the stability of the Earth, than can Copernicus assertions, which concerne the motion of the Earth.[85]

The dialogue goes on to place the machine firmly in a familiar line of descent of automata, reaching back to those dependent on the pneumatics of Hero of Alexandria. Tymme states that the *perpetuum mobile* was operated 'By extracting a fiery spirit'.

Before we consider Drebbel any further we must define his relationship to the Prince's circle. Two substantial payments to him exist, one in December 1609 and the second in March 1610, both of £20.[86] The third piece of evidence is undated but it must precede Salisbury's death in May 1612. It is a petition from the impecunious Drebbel to the Prince, following a refusal by the Lord Mayor to allow him to hold a lottery within the City and begging Henry to use his influence with the Treasurer to have one outside its jurisdiction.[87] In addition to these facts Drebbel's perpetual motion machine figures in Henry Peacham's *Sights and Exhibitions in England*, prefixed to Thomas Coryat's *Crudities* (1611). All this indicates that in Drebbel we have a figure in whom the interest of the King's and Prince's courts overlapped.

Drebbel also provides a link between the court of Rudolf II and the Jacobean courts because, in 1610, James I gave him leave to go to Prague. He was back in England again in 1612 after the Emperor's death. One wonders whether there could be any connection between this and the arrival of another Dutchman, who was also supposed to have served the imperial court: Abraham van der Doort. Putting that hypothesis to one side, Drebbel is a typical product of his period, in which the rational and practical side of his activities cannot in any way be disentangled from the irrational, with their deep roots in the prevailing magico-hermetic view of the cosmos. So many of his inventions, however, reflect exactly the St James's court. He built the earliest submarine, which he demonstrated in a voyage from Westminster to Greenwich. He could apparently induce changes of atmosphere and weather and on one occasion made Westminster Hall so cold in summer that James and his court were forced to withdraw. His activities went on to include some sort of incubator and a kind of magic lantern: 'there was no painter or painter's work to be seen, so that you saw a picture in appearance, but not in reality'. And like de Caus he was fascinated with the use of mirrors and the effects of reflection.

Drebbel was working directly in the tradition of the 'arts mathematicall' of the Renaissance magus. Under 'Pneumatithmie', Dee discusses the power of a vacuum and states that by understanding its force 'two or three men together, by keping Ayre under a great Cauldron, and forcying the same downe, orderly, may without harme descend to the sea bottome: and continue there a tyme &c.'[88] This is Drebbel's submarine, just as, in the same way, we can place his *perpetuum mobile* machines by Tymme's references to mechanical wonders such as the moving images of Mercury and the speaking brazen head made by Albertus Magnus; the latter were generally regarded in the Renaissance as magical and are listed among the examples by Dee in his discussion of 'Thaumaturgike'. In that section Dee lists the source of inspiration for all such mobile representations of the heavens, that of Archimedes. In short, Drebbel's model of the heavens was a typical manifestation of late Renaissance hermetic magic. It was a 'fiery spirit' which animated the machine and, when it ceased to revolve, it was deemed that the spirit was either tired or had left. Tymme in fact refers to Dee's preface where the magus records that he and Cardanus had together seen such a perpetual motion machine presented to the Emperor Charles V. Drebbel is one aspect of the Prince's interest in the 'arts mathematicall'; so too is his dedication to the arts of navigation.

In the words of David W. Waters, 'Recent researches make it clear that the credit for first grasping the possibilities of arithmetical navigation, for doing the pioneer work on it, and for teaching its potentialities to both navigators and to younger mathematicians lies with Dr John Dee.'[89] It was his instruction and example that blazed the path for the generations of mathematicians in late Elizabethan and Jacobean

England who were to solve mathematically a great number of the outstanding problems of navigation.

Of these the most prominent was William Gilbert (1540–1603), a Colchester physician, whose work *De Magnete, magneticisque corporibus* is generally recognized to be the first wholly English scientific treatise.[90] The major part of the book deals with magnetism and electricity, but in the later chapters he tackles the practical application of his solutions to navigational problems. On the accession of James I he was appointed a royal physician and shortly before he died in November 1603 he dedicated a manuscript treatise to Prince Henry: *De mundo nostro sublunari philosophia nova*. The line of descent to the Prince is direct: two members of Gilbert's intimate circle, Edward Wright and William Barlow, were not only to teach him but also to hold places in his household.

Edward Wright (1558–1615) is famous for having 'set the seal on the supremacy of the English in the theory and practice of navigation at this time'.[91] In 1589, in the aftermath of the defeat of the Spanish Armada, he was 'called forth to the public business of the nation, by the Queen' to help as a mathematician and cosmographer in improving the art of navigation. Wright worked for George Clifford, Earl of Cumberland, and eventually he published his findings in 1599 as *Certaine Errours in Navigation, Detected and Corrected*. He described it as an application of 'Mathematicall Studies to the use of Navigation' and it was to be the most influential and oft-quoted treatise on nautical practice of the age. Wright was also a maker of instruments, some of which were for Prince Henry, to whom he gave mathematical instruction and to whom he dedicated his 1610 edition of *Certaine Errours*. He was destined to have been the Prince's librarian had the tragic events of 1612 not taken place. In their aftermath comes the pathetic entry: 'Mr Wright the Keeper of the librarie, an excellent Mathematitian, & Navigator, & a very poor man – 30^{li}.8.'[92] Shortly before that, he had been in the employ of Sir Hugh Myddleton, undertaking surveying in relation to the New River project. He also lists among his services rendered to Prince Henry preparing a plan to show how water could be brought from Uxbridge for the use of the household. With him we touch a major figure in the mathematical revolution begun under the aegis of Dee, and one who not only assisted Gilbert on his *De Magnete* but was also an intimate of the first Gresham Professor of Geometry, Henry Briggs.

William Barlow (1544–1625) was also close to Gilbert and was later to fall out with Wright.[93] Son of the Bishop of Chichester, he had been educated at Balliol College, Oxford, and subsequently held various ecclesiastical appointments at Winchester and Salisbury. As a young man he had abhorred the sea, but discovering its relation to mathematics, he perfected himself in the art of navigation 'with some of the skilful-lest navigators of our land'. In 1597 he published what was to be his major work: *The Navigator's Supply,* dedicated to Essex. It dealt with the compass in general, the compass of variation, the Traveller's Jewel, the pantometer, the hemisphere and the traverse board. Barlow, in fact, de-vised a better model of compass, which 'with its improved needle mounting, its verge ring and its sight bar, marked a definite step for-ward in the art of navigation.' He was tutor to the Prince for no fewer than seven years and employed his own workman at Winchester to construct instruments, including ones presented to his pupil. These were a model astrolabe, and a model pantograph, besides a number of maps. Barlow, while he was in the Prince's service, wrote *Magneticall Advertisements,* the manuscript version of which is dated 1609 and is dedicated to Sir Thomas Chaloner. It was not published until 1616. Both of these books firmly belong in the popularizing tradition of Dee, for Barlow wrote his books in the vernacular, aiming less at profes-sional seamen than at young gentlemen sent off to sea in total ignor-ance of the laws of navigation.

These figures are all part of the tradition from which the Prince sprang. They need to be placed side by side with Salomon de Caus, In-igo Jones and Constantino de' Servi, for they all belong to the same thought context, that of Dee's magico-hermetic universe, with its quest to harness powers and secrets, stemming from a pervasive view of the cosmos as governed by occult influences to which the key lay in num-ber. That alliance of art, science and the monarchy snapped in 1612, not to be re-established until after the Restoration, with the foundation of the Royal Society. Prince Henry's renaissance was a unique fusion of all that was most advanced in the arts and sciences in late Mannerist Europe, aligned to a fiercely Protestant stance. That was not to be re-peated, for when the theme was taken up again by his brother in the 1620s it was no longer based on the 'arts mathematicall'. The approach henceforth was to be wholly aesthetic and one of the gentleman virtu-oso. It was to be linked, too, with James's *via media* policy, first in the quest for a Spanish marriage and later in the match of Charles with Henrietta Maria. In the mind of the Protestant populace the arts as cul-tivated at the court of Charles I were to be linked with concessions to Catholicism, an association fatal for the crown. They were to be asso-ciated, too, with England turning its back on its Protestant allies in nor-thern Europe in the great struggle against the Habsburgs and Catholi-cism which broke out in 1618. How different would have been the course of events, many must have mused, had James I been succeeded by Henry IX.

Epilogue: Our Rising Sun is Set

The death of the Prince of Wales was wholly unexpected. Nothing would have led anyone to believe that this athletic and masculine figure would succumb to illness and die in his nineteenth year.[1] At the beginning of October 1612 there were the first signs of an approaching fever, but Henry ignored them and was present at all the public occasions that lent support to the Palatine marriage. The details of this he worked on constantly, until forced to take to his bed on Sunday 25 October. Even then he got up the next day, revived enough even to play cards with his brother and Count Henry of Nassau: 'yet his Highness for all this looked ill and pale, spake hollow, and somewhat strangely, with dead sunk eyes'. The arrival of Dr Theodore de Mayerne on 27 October was a prelude to the final eleven days, during which a whole team of doctors was called upon in vain to stem the tide of disease. Two centuries later their observations enabled a physician to diagnose a classic case of typhoid fever. No one at the time knew that, and the detailed account of the Prince's last days makes painful reading, as the expedients resorted to, in an attempt to save his life, became more and more macabre. On Sunday 1 November he was visited by the entire royal family, and by his father again on the following day. That earlier occasion must have been the one when little Prince Charles pressed into his dying brother's hands Giovanni Bologna's bronze horse. No picture could be more poignant. The Prince finally died on the evening of 6 November.

Never before had there been such universal grief. His family was overwhelmed, especially the Queen and the two remaining children. Anne of Denmark wept alone in her room and even in April 1613 the Venetian Ambassador was warned not to offer his condolences, 'because she cannot bear to hear it mentioned; nor does she ever recall it without tears and sighs'.[2] Four years later she was to absent herself from the sad ceremonies which created Charles the new Prince of Wales, because she could not face the memories that such a ritual would evoke. In January the King was still recovering from his grief, although it would suddenly come over him and he would burst out crying, 'Henry is dead, Henry is dead.'[3]

The flood of literature that attended his departure far exceeded that for Gloriana in quantity, and in theme it matched that which mourned the passing of another quintessential perfect Protestant Knight, Sir Philip Sidney.[4] No one who put pen to paper, whether in verse or in private communication, demurred from the view that a major figure had indeed gone from the stage. 'To tell you that our Rising Sun is set ere scarce he had shone, and that all our glory lies buried', wrote the Earl of Dorset to Sir Thomas Edmondes, 'you know and do lament as well as we, and better than some do, and more truly, or else you were not a man, and sensible of this kingdome's loss', a sentiment which was echoed in many a correspondence.[5]

That a substantial biography can be written of a man who died before his nineteenth birthday, and whose period of public activity barely exceeded five years, is some measure of his stature. In comparison, his brother was to remain a pale pathetic shadow for many years. Henry was a man of definite convictions, with qualities which sometimes strike one as utterly contradictory. Austere, withdrawn, and slow of speech, he ruled, martinet-like, over a household which was a monument to the Protestant virtues and where even swearing was punishable by fine. So pious was he that, having heard the sermon at St James's on a Sunday morning, he would cross the park to listen to that at his father's palace of Whitehall. Although during the last months of his life there are allusions to courtly dalliance, even perhaps with that most notorious of beauties, the Countess of Essex, his sexual abstinence and seeming disinterest in women up to that point take on a chill, repressive quality. And yet he clearly abhorred the homosexuality of his father. Human emotion for him found its outlet only in his devotion to his mother and above all in his passion for his sister. Chamberlain records that 'the last wordes he spake in good sense (they say), were, Where is my deare sister?'[6] This inability to express emotion in human relationships is perhaps one of the keys to his character; it also becomes sublimated in the cultivation of animals and of things. When it came to them his reaction was spontaneous and sensual, the frigid mask dropped and he acted in a way that is quite surprising, seizing, for instance, a painting by Beccafumi and carrying it to another room for his personal enjoyment, or picking up and arranging himself the Giovanni Bologna bronzes, objects whose appeal lay essentially in their tactile value and whose subjects were often overtly erotic. The collections gave the Prince an emotional fulfilment he deliberately denied himself in other forms.

As a character he emerges, too, as one of the earliest instances of the spell exerted over the cold Protestant north by the warm Catholic south. Although he cast himself as a forerunner of Gustavus Adolphus, leading the troops of Protestant chivalry to victory over Catholicism and the Habsburgs, yet there are elements in his make-up which recall the Swedish King's daughter, Christina, whose surrender to the lure of the south led to the abandonment of a kingdom and her faith and the great journey to Italy. We catch glimpses of this streak in the cultural milieu of the court at St James's which, at times, began to resemble that of a Counter-Reformation ruler of a petty Italian state.

So much religiosity but aligned to so much egotism, for like Elizabeth I, he revelled in public appearances and was obsessed by his own image, whether in the form of festival or portrait. It was relentlessly fabricated as part Roman Emperor, Spenserian knight, St George, the heir of Arthur and of the Trojan king, Brutus, Oberon, the Fairy Prince and Meliadus, the Soldier to God. It is Henry who, without doubt, laid down the content of each masque, tournament and portrait, visions blunted by lack of funds, by an inability to recruit the necessary personnel and by a father whose policy was one of appeasement. In Henry, as a result, we witness the paradox of a Prince who epitomized the revival of the aims and ideals of the last Tudor queen in her role as an apocalyptic ruler of the Last Days, the vanquisher of the mighty Armada of Spain, but attired in the new robes of Renaissance art.

Bacon wrote, 'In his court no person was observed to have any ascendant over him, or strong interest with him ...'. That we know to be true, and yet these desires for the new architecture, for pictures and bronzes, for coins and medals, for splendid court festivals must have owed their impulse to those around him who stimulated this Prince with their accounts of Medicean Florence or the court of Henri IV. The passion for ships, navigation, the arts of war and horsemanship belong to the native tradition nurtured by his relationship with the hero of the Armada, Charles Howard, Lord Howard of Effingham and Earl of Nottingham, with the shipwright Phineas Pett or that flower of chivalry, Sir Henry Lee. They were reinforced by those who taught him, Edward Wright, William Barlow or Monsieur de St Antoine. But the sympathy for art is more difficult to explain. It must, of course, have owed much to his mother, of whom it was written that she preferred the company of pictures to that of people. But she never essayed so coherent a programme as that inaugurated by her son, whose attitudes would be more easily explained if he had travelled abroad like so many of his friends and those of the older generation around him. And yet it is to them that we must attribute the awakening that led to this short-lived flowering. Salomon de Caus, who taught him drawing and the art of perspective at the age of thirteen, must have made a major impression on him. In the Italian correspondence, when anything connected with the arts comes to the surface, two people always emerge well to the fore, his Chamberlain, Sir Thomas Chaloner, and the soldier, Sir Edward Cecil. Both had travelled and lived abroad for considerable periods of time. So had Inigo Jones, Robert Dallington, Sir John Holles and Arundel. Their input into this young mind is difficult to gauge. More certain is the impact of Constantino de' Servi, whose influence over the Prince grew the longer he was in England. There is no doubt that he was on terms of intimacy with him and he was a man with first-hand knowledge of the courts of Florence, Prague and Paris, besides having the ability to draw and make *modelli* to show his patron the new ideals. But these people could only flourish because they were tilling fertile soil, the mind and eye of a man whose mainspring was to culti-vate all those abilities and characteristics which his father either des-pised or lacked.

To all of this we must add a final and vital ideological line of descent into which he should firmly be placed. That line runs as follows: Eliza-beth I's first favourite, Robert Dudley, Earl of Leicester; secondly his nephew, Sir Philip Sidney; and finally his stepson and the Queen's last favourite, Robert Devereux, 2nd Earl of Essex. All three acted as a fo-cus of attempts to introduce the fruits of Renaissance civilization while maintaining an extreme Protestant and anti-Spanish stance. At its head stands Leicester during the 1560s and 1570s, when he was a major pa-tron of the arts with huge building projects at his three houses, Leices-ter House, Wanstead and Kenilworth Castle.[7] His picture inventories reveal a large collection and it was he who was the first major patron of the young Nicholas Hilliard, as well as being instrumental in bringing to England the Roman Mannerist painter, Federigo Zuccaro, in 1575. That year Leicester staged the 'Princely Pleasures' at Kenilworth in ho-nour of the Queen, a somewhat crude attempt to imitate the *magnificences* which represented the cultural apogee of Valois court civilization. To all this we can add a massive and calculated patronage of literature in the Puritan interest. And in 1585 it was Leicester who led the flower of Eng-lish chivalry to the Low Countries to fight against Spain.

By that date his mantle had descended onto a younger generation in the shape of Philip Sidney.[8] Sidney's impact on his contemporaries was minimized by his lack of financial resources and his early death, but his influence by way of his posthumous cult was to be decisive in creating the mythology of the ideal Protestant knight, brave on the field of bat-tle, valiant in the spectacle of the tiltyard at Whitehall in homage to his sovereign. To these attributes he added both those of a man of letters who could pen a chivalrous romance or write a sonnet, and those of one whose devotion to the Protestant cause was unshakeable and in whose defence he died.

After his death in 1586 on the field of Zutphen that role passed to Essex, who deliberately cultivated his part as the new Philisides. Sidney, in a symbolic gesture, had left him his sword and the Earl, to cement the identity still further, married the widow. No major study of Essex and the arts has ever been written but he more than any of the others is the one who takes us down to Prince Henry.[9] His role as the ideal Protestant knight is a well-defined one, not only as the dominant figure in the pageantry of the Accession Day Tilts throughout the 1590s but also on the fields of battle in France, Portugal and Ireland. That was all to end in disaster with his rebellion and execution. What is striking, however, is how many figures around the Prince had links either directly or indirectly with the Essex circle. Southampton, who danced in *Oberon,* was one of the Earl's most loyal supporters. Sir Thomas Chaloner, Henry's Lord Chamberlain, had been his agent both in Italy and in France. Sir John Hayward, the Prince's historiographer, looked to Essex as his patron. Lionell Sharpe, one of his chaplains, had also been chaplain to Essex. Inigo Jones and Robert Dallington had been members of the household of another devoted follower, the Earl of Rutland. Samuel Daniel, who wrote the Creation masque, was a protégé of Philip Sidney's sister, Mary, Countess of Pembroke. Francis Bacon, who dedicated his *Essays* to Henry, was secretary to Essex, and Sir Arthur Gorges, who was a Gentleman of the Privy Chamber, had voyaged with him on the Azores expedition. Sir Henry Lee, who looked to the young Prince as his last 'son in chivalry', was close not only to Sidney but also to Essex. It was the Earl who achieved the elevation of Lee to Knight of the Garter in 1597. Lee too may be the vital connection for Essex's patronage of the visual arts, for he had been the major sponsor of the young Marcus Gheeraerts, who was to paint the Earl shortly after 1596 at the same time as he abandoned Hilliard for Isaac Oliver.

In this way it can be argued that Prince Henry takes his place as the final figure in a series of still-born renaissances. Sidney was killed at thirty-two, Essex was executed at thirty-five, Prince Henry died at eighteen. In the case of the last, what is interesting is how he was also able to draw to himself devotees of the rival camp: Essex's enemy Raleigh and, even more significantly, Robert Cecil. Still more striking is how the crown stands quite apart, under both Elizabeth and James, from these major thrusts forward in the arts. How different from the pattern across the channel, where the alliance at the Valois and Bourbon courts of the monarchy and the arts in a perpetual manifestation of golden age *renovatio* was an act of state. It explains at once the diffuse and disjointed nature of English Renaissance culture, its lack of focus and often intangibility. That would have been reversed if Henry had lived to succeed.

The writing of history must always take into account lost visions and lost hopes, the world that might have been but never was. That is what this book has set out to evoke, a vanished, shortlived ethos, the achievements and aspirations of one minor late Renaissance court. Of all the laments on Prince Henry's death one letter catches more than any other the spirit of what was lost. It was written to William Trumbull by Beaulieu, from Paris, just six days after the tragic event:

I now begin ... by pouring out my Heart into the Bosom of my dearest Friend, the Torrent of Grief wherewith it is ready to burst out for *that wofull and unexpected News which we had yesterday night of the untimely Death of that brave Prince* of Wales; *the Flower of his House, the Glory of his Country, and the Admiration of all Strangers*; which in all Places had imprinted a great Hope in the Minds of the well affected, *as it had already stricken Terrour into the Hearts of his Enemies ... whose extraordinary great Parts and Vertues,* made many Men hope and believe, that God had reserved and destined him *as a chosen Instrument to be the Standard-bearer of his Quarrell in these miserable Times, to work the Restoration of his Church and the Destruction of the* Romish *Idolatry.*[10]

No truer epitaph for Henry IX was ever written.

Appendix

Memoirs of Henry, Prince of Wales

Apart from Francis Bacon's short *The Praise of Henry, Prince of Wales*, there are three main contemporary or near-contemporary sources for his life. As there has been confusion between these, as well as misattribution in respect of authorship, I list them here in order of compilation:

1 John Hawkins, A life starting 'Know then: that the Kings Majesty and the Quene ...', BL Add. MS 30075.

This was published in 1641 as *The Life and Death of our late most incomparable and heroic Prince, Henry, Prince of Wales ... Written by Sir Charles Cornwallis, Treasurer of His Highness's Household*. In 1751 this was reprinted under the title *An Account of the Baptism, Life, Death and Funeral of the most incomparable Prince, Frederick Henry, Prince of Wales, by Sir Charles Cornwallis, knight, his highness's treasurer*.

There is no reason to assign this to Cornwallis, who wrote his own account in 1626, or to doubt that the author was a certain John Hawkins. Although it was written by someone close to the Prince, or with access to persons close to him, the identity remains uncertain. A possible John Hawkins is referred to as having the grant in reversion of the office of Whiffler, and one of the Gunners of the Tower in March 1608 (*CSP Domestic, 1603–10*, p. 415). This at least would fit in with the militaristic content of the life. Hawkins must have written it soon after Henry's death, as a copy of it (BL Add. MS 11532) is dated 1613.

2 *A Discourse of the most illustrious prince, Henry, late Prince of Wales. Written Anno 1626 by Sir Charles Cornwallis, knight, sometime treasurer of his highness*, London, 1641.

This also exists in manuscript amidst the papers of the author's son (BL Add. MS 39853, ff. 26^v–29) and was reprinted in the *Harleian Miscellany*, IV, pp. 333–40.

3 W. H., *The Trve Picture and Relation of Prince Henry ...*, Leiden, 1634.

W. H. is almost certainly William Haydon, the senior groom of the Prince's bedchamber (Birch, *Henry*, p. 451). This was first suggested by W. B. Rye in *England as Seen by Foreigners in the Days of Elizabeth and James the First*, London, 1865, p. 451. It would fit exactly with W. H.'s statement that he 'had the honour to bee one of the most illustrious Prince HENRY his servants' (*True Picture*, p. 2).

Notes

Abbreviations

AO
 Audit Office
ASF
 Archivio di Stato, Florence
Birch, *Henry*
 Thomas Birch, *The Life of Henry Prince of Wales, Eldest Son of King James I*, London, 1760
BL
 British Library
Boderie, *Ambassades*
 Antoine la Fèvre de la Boderie, *Ambassades de Monsieur de la Boderie en Angleterre (1606–1611)*, Paris, 1750
Chamberlain, *Letters*, ed. McClure
 The Letters of John Chamberlain, ed. N. E. McClure, Philadelphia, 1939
Chambers, *Elizabethan Stage*
 E. K. Chambers, *The Elizabethan Stage*, Oxford, 1923 (1951 edn)
Complete Peerage
 G. E. C., *The Complete Peerage of England, Scotland, Great Britain and the United Kingdom, Extant, Extinct or Dormant*, Alan Sutton reprint, 1982
Cornwallis, *Account*
 Sir Charles Cornwallis, *An Account of the Baptism, Life, Death and Funeral of the most incomparable Prince, Frederick Henry, Prince of Wales...*, London, 1751
Cornwallis, *Discourse*
 Sir Charles Cornwallis, *A Discourse of the most illustrious Prince, Henry, late Prince of Wales*, 1626, reprinted in *Harleian Miscellany*, IV, pp. 333–40
CSP
 Calendar of State Papers
DNB
 Dictionary of National Biography
Garganò, *Scapigliatura*
 G S Garganò, *Scapigliatura Italiana a*

Londra sotto Elisabetta e Giacomo I, Florence, 1923
HMC
 Historical Manuscripts Commission
Nichols, *Progresses*
 John Nichols, *The Progresses, Processions, and Magnificent Festivities of King James I*, London, 1828
Orgel and Strong, *Inigo Jones*
 Stephen Orgel and Roy Strong, *Inigo Jones. The Theatre of the Stuart Court*, Sotheby's and the University of California, 1973
PRO
 Public Record Office, London
Smith, *Wotton*
 Logan Pearsall Smith, *The Life and Letters of Sir Henry Wotton*, Oxford, 1907
SP
 State Papers
W. H., *True Picture*
 W. H., *The Trve Picture and Relation of Prince Henry...*, Leiden, 1634
Williamson, *Myth*
 J. W. Williamson, *The Myth of the Conqueror. Prince Henry Stuart, a Study in 17th Century Personation*, New York, 1978
Wilson, *History*
 Arthur Wilson, *The History of Great Britain, being the Life and Reign of King James the First...*, London, 1653
Wilson, *Henry*
 Elkin Calhoun Wilson, *Prince Henry and English Literature*, Cornell U. P., 1946
Winwood, *Memorials*
 Edmund Sawyer, *Memorials of Affairs of State... Collected from the Original Papers of the Right Honourable Sir Ralph Winwood*, London, 1725

Portrait of a Prince (pp. 7–70)

1 For descriptions of the funeral see PRO, SP 14/71, ff. 104–15; BL Cotton MS Vespasian. CXIV. ff. 216–17; *The Funeral of the High and Mighty Prince Henry ...*, printed in Nichols, *Progresses,* II, pp. 493–503; Cornwallis, *Account,* pp. 44 ff.; Chamberlain to Carleton, 17 December 1612, *Letters,* ed. McClure, I, p. 396; Dispatch of Foscarini, 29 December 1612, *CSP Venetian, 1610–13,* pp. 467–9. For the sermons preached by his chaplain leading up to the funeral see Daniel Price, *Lamentations for the Death of the late illustrious Prince Henry and the dissolution of his religious familie. Two sermons: Preached in his Highnesse Chappell at Saint Iames, on the 10. and 15. day of Nouember ...*, London, 1613; *Teares shed ouer Abner. The Sermon Preached on the Sunday before the Prince his funeral in St Iames Chappell before the Bodie,* Oxford, 1613; *Sorrow for the Sinnes of the Time. A Sermon Preached at St Iames on the third Sunday after the Prince his death,* Oxford, 1613.

2 Isaac Wake to Lady Carleton, 19 December 1612, PRO, SP 14/71, f. 128.

3 *HMC Portland,* IX, pp. 8, 11, 14, 28, 33–40.

4 *Ibid.,* pp. 8–11.

5 The best account of Henry's early years is in Walter W. Seton, 'The Early Years of Henry Frederick, Prince of Wales and Charles, Duke of Albany (Charles I) 1593–1605', *Scottish Historical Review,* XIII, 1915–16, pp. 366–8. See also Birch, *Henry,* pp. 1ff.; E. C. Williams, *Anne of Denmark,* London, 1970, pp. 46–57, 70–73; Williamson, *Myth,* pp. 1–26.

6 *Ben Jonson,* ed. C. H. Herford and P. and E. Simpson, Oxford 1941, VII, p. 131.

7 Nichols, *Progresses,* I., pp. 193–4.

8 *Ibid.,* I, p. 416.

9 Wilson, *History,* p. 12.

10 Nichols, *Progresses,* II, p. 33.

11 *Ibid.,* p. 80.

12 See letter of Lady Lumley to Lady Shrewsbury, 3 October 1604, *ibid.,* I, p. 459.

13 See Appendix. For Bacon's account see *The Moral and Historical Works of Lord Bacon ...*, ed. Joseph Devey, London, 1866, pp. 493–5.

14 W. H., *True Picture,* p. 31. See also the description of him in Cornwallis, *Account,* pp. 50–51 and Lionel Sharpe, *Oratio funebris ...*, quoted Birch, *Henry,* p. 376.

15 Cornwallis, *Account,* p. 26.

16 Chamberlain to Carleton, 6 November 1611, *Letters,* ed. McClure, I, p. 313.

17 Cornwallis, *Discourse,* p. 339.

18 The Prince's wardrobe is very fully documented and would make a study in itself. The wardrobe accounts by Sir David Murray covering 1610–12 are in PRO, E 35/3085; some items appear in the Privy Purse account, SP 14/57, ff. 142–4; see also William Bray, 'Extracts from the Wardrobe Account of Prince Henry, eldest son of King James I', *Archaeologia,* XI, 1794, pp. 88–96. Sir Arthur Gorges cites Henry and his court as examples of moderation in dress as opposed to 'extreame excess and pride of Apparell' in his *A Breefe Discourse tending to the wealthe and strength of this Kingdome of Great Brittayne* in Cambridge, Trinity College MS R.7.23* (3), f. 6.

19 W. H., *True Picture,* 9.

20 Dispatch 10 March 1611, *CSP Venetian, 1610–13,* pp. 122–3.

21 Lotti to Vinta, 3 March 1611, ASF 4189.

22 Lotti to Vinta, 12 August 1611, *ibid.*

23 Quoted in Williams, *Anne of Denmark,* p. 54.

24 Nichols, *Progresses,* I, p. 304.

25 Letters of Henry to the King, BL

Harleian MS 7007, f. 14 (1603), 25 (1604), 171 (1607/8), Latin oration to, ff. 229–31. Nichols, *Progresses*, II, pp. 161–2, 213 prints a few.

26 Nichols, *Progresses*, I., p. 556.

27 *Relazione* of 1607 by Nicolo Molin, *CSP Venetian, 1603–7*, pp. 513–14

28 W. H., *True Picture*, p. 3.

29 Dispatch, May 1611, *CSP Venetian, 1610–13*, p. 142.

30 Godfrey Goodman, *The Court of King James the First*, ed. J. S. Brewer, London, 1839, I, pp. 250–51.

31 *Ibid.*, p. 251.

32 Prince Henry to the King, December 1609, BL Harleian MS 7007 f. 316, printed Nichols, *Progresses*, II, pp. 265–6.

33 Dispatch, 20 May 1609, *CSP Venetian, 1607–10*, p. 276.

34 W. H., *True Picture*, p. 4.

35 Letters from the Prince to his sister are in BL Harleian MS 7007, ff. 21, 22 (undated), 62, 63, 64 (probably all 1605), 143, (30 June 1607), 284 (20 August 1609). Gifts from Elizabeth to her brother are recorded in PRO, SP 14/57, f. 139ᵛ (13 September 1610, a cabinet), E 351/2794 (New Year's gift for 1612, an ebony cabinet with silver mounts).

36 Birch, *Henry*, p. 231; Nichols, *Progresses*, I, pp. 460–61. For Henry and Prince Charles see Pauline Gregg, *King Charles I*, London, 1981, ch. 2, 3.

37 On the Great Contract see *CSP Venetian, 1610–13*, pp. v-vii; D. H. Willson, *James I and VI*, London, 1956, pp. 44 ff.; Robert Ashton, 'Deficit Finance in the Reign of James I', *Economic History Review*, 2nd Series, X, 1957, pp. 15–29.

38 Dispatch, 25 November, 1609, *CSP Venetian, 1610–13*, pp. 79–80.

39 For lists of the household see PRO, SP 14/72 ff. 189, 190ᵛ, 196; Birch, *Henry*, p. 218.

40 Lotti to Vinta, 29 March 1610, ASF 4189.

41 Cornwallis, *Discourse*, p. 336.

42 Roger Coke, *A Detection of the Court and State of England*, London, 1694, I, p. 61.

43 For Chaloner see Birch, *Henry*, pp. 32–4; Nichols, *Progresses*, I, p. 204 note 1; *DNB*; P. W. Hasler, *The House of Commons 1558–1603*, HMSO, 1981, I, pp. 588–9.

44 For Newton see Birch, *Henry*, pp. 14–15; *DNB*.

45 Henry Peacham, *Minerva Britanna*, London 1612, p. 39.

46 John Summerson, *Architecture in Britain 1530–1830*, 4th edn, London, 1963, pp. 43–4; Olive and Nigel Hamilton, *Royal Greenwich*, 1969, p. 157.

47 P. Ganz, *The Paintings of Hans Holbein*, London, 1950, p. 229 (no. 36).

48 Cornwallis, *Account*, p. 41. For Murray see *DNB*.

49 Lord Roos to David Murray, 25 November 1612, Birch, *Henry*, p. 321.

50 B. H. Newdigate, *Michael Drayton and his Circle*, Oxford, 1961, pp. 196–7.

51 On Stirling see *DNB*; *Complete Peerage*, s. v. Stirling.

52 For Holles see *DNB*; Arthur Collins, *Historical Collections of the Noble Families of Cavendish, Holles, Vere, Harley, ...*, London, 1752, pp. 80 ff.; Nichols, *Progresses*, II, p. 374 note 2; *HMC Portland*, IX, pp. v-viii.

53 Northumberland to Holles, undated, *HMC Portland*, IX, p. 152; on the return of the books, *ibid.*, pp. 115–16.

54 For Cornwallis see *DNB*.

55 Sir Charles Cornwallis to the Prince, 7/17 April 1609, BL Harleian MS 7007, f. 255; printed in Winwood, *Memorials*, III, pp. 9–10.

56 The Prince to Sir Charles Cornwallis, 24 May 1609, BL Harleian MS 7007, f. 266.

57 Wilson, *History*, p. 52.

58 BL Harleian MS 7009, f. 5.

59 Biographies of all these are either in the *DNB* or *Complete Peerage*. For Carey see Hasler, *House of Commons*, II, pp. 545–6.

60 Karl Josef Höltgen, 'Sir Robert Dallington (1561–1637), Author, Traveller and Pioneer of Taste' (forthcoming). I am most grateful to the author for sending me a copy of the typescript of this article.

61 *HMC Hatfield*, XXI, p. 171.

62 For Danvers see Roy Strong, *The Renaissance Garden in England*, London, 1979, pp. 176–81.

63 John Aubrey, *The Natural History of Wiltshire*, ed. J. Britton, Wiltshire Topographical Society, 1847, p. 93.

64 Warrant to pay him £1000 p. a. as Keeper of the Privy Purse, *CSP Domestic*, 1611–18, p. 206.

65 On Byfleet see John Harris, Stephen Orgel and Roy Strong, *The King's Arcadia. Inigo Jones and the Stuart Court*, Arts Council exhibition, 1974, pp. 95, 98 (176); H. M. Colvin, John Summerson, Martin Biddle, J. R. Hale and Marcus Merriman, *The History of the King's Works*, ed. H. M. Colvin, IV, 1485–1660 (Part II), HMSO, 1982, pp. 58–9; L. R. Stevens, 'Byfleet House', *Surrey Archaeological Collections*, I, 1946–7, p. 99 which also reproduces Aubrey's drawing from Bodleian MS Aubrey 4, f. 196.

66 On Ancrum see *DNB; Complete Peerage*, s. v. Ancrum.

67 Oliver Millar, *Abraham van der Doort's Catalogue of the Collections of Charles I*, Walpole Society, XXXVII, 1960, pp. 11, 55, 56, 57, 60, 85, 128, 144.

68 On Gorges see *The poems of Sir Arthur Gorges*, ed. H. E. Sandison, Oxford, 1953. See the undated letter from Gorges to the Prince, BL Harleian MS 7007, f. 440; and one dated 29 April 1610, *ibid.*, f. 357.

69 Gorges, *Poems*, ed. Sandison, *op. cit.*, pp. lv-lvi.

70 Mary S. Hervey, *The Life, Correspondence and Collections of Thomas Howard, Earl of Arundel*, Cambridge, 1921, p. 465.

71 For Essex see Vernon F. Snow, *Essex the Rebel. The Life of Robert Devereux, the Third Earl of Essex 1591–1646*, University of Nebraska, 1970.

72 For Lord Harington see Birch, *Henry*, pp. 117–26; *Complete Peerage*, s. v. Harington. For letters see BL Harleian MS 7007, f. 189; 7008, ff. 235, 295; Birch, *Henry*, pp. 323–5.

73 There is also a poem by Gorges, see *Poems*, ed. Sandison, pp. 130–31.

74 Sir James Whitelocke, *Liber Familicus*, quoted *Complete Peerage*, s. v. Harington of Exton, VI, p. 322 note b.

75 The Prince to Harington, 4 March 1608/9, BL Harleian MS 7007, f. 241.

76 Logan Pearsall Smith, *The Life and Letters of Sir Henry Wotton*, Oxford, 1907, I, p. 441 note 2.

77 Report of 13 January 1608/9, *CSP Venetian, 1607–10*, pp. 215–16.

78 Harington to the Prince, 11/21 November 1608, wondering whether his letters had arrived and stating that he had written from Frankfort, Heidelberg and Basle, BL Harleian MS 7007, f. 215. Undated but from Florence, *ibid.*, f. 221 and two other letters, ff. 223, 224.

79 Nichols, *Progresses*, II, p. 268.

80 Arthur M. Hind, *Engraving in England in the Sixteenth and Seventeenth Centuries*, Part II, *The Reign of James I*, Cambridge, 1955, pp. 156, 176–7, 375.

81 John Harington, *Nugae Antiquae*, London, 1779, pp. 155–6. Harington is virtually duplicated in Richard Stock, *The Churches Lamentation for the losse of the Godly ...*, London, 1614. This was Lord Harington's funeral sermon.

82 On Cranborne see *Complete Peerage,* s. v. Salisbury; Charles Dalton, *Life and Times of General Sir Edward Cecil, Viscount Wimbledon,* London, 1885, I, p. 204 note 1. I am indebted for information communicated by Mr Robin Harcourt-Williams from the Hatfield archives.

83 *HMC Bath,* II, p. 56.

84 *HMC Hatfield,* XXI, pp. 19, 35.

85 The journal covers 29 July/ 8 August 1609 and 20/30 October 1610, HMC Hatfield, XXI, pp. 104–13, 237–49. There are several references to his travels in Chamberlain, *Letters,* ed. McClure, I, pp. 273, 278, 301, 302. The assassination of Henri IV led to his return.

86 *HMC Hatfield,* XXI, p. 242.

87 Chamberlain to Carleton, 6 November 1611, *Letters,* ed. McClure, I, p. 369.

88 See Michael Strachan, *The Life and Adventures of Thomas Coryate,* Oxford University Press, 1962; the pension of £10 p. a. is listed in PRO E351/2794; AO/2021 no. 2.

89 For Edward Cecil see Dalton, *op. cit.*

90 *Ibid.,* p. 193.

91 Lotti to Vinta, 3 March 1610/11, ASF 4189.

92 Chamberlain to Carleton, 11 March 1612, *Letters,* ed. McClure, I, p. 339.

93 Chamberlain to Carleton, 25 March 1612, *ibid.,* I, p. 343.

94 *King's Arcadia, op. cit.,* p. 106 (190).

95 On Southampton see C. C. Stopes, *The Life of Henry Third Earl of Southampton, Shakespeare's Patron,* Cambridge, 1922, pp. 340, 345, 348, 355, 358.

96 See below, p. 120.

97 For Arundel during this period see Hervey, *Arundel, op. cit.,* pp. 33, 52–9.

98 D. Lloyd, *Memoires of ... those that suffered,* London, 1677, p. 248.

99 Hervey, *Arundel,* p. 465.

100 On Fanshawe see *Memoirs of Lady Fanshawe ...,* London, 1829; pp. 13, 16; Strong, *Renaissance Garden, op. cit.,* pp. 123–4.

101 On Harington see A. L. Rowse, 'Elizabeth I's Godson: Sir John Harington' in *Eminent Elizabethans,* London, 1983, pp. 107–52. See also Nichols, *Progresses,* II, pp. 102, 197–9, 268. On 1 August 1608 the Prince gave Harington 'a ring with 32 dyamants'; see Leila Parsons, 'Prince Henry (1594–1612) as a Patron of Literature', *Modern Language Review,* 47, 1952, p. 504.

102 Lucy Gent, *Picture and Poetry 1560–1620,* Leamington Spa, 1981, pp. 9–10, 24, 25, 69.

103 On Peacham see Alan R. Young, *Henry Peacham,* Boston, 1979; Margaret C. Pitman, 'Studies in the Work of Henry Peacham', *Bulletin of the Institute of Historical Research,* XI, 1933–4, pp. 189–92; same author's 'The Epigrams of Henry Peacham and Henry Parrot', *Modern Language Review,* XXIX, 1934, pp. 129–36; R. R. Cowley, *Henry Peacham, His Contribution to English Poetry,* 1971; F. J. Levy, 'Henry Peacham and the Art of Drawing', *Journal of the Warburg and Courtauld Institutes,* XXXVII, 1974, pp. 174–90.

104 Peacham, *Minerva Britanna,* p. 210.

105 On Raleigh and the Prince see Williamson, *Myth,* pp. 56–8. All the Raleigh literature refers to the Prince, but by far the best account is Pierre Lefranc, *Sir Walter Raleigh, Écrivain. L'Oeuvre et les Idées,* Université de Laval, 1968, pp. 37ff.; 53, 254ff.; 586ff.

106 *Aubrey's Brief Lives,* ed. Oliver Lawson Dick, London, 1962 edn, p. 321.

107 Roger Coke, *Detection of the Court and State of England,* London, 1694, I, p. 61.

108 There is a large literature on the Prince and Raleigh's *History of the World,* but see F. Smith Fussner,

The Historical Revolution. English Historical Writing and Thought, 1580–1640, Westport, Connecticut, 1976 edn., pp. 191–210; Leonard Tennenhouse, 'Sir Walter Raleigh and the Literature of Clientage', in *Patronage in the Renaissance*, ed. G. F. Lytle and S. Orgel, Princeton UP, 1981, pp. 235–58.

109 Williamson, *Myth*, pp. 58–60.

110 Cornwallis, *Account*, p. 52.

111 *Ibid.*, p. 51. W. H., *True Picture*, p. 2 writes of 'rare tokens of a religious and vertuous disposition'; Bacon also refers to him as 'firm to the course of religion'.

112 *Funerall Notes Upon my Patron, Sir Augustine Nicolls, Knight, ...*, printed as an appendix to Robert Bolton, *Foure Last Things*, London, 1633, pp. 53 ff.

113 For more anti-papal literature dedicated to the Prince see William Tooker, *Duellum siue singulare certamen cum Martino Becano Jesuita ...*, 1611; John Gordon, *Anti-bellarmino-tortor siue Tortus Retortus*, London, 1611; George Hakewill, *Scutum Regium*, 1612. It is interesting that Harington sent the Prince from Venice 'le pourtrait d'Alessandre iii ce mettant le pied su le col de l'Empereur' as it was depicted in the Doge's palace, undated letter, 1609, BL Harleian MS 7007, f.319.

114 Holles to the Prince 23 June 1611, *HMC Portland*, IX, pp. 47–9. For his proposal to the King to take on the forfeitures by recusants see BL Harleian MS 7009 f. 20–30.

115 Letter from Sharpe to the Prince, undated, sending his *Speculum Papae*, BL Harleian MS 7008, f. 233.

116 Northampton to Cornwallis, 10 August 1612, *CSP Domestic, 1611–18*, p. 143; Linda Levy Peck, *Northampton; Patronage and Policy at the Court of James I*, London, 1982, pp. 61–2.

117 In 1610 Price dedicated to the Prince his *The Defence of Truth*, in which he wrote: 'The eies, and harts, and hopes of all the Protestant world, be fixed upon your Highnesse.'

118 Frank Livingstone Huntley, *Bishop Joseph Hall 1574–1656. A Biographical and Critical Study*, D. S. Brewer, Cambridge, 1979.

119 For Sylvester see Parsons, 'Prince Henry as a Patron of Literature', *op. cit.*, For his salary of £15 see PRO, E 351/2794.

120 The Prince translated this into Latin for presentation to his father but never completed the task, Cambridge Trinity College MS R.7.23* (VII).

121 Daniel Price, *Prince Henry His First Anniversary*, Oxford, pp. 4, 6.

122 Although he does not touch on the relationship of the Prince and Somerset the best study is P. R. Seddon, 'Robert Carr, Earl of Somerset', *Renaissance and Modern Studies*, XIV, 1970, pp. 48–68. See also Williams, *Anne of Denmark*, pp. 133 ff.

123 Williamson, *Myth*, pp. 58–60.

124 Wilson, *History*, pp. 55–6. See also Roger Coke, *A Detection of the Court and State of England*, London, 1694, I, p. 60.

125 *The Secret History of the Reign of King James I in the Autobiography and Correspondence of Sir Simonds D'Ewes, Bart.*, ed. J. O. Halliwell, London, 1845, pp. 351–2.

126 Snow, *Essex the Rebel*, pp. 42–3; Robert Codrington, *The Life and Death of the illustrious Robert, Earl of Essex ...*, 1646, printed in *Harleian Miscellany*, I, pp. 218–19. Codrington, who is sole source for this incident, does not connect it with the Countess.

127 Wilson, *History*, p. 55.

128 *HMC Mar & Kellie*, pp. 40–41.

129 Robert Johnston, *Historia Rerum Britannicarum*, Amsterdam, lib. xv, pp. 468–9.

130 Wilson, *History*, p. 63.

131 Sir A(nthony) W(eldon), *The Court*

and Character of King James, London, 1817, p. 27.

132 Birch, *Henry*, pp. 38–9; Nichols, *Progresses*, I, p. 425; *The Autobiography of Phineas Pett*, ed. W. G. Perrin, Navy Records Society, 1918, pp. 22–3; Williamson, *Myth*, pp. 49–51.

133 Birch, *Henry*, pp. 96–7; Pett, *Autobiography, op. cit.*, pp. 31–2.

134 On the navy in the Jacobean period see M. Oppenheim, *A History of the Administration of the Royal Navy and of Merchant Shipping in relation to the Royal Navy*, London, 1896, I, pp. 184ff.

135 On the building of the *Prince Royal* see PRO, SP 40, 24 November 1610; BL Harleian MS 7009 f. 50, 21 November 1610: 'The reasons of the surcharge of his Majesties shipp the Prince Royall'; Pett, *Autobiography*, pp. lxvi–lxxxii; Oppenheim, *Royal Navy, op. cit.*, pp. 203–5; R. C. Anderson, 'The Prince Royal and other Ships of James I', *Mariner's Mirror*, III, 1913, pp. 272–5, 305–7, 341–2; Williamson, *Myth*, pp. 54–5.

136 Nichols, *Progresses*, II, pp 249–57.

137 Pett, *Autobiography*, p. 62.

138 *Ibid.*, p. 66.

139 On the launching see *ibid.*, pp. 79–84; dispatch of 7 October 1610, CSP Venetian, 1610–13, p. 52.

140 E. Croft-Murray, *Decorative Painting in England 1537–1837*, London, 1962, I, p. 204 (b).

141 For *Trades Increase* and the *Peppercorn* see dispatches of February and 20 May, *CSP Venetian, 1607–10*, pp. 47, 275; Chamberlain to Winwood, 13 January 1610, *Letters*, ed. McClure, I, p. 294; Birch, *Henry*, pp. 181–2; Nichols, *Progresses*, II, pp. 268–9.

142 On the *Phoenix* see Pett, *Autobiography*, pp. 96, 104.

143 Cornwallis, *Account*, pp. 25–6.

144 Pett, *Autobiography*, p. 88.

145 On the visit to the navy see Birch, *Henry*, pp. 242–4.

146 Pett, *Autobiography*, p. 90.

147 Cornwallis, *Discourse*, p. 336.

148 Pett, *Autobiography*, p. 92.

149 *Ibid*, p. 95; Birch, *Henry*, pp. 257/64.

150 Pett, *Autobiography*, p. 95.

151 Goodman, *The Court of James the First*, I, p. 250.

152 Dispatch of 21 October 1611, *CSP Venetian, 1610–13*, p. 227.

153 Dispatch of 25 November, *ibid.*, p. 240; see the further report on the Prince's proposed reforms in 30 December, *ibid.*, pp. 264–5. This may connect with undated items concerning projects to cut the costs of shipbuilding in BL Harleian MS 7009, ff. 30–47.

154 Edward Wright, *Certaine Errours in Navigation*, London, 1610, dedication.

155 Robert Tindall to the Prince, 22 June 1607, BL Harleian MS 7007, f. 139.

156 For the resurgence in colonization plans see James S. M. Anderson, *The History of the Church of England in the Colonies and Foreign Dependencies of the British Empire*, London, 1845, I, pp. 193ff.; 229ff.; 241–2; Edward D. Neill, *History of the Virginia Company of London ...*, 1869.

157 Dispatch of 27 February 1609, *CSP Venetian, 1607–10*, p. 237; Williamson, *Myth*, pp. 51–2.

158 *The Works of Michael Drayton*, ed. J. W. Hebel, Oxford, 1961, II, p. 363.

159 On Dale see Neill, *History*, pp. 73–77.

160 *HMC Hatfield*, XXI, p. 276.

161 For the North-West Passage see dispatch of 4 November 1611, *CSP Venetian, 1610–13*, p. 233; and introduction, pp. xxvi–xxvii; Birch, *Henry*, pp. 264–5; G. M. Asher,

Henry Hudson, the Navigator, Hakluyt Society, 1860, pp.255–60; Williamson, *Myth*, p.53. See the petition of the Merchant Discoverers of the North-West Passage, BL Harleian MS 7009, f. 168 (undated).

162 *CSP Domestic*, 1611–18, p.139.

163 Chamberlain to Carleton, 4 December 1611, Letters, ed. McClure, I, pp.321–2.

164 Dispatch of 31 December 1611, *CSP Venetian, 1610–13*, p.265.

165 See dispatches of 1 March, 19 April and 24 May, 1612, *ibid.*, pp.299–300, 333, 361.

166 See *Voyage of Sir Thomas Button* in Thomas Rundall, *Narrative of Voyages towards the North-West in Search of a Passage to Cathay and India*, Hakluyt Society, 1849, pp.81–94.

167 Dispatch of 1 September 1604, *CSP Venetian, 1603–7*, pp.178–9.

168 For St Antoine see W. B. Rye, *England as Seen by Foreigners in the Days of Elizabeth and James the First*, London, 1865, p.253 note 102. On the movements of St Antoine to and from France see the Prince to Henri IV, 28 November 1608, BL Harleian MS 7007, f.163; Sir George Carew to the Prince, 1 April 1608, *ibid.*, f.180.

169 Lotti to Vinta, 15 April 1610, ASF 4189.

170 See *The History of the King's Works*, ed. Colvin, *op. cit.*, pp.244–5; Mark Girouard, 'The Smythson Collection of the RIBA', *Architectural History*, V, 1962, p.33.

171 *Royal Commission on Historic Monuments, Dorset*, III, Part i, 1970, pp.69–70. On Trenchard see Hasler, *The House of Commons*, III, p.527.

172 Mark Girouard, *Robert Smythson and the Elizabethan Country House*, Yale UP, 1983, pp.251–3.

173 Godfrey Trease, *Portrait of a Cavalier, William Cavendish, First Duke of Newcastle*, London, 1979, pp.28–9.

174 Oliver Millar, *The Tudor, Stuart and Early Georgian Pictures in the Collection of H. M. The Queen*, London, 1963, I, p.93 (143).

175 W. H., *True Picture*, pp.26–7.

176 Landesbibliothek Kassel, MS Hass. 18, f.79ᵛ.

177 Cornwallis, *Account*, p.26, See PRO, E 351/3085 for Polonian and Barbary horses. The accounts are full of purchases of horses, e.g. 12 February 1609/10; 'to four groomes who brought horses out of france for his highness', PRO, SP 14/57.

178 The gifts of horses exceed any other type of presentation to the Prince. Ones presented by the Duke of Lorraine, the King of Denmark, Prince Radziwill and the Comte de Vaudemont are recorded in *CSP Venetian, 1603–7*, p.416; *1607–10*, p.210; *1610–13*, p.227. Other gifts of horses occur in the following: Birch, *Henry*, p.100 (Prince de Joinville); BL Harleian MS 7007, ff.193, 196 (Duc de Bellegarde, Henri IV's Master of the Horse); *ibid.*, f.324 (Lord Salisbury); *ibid.*, f.429 (the Prince of Anhalt); Harleian MS 7008, f.232 (Count of Emden); Lotti to Vinta, 15 April 1610, ASF 4189 (Duc de Rohan); 23 June 1610, *ibid.* (Grand Duke of Tuscany). Further records of gifts from the Prince de Joinville, the Landgrave of Hesse and Madame de Nassau are in PRO, E 351/2794.

179 *CSP Venetian, 1607–10*, pp.295, 433; Smith, *Wotton*, I, p.458 note I; 470.

180 Sir David Murray to Salisbury, 12 July 1609, *HMC Hatfield*, XXI, p.84.

181 Dispatch of 11 August, 1611, *CSP Venetian, 1610–13*, p.194.

182 Nichols, *Progresses*, II, p.80. For a medieval manuscript on tournaments which was in his collection see Albert Way, 'Illustrations of Medieval Manners and Costume from Original Documents', *Archaeological Journal*, IV, 1847, pp.226–9;

Viscount Dillon, 'On a MS. Collection of Ordinances of Chivalry of the Fifteenth Century belonging to Lord Hastings', *Archaeologia*, LVII, pt. i, 1900, pp. 29–70.

183 Cornwallis, *Account*, p. 18.

184 Birch, *Henry*, p. 16.

185 Letter of La Boderie 31 October 1606 quoted *ibid.*, pp. 75–6.

186 Roy Strong, *Artists of the Tudor Court*, V & A Exhibition Catalogue, 1983, pp. 148–9 (nos. 245, 246).

187 On Lee see E. K. Chambers, *Sir Henry Lee*, Oxford, 1936, pp. 211–12; Nichols, *Progresses*, II, pp. 209–10. The armour is that reproduced in Sir Guy F. Laking, *A Record of European Arms and Armour through Seven Centuries*, London, 1922, V, pl. 1435.

188 Lee to the Prince, undated, BL Harleian MS 7008, f. 279; printed in Chambers, *Lee*, p. 212.

189 Peacham, *Minerva Britanna*, p. 17.

190 Williamson, *Myth*, pp. 34–5.

191 Cornwallis, *Account*, p. 26.

192 Maurice of Nassau to the Prince, 8 December 1611, BL Harleian MS 7008, f. 112. Van Nyvelt's pension is listed in Harleian 7009, ff. 1–2 dated as from June 1612. For van Nyvelt see J. Gaillard, *Maison de Zuylen, Histoire et Geneographie*, Bruges, 1863, I, p. 72; F. J. G. ten Raa and F. de Bas, *Het Staatsche Leger*, Breda, 1913, II, p. 414; N. Japikse and H. H. P. Rijperman, ed., *Resolutiën der Staten-Generaal van 1576 tot 1609*, The Hague, 1915–70, XII, pp. 546 note 7 547 note 1, 570, 680, 684, 705; XIV, pp. 176, 181–2; A. T. van Deursen and J. G. Smits, ed., *Resolutiën der Staten-Generaal*, Niewe Reeks, 1610–70, The Hague, 1971, I, p. 269, I am much indebted to Miss M. J. Poort for these references.

193 PRO, E 351/2794; AO, 1/2021 no. 2.

194 On the purchase of Kenilworth see

Arthur Gould Lee, *The Son of Leicester, The Story of Sir Robert Dudley*, London, 1964, pp. 142ff. Thomas Chaloner had been Dudley's tutor at Oxford and through him it was hoped to obtain a restoration to favour via the sale to Henry of the castle. See also George Adlard, *Amye Robsart and the Earl of Leicester*, London, 1870, pp. 289ff.

195 *The History of the King's Works*, ed. Colvin, pp. 367ff. gives the Tudor background but there is no study of the Jacobean period.

196 Boderie to M. de Pinsieuse, 21 June 1607, *Ambassades*, Paris, 1750, II, p. 289; Birch, *Henry*, pp. 86–7.

197 Dispatch of 11 August 1611, *CSP Venetian, 1610–13*, p. 194.

198 Anna E. C. Simoni, 'A Present for a Prince' in *Ten Studies in Anglo-Dutch Relations*, ed. Jan van Dorsten, Publications of the Sir Thomas Browne Institute, General series, no 5, Leiden, 1974, pp. 51–71.

199 I am much indebted to Mr Claude Blair for elucidation in the matter of Prince Henry's various armours. These are: (i) Armour given by Henri IV, 1607: Birch, *Henry*, pp. 87–90; Henri IV to the Prince 9 June 1607, BL Harleian MS 7007, f. 132, reproduced Laking, *Record*, V, pl. 1446; (ii) Armour given by the Prince de Joinville, although its real donor may have been the Dauphin, see La Boderie, *Ambassades*, I, s. v. letter dated 31 May 1606, reproduced Laking, *Record*, V, pl. 1425–6; (iii) Armour presented by Sir Henry Lee, 1608, see note 187; (iv) Armour presented by Maurice of Nassau. This is recorded in the visit of 'Counte Maurice his Armourer' in PRO, E 51/2794 of 1611–12. Mr Blair believes this to be Laking, *Record*, II, pl. 91; (v) Armour made, 1609: 13 October 1609: 'To the Armorer who came with a new sute of Armer to his highnes be comand', £3, PRO, SP 14, f. 129. There is another payment of 10 shillings to the ar-

mourer on 3 February 1609/10, *ibid.*, f. 133ᵛ.

200 Sir Edward Cecil [to Thomas Murray], 21 October 1612, *CSP Domestic, 1611–12*, p. 153; see Dalton, *Cecil*, pp. 234–6. They had been used by Prince Maurice.

201 Oliver Millar, *The Inventories and Valuations of the King's Goods 1649–51*, Walpole Society, XLIII, 1972, pp. 153–4. See also the extraordinary letter on military machines from Edward Helwis to the Prince, undated, BL Harleian MS 7007. f. 10. Helwis had been with Henry VIII at Boulogne and 'contryved certaine engins'.

202 Birch, *Henry*, pp. 86–7; Williamson, *Myth*, p. 61.

Princely Policy (pp. 71–85)

1 The best introduction to James's foreign policy is Maurice Lee Jr, *James I and Henri IV. An Essay in English Foreign Policy*, University of Illinois Press, 1970.

2 Cornwallis, *Discourse*, p. 336.

3 *Ibid., loc. cit.*

4 La Boderie was instructed to cultivate the Prince; Birch, *Henry*, pp. 41–2, 67. See Prince Henry to Henri IV, August 1606, acknowledging his 'affection vrayement paternelle', BL Harleian, MS 7007, f. 103.

5 See below, p. 191.

6 See Roland Mousnier, *The Assassination of Henri IV*, London, 1973; pp. 110ff. on Henri IV's foreign policy; see also Corrado Vivanti, 'Henry IV, the Gallic Hercules', *Journal of the Warburg and Courtauld Institutes*, XXX, 1967, pp. 176ff.

7 Conway to Newton, 2 June 1611, BL Harleian MS 7002 ff. 105–6. See Jan van Dorsten, 'Garter Knights and Familists', *Journal of European Studies*, 4, 1974, pp. 178–88.

8 Joel M. Rodney, 'The Earl of Salisbury and Henry Frederick, Prince of

Wales', *Washington State University, Research Studies*, XXX, 1965, pp. 56–63. The most important cache of letters, nearly all to Newton, establishing their relationship, is in BL Harleian MS 7002, ff. 136–37ᵛ (6 August, no year), 138–39ᵛ (undated), 97–98ᵛ (2 August, no year), 89–90ᵛ (undated), 91–92ᵛ (undated), 93–94ᵛ (undated), 95–96ᵛ (undated), 86–86ᵛ (endorsed 1612), 87–88ᵛ (endorsed 1611), 84 (undated), 83–83ᵛ (30 April 1611).

9 Salisbury to Newton, undated, BL Harleian MS 7002, ff. 95–96ᵛ. See Sir Thomas Lake to Salisbury, 1 August 1906: 'I would have sent you the letter out of France but that the Prince has not done with it', *HMC Hatfield*, XXI, pp. 113–14; Salisbury to ?Lake, July, undated: 'I left a letter from our agent in Spain either with the King or with the Prince', *ibid*, p. 230; Salisbury to Newton, 30 April 1611: 'I send you the copie of a letter...I sent the original to the King' (BL Harleian MS 7002, ff. 83–83ᵛ).

10 See Trumbull to the Prince, Brussels, 28 August 1612: 'to have the happines of being known to your Highness and employed in your gratious Commissyons while I resyde in these partes', BL Harleian MS 7008, f. 207.

11 Thomas Birch, *An Historical View of the Negotiations between the Courts of England, France and Brussels*, London, 1749, pp. 327–8.

12 John Walter Stoye, *English Travellers Abroad 1604–1667*, London, 1952, pp. 51–2. The Lorkin correspondence is in BL Harleian MS 7002, ff. 147ff.; the Forboyst is in Harleian 7015, ff. 240ff.

13 Smith, *Wotton*, I, pp. 78ff.; Frances A. Yates, 'Paolo Sarpi's History of the Council of Trent', *Journal of the Warburg and Courtauld Institutes*, VIII, 1944, pp. 123–43.

14 Dispatch, 28 September 1606, *CSP Venetian, 1603–7*, p. 404.

15 The Prince to the Doge, February

1607, BL Harleian MS 7007, f.117; dispatch, 7 May 1607, *CSP Venetian, 1603–7*, p.2.

16 Wotton to the Prince, 24 April 1608, BL Harleian MS 7007, f. 185; printed, Smith, *Wotton*, I, pp.425–7.

17 See John Lievsay, 'Paolo Sarpi's Appraisal of James I', in *Essays in History and Literature*, ed. Heinz Blohm, Chicago, 1965, pp. 109–17.

18 For the Julich-Cleves crisis see the introduction to *CSP Venetian 1607–10*; Boderie, *Ambassades*, V, pp. 1–29; Lee, *James I and Henry IV*, pp. 142ff.; Mousnier, *Assassination*, pp. 116ff.

19 Georges Ascoli, *La Grande-Bretagne devant l'Opinion Française au XVIIᵉ Siècle*, Travaux et Mémoires de l'Université de Lille, Droit-Lettres, Nouvelle série, fasc. 13, Paris, 1930, p. 27. See also Birch, *Henry*, pp. 189–90.

20 *CSP Venetian, 1607–10*, p. 506.

21 Dispatch of 25 May 1611, *CSP Venetian, 1610–13*, pp. 153–4.

22 For Frederic Ulric see Rye, *England as seen by Foreigners in the Days of Queen Elizabeth and James the First*, London 1865, pp. 224–5, note 72.

23 The large number of letters testify to the rapport between the two; the Prince to Frederic Ulric, 7 February 1604/5, BL Harleian MS 7007, f.56; 1609, *ibid.*, ff.277, 287, 305; 1610, *ibid.*, ff.360, 443; 1611, Harleian 7008, ff.7, 49, 57, 60, 93; undated, *ibid.*, f.270.

24 On the visit see SP 40, 17 May 1610 warrant for entertaining; Nichols, *Progresses*, II, p. 307–8; Lotti to Vinta, 15 April 1610, ASF 4189; Beaulieu to Trumbull, 29 March, Nichols, *Progresses*, II, p.290; *CSP Venetian, 1607–10*, pp.453, 461, 465.

25 Frederic Ulric to the Prince, 13 May 1610, BL Harleian MS 7007, f.360.

26 Frederic Ulric to the Prince, 12 June 1611, BL Harleian MS 7008, f.60.

27 Letters from Christian, BL Harleian MS 7007, f.396; 7008, ff.63, 155.

28 On the armour see Claude Blair, 'The Brunswick Armour', *Christie's Review of the Season*, 1982, Oxford, 1982, pp. 404–7.

29 On the visit of the Prince of Hesse see Nichols, *Progresses*, II, p.424; dispatch of 11 August 1611, *CSP Venetian, 1610–13*, p.196; Rye, *England as seen by Foreigners in the Days of Queen Elizabeth and James the First*, pp. 143 ff.; letters from the Prince of Hesse in BL Harleian MS 7008, ff.81–2, 89, 138.

30 There was a considerable interchange of emissaries between Heidelberg and the Prince from the inception of the match, as the letters bear testimony: BL Harleian MS 7007, ff. 338, 343, 359; 7008, ff. 43, 44, 140, 144, 147, 181, 192, 203, 211, 215, 216, 219, 221, 239, 245.

31 Dispatch of 11 February 1610, *CSP Venetian, 1607–10*, p. 420.

32 Dispatch of September 1610, *CSP Venetian, 1610–13*, p.31; dispatch of 21 October 1610, *ibid.*, p. 51, with mention that if it happened it would take place in a year.

33 Dispatches of 11 October and 20 November 1611, *ibid.*, pp. 234, 239.

34 Beaulieu to Trumbull, 23 January 1612: 'for as much as I can perceive, his Majesty's Mind is determinately fixed', Winwood, *Memorials*, III, p. 327.

35 Dispatch of 20 January 1612 refers to the Duke of Württemberg frequenting the Prince's company, *CSP Venetian, 1610–13*, p. 278. Anne of Denmark's froideur returned in August; Chamberlain, *Letters*, I, pp. 375, 376.

36 On this embassy see dispatches of 19 April and 4 May, *CSP Venetian, 1610–13*, pp.332, 344; Chamberlain, *Letters*, ed. McClure, I, pp. 345, 347–8; Winwood, *Memorials*, III, pp. 340–42, 357.

37 BL Harleian MS 7008, f.196 and his reply, f.236. A similar letter of grati-

tude was sent by John, Count Palatine, *ibid.*, f.194, and Frederick, f.198.

38 For an account of Prince Henry's various marriage negotiations, see *CSP Venetian, 1610–13*, introduction, pp. vii ff.

39 Cornwallis, *Discourse*, p.337.

40 For the Spanish match see Sir Charles Cornwallis, 'A Relation of the Carriage of the Marriages that should have been made between the Prince of England, and the Infanta Major, as also after with the younger Infanta', in John Gutch, *Collectanea Curiosa*, Oxford, 1781, pp.133–55; Albert J. Loomie, 'Sir Robert Cecil and the Spanish Embassy', *Bulletin of the Institute of Historical Research*, XLII, 1969, pp.30–57.

41 For the Medici match see J. R. Galluzzi, *Istoria del Granducato di Toscano sotto il Governo della Casa Medici*, Florence, 1781, III, pp.316 ff; Sir Charles Cornwallis, 'A Discourse concerning the Marriage propounded to Prince Henry with a Daughter of Florence' in Gutch, *Collectanea Curiosa, op. cit.*, I, pp.156–60; Garganò, *Scapigliatura*, pp.51 ff.; J. D. Mackie, *Negotiations between King James VI and I and Ferdinand I, Grand Duke of Tuscany*, 1927, pp. 71 ff.; Roy Strong, 'England and Italy: The Marriage of Henry, Prince of Wales' in *For Veronica Wedgwood These: Studies in 17th-Century History*, ed. R. Ollard and P. Tudor-Craig, London, 1986.

42 For the Savoy match see: Domenico Carutti, *Storia Diplomazia della Corte di Savoia*, Turin, 1876, II, pp.106–9; Smith, *Wotton*, I, pp. 113 ff.; Strong 'England and Italy: Prince Henry's Marriage', *op. cit.*

43 Chamberlain to Carleton, 17 June 1612, *Letters*, ed. McClure, I, p.361.

44 Dispatch of 19 August 1612, *CSP Venetian, 1610–13*, p.412.

45 Wake to Carleton, 9 March 1612/13; quoted Smith, *Wotton*, I, pp.124–5.

46 For the French marriage see Birch, *Henry*, pp.269–71, 289, 303–15; *CSP*

Venetian, 1610–13, pp. 171, 217, 339, 342, 348, 359.

47 Sir Thomas Lake to Carleton, 19 May 1613, *CSP Domestic, 1611–18*, p.185.

48 Raleigh, 'Touching a Marriage between Prince Henry of England and a Daughter of Savoy' in *Works*, London, 1829, VIII, pp.237–52.

49 Cornwallis, 'A Discourse ...', in Gutch, *Collectanea Curiosa, op. cit.*

50 Wake to Carleton, undated 1612, quoted S. R. Gardiner, *History of England 1603–1642*, London, 1884, II, p.57; Newton to Winwood, 17 November 1612 writes ' Sir Henry Neville told me, *he had vowed that never Idolater should come into his Bed*', Winwood, *Memorials*, III, p.410.

51 *Ibid., loc. cit.* Also Chamberlain to Carleton, 12 November 1612, *Letters,* ed. McClure, I, p.390.

52 Chamberlain to Carleton, 19 November 1612, *ibid.*, pp.390–92.

53 Dispatches of 20 and 23 November, 30 December 1612, *CSP Venetian 1610–13*, pp.450, 453–4, 470.

Art and Artists (pp. 86–137)

1 On Buontalenti see Ida Maria Botto, *Mostra di Disegni di Bernardo Buontalenti (1521–1608)*, Gabinetto Disegno e Stampe degli Uffizi, XXVIII, 1968; and especially Luciano Berti, *Il Principe dello Studiolo. Francesco dei Medici e la fine del Rinascimento fiorentino*, Florence, 1967, ch. VI.

2 R. J. W. Evans, *Rudolf II and His World. A Study in Intellectual History 1576–1612*, Oxford, 1973, ch. V–VII.

3 The only account in any detail of de' Servi is in Garganò, *Scapigliatura*, pp. 133 ff.

4 See Berti, *Il Principe dello Studiolo, op. cit.*

5 G. Gaye, *Carteggio inedito d'Artisti*, Florence, 1840, III, pp. 473–6.

6 Eve Barsook, 'Art and Politics at the Medici Court IV: Funeral Decor for Henry IV of France', *Mitteilungen des Kunsthistorischen Instituts in Florenz*, 1969, II, pp. 205–6; See André Valladier, *Labyrinthe Royal de l'Hercule Gaulois Triomphant*, Avignon, 1601, 3rd unnumbered page; see also Corrado Vivanti, 'Henry IV, the Gallic Hercules', *Journal of the Warburg and Courtauld Institutes*, XXX, 1967, pp. 176–97.

7 Lotti to Vinta, 30 September 1610, ASF 4189.

8 For the Francini see Albert Mousset, *Les Francine*, Paris, 1930; Margaret M. McGowan, *L'Art du Ballet de Cour en France 1581–1643*, CNRS, Paris, 1963, pp.81 note 40, 82, 87, 89, 90, 91, 92, 104, 111, 119, 130, 150.

9 Lotti to Vinta, 1 June 1611, ASF 4189 refers to de' Servi's late arrival, to the Prince securing the services of a Frenchman (de Caus) by way of the French ambassador, la Boderie, and to Thomas Chaloner's courtesy.

10 Lotti to Vinta, 9 June 1611, ASF 4189 which also refers to the favour of Sir Edward Cecil.

11 De' Servi to Cioli, 9 June 1611, ASF 4189.

12 Lotti to Vinta, 15 June 1611, ASF 4189.

13 De' Servi to Cioli, 23 June 1611, ASF 4189.

14 Lotti to Vinta, 13 July 1611, ASF 4189.

15 Lotti to Vinta, 27 July 1611, ASF 4189.

16 De' Servi to Cioli, Richmond 16 August 1611, ASF Mediceo 1348, f. 194.

17 De' Servi to Cioli 23 August 1611, ASF Mediceo 1348, f.213.

18 Lotti to Vinta 1 September 1611, ASF 4189; see also PRO, 'Mr Constantyne to Woodstocke beinge sent for by the Prince lv^s'; same payment in E 351/2794 1611–12.

19 De' Servi to Cioli, 22 September 1611, ASF Mediceo 1348, f.233.

20 Lotti to Vinta 29 September 1611, ASF 4189.

21 References to these financial difficulties are various: BL Harleian MS 7009 ff.6–7 'Sr John Hollis his remembrances', probably March 1612, gives a long list of financial claims by de' Servi including a 'Mem. Constantino coveteth sum lodging near St James, that he might faul in hand with his models etc.'; f.34 'Remembrances for certeyne privy seales to be allowed' includes de' Servi, who is without money, needs a lodging and an allowance for diet. See also PRO 101/433 No. 15 for money given to de' Servi in September 1611 which came from a merchant, John Brown, at the behest of Sir John Holles.

22 Here I list various payments to de' Servi: BL Harleian MS 7009 ff. 1–2 lists his salary as £200 p. a.; PRO, AO 1/2021 No. A: 'Constantyne de Servye a fflorentyne for his pencõn at CC^li per annum payable quarterlie ... l^li'; later under gifts and rewards £70 for diet, lodging and other expenses covering 1 August 1610 to 1 June 1612 and £100 'by way of his highnes guifte for recompense of his service for one yeare ended at Midsomer 1612 ...'. He reappears under Debts after the Prince's death, PRO E 101/433 No. 15 and as paid, along with Angelo Notari, in March 1613, PRO, AO 1/2021 No. 3.

23 Sir John Holles to Prince Henry, 9 December 1611, BL Additional MS 32464, ff.52–52^v.

24 Cioli to Vinta 24 July 1612, ASF 4190, f.52.

25 Cioli to Vinta 29 July 1612, ASF Miscell. Medicea, 293 inserto 28: No. 39.

26 De' Servi to Vinta 9 August 1612, ASF Mediceo 1229, f.286.

27 BL Harleian MS 7009, ff. 87–9,

three sheets in Italian addressed to the Prince. It is not signed but it could only be de' Servi and the date 1612.

28 Garganò, *Scapigliatura*, p. 146.

29 Undated, but there is no need to assume, as Orrell does, that the wedding referred to is the Somerset one of 1613. See John Orrell, 'The London Stage in the Florentine Correspondence, 1604–1618', *Theatre Research International*, 3, pp. 170–71.

30 De' Servi to Cioli, 7 December 1612, ASF Mediceo 1349 unnumbered folio. He states that he was to assemble materials 'delle sue fabriche' in Florence and Livorno.

31 For a letter from Lotti describing this, see Garganò, *Scapigliatura*, pp. 81–3.

32 De' Servi to Cioli 13 June 1613, Mediceo 1350 unpaginated.

33 For the *Masque of Squires* see Chambers, *Elizabethan Stage*, III, pp. 245–7.

34 Thomas Campion, *The Works*, ed. Walter R. Davis, London, 1969, p. 268.

35 Chamberlain to Carleton, 30 December 1613, *Letters*, ed, McClure. I, p. 496.

36 John Orrell, 'The agent of Savoy at *The Somerset Masque*', *Review of English Studies*, 28, 1977, pp. 301–4.

37 Campion, *Works*, ed. Davis, pp. 268, 269.

38 *Ibid.*, p. 269.

39 On the Tilt see *Ben Jonson: The Complete Masques*, ed. Stephen Orgel, Yale U. P., 1969, pp. 198–205; *Ben Jonson*, ed. C. H. Herford, P. and E. Simpson, Oxford, 1950, X, pp. 537–8.

40 A. M. Nagler, *Theatre Festivals of the Medici 1539–1637*, Yale U. P., 1964, p. 125.

41 See Roy Strong, *Art and Power. Renaissance Festivals 1450–1650*, London, 1984, part II, ch. IV.

42 This account of de Caus is based on Roy Strong, *The Renaissance Garden in England*, London, 1979, pp. 73–112, and p. 227 note 1 for bibliography.

43 PRO, E 179/146/369 Lay subsidy roll for 39 Elizabeth under the parishes of St George and St Margaret: 'Straungers': 'Salomon de Vaute…Liijˢ.iiijᵈ'. Such a large sum could imply a double assessment covering two years.

44 I list here the payments to de Caus: BL Harleian MS 7009 ff. 1–2 annual pensions from June 1610 to November 1612. The one to de Caus is dated as from March 1610/11; f. 3, a petition for his allowance; PRO, E 351/2793 1611–12 pension for one year, also recorded in AO 1/2021 No. 1A; AO 1/2021 No. 2, 1 October 1610 to 6 November 1612: 'Mounʳ du Caus clviiˡⁱ'; also 'Sondrye prouicons had from Mouns de Cawse, and others … xxxvˡⁱ'; also to the nurse and midwife of de Caus, 40s and a gift of plate costing £ 6.17.9d; PRO, AO 1/2021 No. 3 March 1612/13 debts include £ 50 for a half-yearly salary to de Caus; repeated in E 101/433 No. 15. More payments, repetitions of these, are in BL Lansdowne MS 164, ff. 188–9, 224–5, 236–7.

45 See Strong, *Renaissance Garden*, pp. 97–103; H. M. Colvin, John Summerson, Martin Biddle, J. R. Hale and M. Merriman, *The History of the King's Works*, ed. H. M. Colvin, IV, 1485–1660, London, 1982, II, pp. 231–2.

46 See PRO, SP 14/63 ff. 84, 121, 172.

47 PRO, AO 1/2021 No. 3. The payment made up one in all of £ 60.

48 Strong, *Renaissance Garden*, pp. 125 ff.

49 Estimate for work at Richmond, May 1611: PRO, SP 63/85. For other payments see PRO, AO 1/2021 Nos 3 and BL Harleian MS 7009 f. 6 which includes £ 1,000 for lead; and E 101/433 No. 15.

50 *King's Works, op. cit.*, p. 231. There is a reference to work stopping in August 1611 in a letter from Sir Charles Cornwallis to Cecil (?) 25 August 1611, PRO, SP 14/65, f. 132.

51 *Les Raisons des Forces Mouvantes*, Paris, 1624. Part I is dedicated to Louis XIII and Part II to Elizabeth of Bohemia (1 January 1615/16).

52 This has recently been the subject of two reprints: *Hortus Palatinus. Die Entwürfe zum Heidelberger Schlossgarten von Salomon de Caus, 1620*, Worms, 1980; *Le Jardin Palatin*, ed. Michel Conan, Paris, 1981.

53 Richard Patterson, 'The "Hortus Palatinus" at Heidelberg and the Reformation of the World', *Journal of Garden History*, I, 1981, pp. 67–104, 179–202.

54 Salomon de Caus, *La Perspective avec la Raison des Ombres et Miroirs*, London, 1612, dedication.

55 *Ibid., loc. cit.* On de Caus and shadows see Thomas Da Costa Kaufman, 'The Perspective of Shadows: the History of the Theory of Shadow Projection', *Journal of the Warburg and Courtauld Institutes*, XXXVIII, 1975, pp. 278–9.

56 Alan R. Young, *Henry Peacham*, Boston, 1979, p. 24.

57 On books on perspective in English libraries see Lucy Gent, *Picture and Poetry 1560–1620*, Leamington Spa, 1981, pp. 74–5.

58 The basic biographical and bibliographical information remains that assembled in John Harris, Stephen Orgel and Roy Strong, *The King's Arcadia. Inigo Jones and the Stuart Court*, Arts Council Exhibition catalogue, 1973.

59 Communicated by G. B. Bredgade to John Harris. The reference comes in the diary of Sivert Grabbe to a dinner held on 10 July 1603 which lists the guests, Copenhagen, Royal Library MSS, Uldallske sams. 499, f. 147.

60 For all these see Orgel and Strong, *Inigo Jones*, I, pp. 89–157; II, pp. 823–5.

61 Lawrence Stone, 'Inigo Jones and the New Exchange', *Archaeological Journal*, CXIV, 1957, pp. 106–21; *King's Arcadia, op. cit.*, pp. 29–31 (28–30).

62 Lawrence Stone, 'The Building of Hatfield House', *Archaeological Journal*, CXII, 1956, pp. 100–128.

63 I list here all the payments to Jones while in the Prince's service; PRO, AO 1/2021 No. 1A payment of £88.2.6d for the period 13 January 1611 to 29 September 1612; AO 1/2021 No. 2 and E 351/2794 October 1610 to November 1612: 'Inigoe Jones the Princes Surveyor xxx[li]'; AO 1/2021 No. 3 and E 101/433 No. 15 October to November 1612, £5.11sh.

64 *King's Arcadia*, p. 36.

65 Gordon Higgott, 'Inigo Jones in Provence', *Architectural History*, XXVI, 1983, pp. 24–34.

66 See John Peacock, 'The French Element in Inigo Jones's Masque Designs' in *The Court Masque*, ed. David Lindley, Manchester U.P., 1984, pp. 149–68, with some dubious comparisons.

67 Campion, *Works*, ed. Davis, p. 268.

68 See *King's Arcadia*, p. 52 (70); I. A. Schapiro, 'The "Mermaid Club"', *Modern Language Review*, XLV, 1950, pp. 6–17.

69 *King's Arcadia*, p. 55.

70 On de Critz see Roy Strong, *The English Icon*, London, 1969, pp. 259–68 and bibliography.

71 *Ibid.*, pp. 269–304.

72 *Ibid.*, pp. 225–52.

73 The iconography is discussed in E. E. Gardiner, 'A British Hunting Portrait', *Metropolitan Museum of Art Bulletin*, III, No. 5, 1944, pp. 113–17.

74 Cesare Enrico Bertana, 'Il Ritratto di uno Stuart alle Corte dei Savoia',

Studi piemontesi, XIII, No. 2, 1983, pp. 423–6. The canvas has been reduced on all four sides.

75 PRO, AO 1/2021 No. 2 and E 351/2794 1611–12; other payments to Peake: E 101/433 No. 8: 14 October 1608: 'To Mr Peck for pictures made by his highnes comand li'.

76 Strong, *Icon*, p. 364 (338).

77 See above pp. 91, 95 for 1611 and 1612 Cioli to the Grand Duchess Christina 16 April 1612 describing that Lotti was on his way either carrying or shortly causing to be sent a portrait of Henry by de' Servi: 'un ritratto del Serenissimo Principe, che Io rappresenta al vivo', ASF Miscell. Medicea 295 inserto 26.

78 Birch, *Henry*, pp. 244 ff.

79 *Ibid.*, p. 485.

80 *Ibid.*, pp. 487–8.

81 *Ibid.*, pp. 489–91.

82 *Ibid.*, p. 496.

83 *Ibid.*, p. 499.

84 For Miereveldt see Jakob Rosenberg, Seymour Slive and E. H. ter Kuile, *Dutch Art and Architecture: 1600 to 1800*, Penguin Books, 1979 edn, pp. 314–15.

85 Strong, *Icon*, pp. 300 (306–7), 315 (325–6).

86 PRO, LC 2/4/6. For Oliver see Roy Strong, *The English Renaissance Miniature*, London, 1983, pp. 142–85; same author's *Artists of the Tudor Court*, V & A exhibition catalogue, 1983, pp. 97–116. There is also a dissertation in typescript which has been printed: Jill Finsten, *Isaac Oliver. Art at the Courts of Elizabeth I and James I*, Garland Publication, New York, 1978.

87 Chamberlain to Carleton, 6 November 1611, *Letters*, ed. McClure, I, p. 312.

88 Finsten, *Isaac Oliver*, I, Appendix.

89 Strong, *Renaissance Miniature*, p. 123; *Artists of the Tudor Court*, p. 148 (245).

90 Strong, *Artists of the Tudor Court*, p. 148 (246).

91 *Ibid.*, p. 142 (230); Finsten, *Isaac Oliver*, II, pp. 104–5 (66).

92 Strong, *Artists of the Tudor Court*, pp. 153–4 (257); Finsten, *Isaac Oliver*, II, pp. 98–100 (63) misdated to *c.* 1610.

93 Strong, *Artists of the Tudor Court*, p. 154 (258); Finsten, *Isaac Oliver*, II, pp. 102–3 (65) but not as variants of the large miniature.

94 See below, p. 189.

95 For a discussion of the problem of the drawings see Strong, *Renaissance Miniature*, pp. 143–51; Finsten, *Isaac Oliver*, I, pp. 140–58.

96 Finsten, *Isaac Oliver*, I, p. 158.

97 *Ibid.*, II, pp. 209–56. The signatures on these drawings often present a major problem.

98 Charles II Inventory (temp. 1662–85) MS in the Royal Collection, pp. 19 (327), 22 (369, 371).

99 *A Catalogue of the Collection of Pictures, &c belonging to James the Second...*, London, 1758, pp. 52 (597), 55 (636), 56 (638).

100 F. J. Levy, 'Henry Peacham and the Art of Drawing', *Journal of the Warburg and Courtauld Institutes*, XXXVII, 1974, pp. 174–90; Alan R. Young, *Henry Peacham*, Boston, 1979, ch. 3.

101 Strong, *Artists of the Tudor Court*, pp. 113 (174–5), 115 (179), 116 (181).

102 See Arthur M. Hind, *Engraving in England in the Sixteenth and Seventeenth Centuries*, Part I, The Tudor Period, C.U.P., 1952, pp. 1–38.

103 *Ibid.*, Part II, *The Reign of James I*, C.U.P., 1955, pp. 316–40.

104 Strong, *Artists of the Tudor Court*, pp. 154–5 (259).

105 *Ibid.*, pp. 150–51 (250–52).

106 I made this suggestion to Margery Corbett and R. W. Lightbown, *The Comely Frontispiece. The Emblematic Titlepage in England, 1550–1660*, London, 1979, pp. 113–18.

107 Orgel and Strong, *Inigo Jones*, I, p. 167 (38).

108 Corbett and Lightbown, *The Comely Frontispiece*, pp. 145–50.

109 *Ibid.*, pp. 153–61.

110 PRO, AO 1/2021 No. 2 and E 351/2794 1611–12. Could this be to Boel?

111 PRO, AO 1/2021 No. 2.

112 Hind, *Engraving*, II, pp. 313–15.

113 *Ibid.*, I, pp. 262 (4); 267–8 (10).

114 Frances A. Yates, *Astraea. The Imperial Theme in the Sixteenth Century*, London, 1975, p. 210.

115 Corbett and Lightbown, *The Comely Frontispiece*, pp. 107–11.

116 Hind, *Engraving*, II, pp. 313–14. Hind also assigns to Boel engravings of James I and Anne of Denmark, *ibid.*, pp. 57 (12), 58 (13).

117 Orgel and Strong, *Inigo Jones*, I, p. 169 (41).

118 *The Moral and Historical Works of Lord Bacon*, ed. Joseph Devey, London, 1866, pp. 493–4.

119 *The first Booke of Architecture, made out of Sebastian Serly, entreating of Geometrie*, London, 1611, See Chambers, *Elizabethan Stage*, IV, p. 353.

120 On Bolsover see Mark Girouard, *Robert Smythson and the Elizabethan Country House*, Yale U.P., 1983, pp. 234 ff.

121 John Newman, 'An Early Drawing by Inigo Jones and a monument in Shropshire', *Burlington Magazine*, CXV, 1973, pp. 360–67.

122 Margaret Whinney, *Sculpture in Britain 1530–1830*, Penguin Books, 1964, pp. 26–7.

123 W. H., *True Picture*, p. 31. There is an inexplicable payment of £ 35 to 'Duchemen which came from Rotterdam for Buyldinges', PRO, E 351/2794; AO 1/2021 No. 2.

The Prince's Festivals (pp. 138–183)

1 Lotti to Cioli 3 August 1608, ASF Filza 4188. Harington later writes on his failure to get a copy of the *fêtes* book as he had wanted to be first to send it to him: undated letter to Prince Henry; but after one dated 11 December 1608, BL Harleian MS 7007, f. 221.

2 Lotti to Cioli, 1 January 1608/9, ASF Filza 4188. In one of the surviving letters Harington sends the Prince the speeches for a barriers he saw in Verona, letter to Prince Henry, 28 May 1609, BL Harleian MS 7007, f. 267.

3 See Roy Strong, *Art and Power. Renaissance Festivals 1450–1650*, London, 1984, pp. 149–52 and p. 210 note 25 for sources.

4 *Ben Jonson*, ed. D. H. Herford and E. and P. Simpson, Oxford, 1970 edn, VIII, pp. 280–81.

5 I summarize here what I attempted to synthesize in *Art and Power, op. cit.*

6 For the Accession Day Tilts see Frances A. Yates, *Astraea. The Imperial Theme in the Sixteenth Century*, 1975, pp. 88–111; Roy Strong, *The Cult of Elizabeth. Elizabethan Portraiture and Pageantry*, London, 1977, pp. 129–62.

7 See *Art and Power, op. cit.*, pp. 50–57.

8 See the bibliography in *ibid.*, p. 211 note 1.

9 For the *Barriers* see Chambers, *Elizabethan Stage*, III, p. 393; Orgel and Strong, *Inigo Jones*, I, pp. 159–75 (nos. 36–44); Mary C. Williams, 'Merlin and the Prince: The Speeches at Prince Henry's Barriers', *Renaissance Drama*, N.S., 8, 1977, pp. 221–30.

10 Cornwallis (Hawkins), *Account*, p. 23.

11 Dispatch of 17 December 1609, *CSP Venetian 1607–10*, p. 401.

12 William Drummond of Hawthornden, *Teares, on the Death of Moeliades* in *The Poetical Works of William Drummond of Hawthornden*, ed. L. E. Kastner, Manchester, 1913, I, p. 75.

13 Cornwallis (Hawkins), *Account*, p. 23.

14 Orgel and Strong, *Inigo Jones*, I, p. 160; ll. 32–40.

15 *Ibid.*, l. 100.

16 *Ibid.*, ll. 169–70.

17 *Ibid.*, ll. 195–6.

18 *Ibid.*, ll. 206–8.

19 *Ibid.*, ll. 221–2.

20 *Ibid.*, ll. 290–91.

21 *Ibid.*, I, pp. 185 (no. 52), 169 (nos. 41–4).

22 Cambridge, Trinity College MS R 10.14, f. 182.

23 On Gwinne see: J. Ward, *Lives of the Professors of Gresham College*, London, 1740, pp. 160–65; Chambers, *Elizabethan Stage*, III, pp. 331–2; J. Buxton, *Sir Philip Sidney and the Elizabethan Renaissance*, London, 1954, p. 161; Christopher Hill, *Intellectual Origins of the English Revolution*, London, 1972 edn, pp. 37, 51, 217.

24 Orgel and Strong, *Inigo Jones*, I, p. 160; ll. 170–73.

25 For Sir John Hayward see *DNB*; Sir John Hayward, *Annals of the First Four Years of the Reign of Queen Elizabeth*, ed. John Bruce, Camden Society, 1840; Margaret Dowling, 'Sir John Hayward's Troubles over his Life of Henry IV', *The Library*, 4th series, 1931, pp. 212–24; Norman Scarfe, 'Sir John Hayward: An Elizabethan Historian. His Life and Disappointments', *Suffolk Institute of Archaeology*, 25, 1952, pp. 79–97.

26 W. H., *True Picture*, p. 26.

27 May McKisack, *Medieval History in the Tudor Age*, Oxford, 1971, p. 121.

28 On which see Kevin Sharpe, *Sir Robert Cotton 1586–1631. History and Politics in Early Modern England*, Oxford, 1979, Part I, ch. III.

29 Orgel and Strong, *Inigo Jones*, I, p. 160; ll. 52–9.

30 *Ibid.*, ll. 84–6.

31 Frances A. Yates, *The Theatre of the World*, London, 1969, pp. 80–91; Stephen Orgel, 'Inigo Jones on Stonehenge', *Prose*, III, 1971, pp. 109–24.

32 Ludovico Zorzi, 'Figurazione pittorica e figurazione teatrale' in *Storia dell'arte italiana*, I, *Materiale e problemi*, I, *Questioni e metodi*, Turin, 1979, pp. 440–41.

33 Strong, *Art and Power*, pp. 150–52.

34 Winwood to Salisbury, 7 October 1609, *Memorials*, III, pp. 78–80.

35 C. Pfister, 'Les "Economies Royales" de Sully et le Grand Dessin de Henri IV', *Revue Historique*, LVI, 1894, pp. 43–44; David Ogg, 'Sully's Grand Design of Henry IV', *The Grotius Society Publications*, London, 1921, p. 44.

36 Letter of 13 January 1609/10 Chamberlain, *Letters*, ed. McClure, I, p. 293.

37 For the 1610 Accession Day Tilt see Nichols, *Progresses*, II, p. 287; Orgel and Strong, *Inigo Jones*, I, p. 177 (no. 45).

38 See Strong, *The Cult of Elizabeth*, p. 134.

39 For domestic and especially the parliamentary background see Wallace Notestein, *The House of Commons 1604–10*, Yale U. P!, pp. xi ff.; 255 ff.; *Proceedings in Parliament, 1610*, ed. Elizabeth Read Foster, Yale U. P., 1966; also Correr's dispatches recording the Prince's alarm at the potential surrender of the right of wardship, *CSP Venetian 1607–10*, pp. 227, 439–40, 451.

40 Carleton to Edmondes, undated in Nichols, *Progresses*, II, p. 358.

41 Dispatch of 26 May 1610, *CSP Venetian, 1607–10*, p. 496; Correr restates this in his dispatch of 16 June, *ibid.*, p. 507.

42 Dispatch of 9 June 1610, *CSP Venetian 1607–10*, p. 508; reiterated in his dispatch of 23 June, *ibid.*, pp. 515–16.

43 Wilson, *History*, p. 44.

44 For the entry down the Thames see *London's Loue to the Royal Prince Henrie...* reprinted in Nichols, *Progresses*, II, pp. 315–22; also pp. 324–6. It is worth referring to a provincial pageant in celebration: *Chester's Triumph in Honor of Her Prince* performed on 23 April; printed in Nichols, *Progresses*, II, pp. 291–306 and by *The Chetham Society*, III, 1844 with an introduction.

45 See Nichols, *Progresses*, II, p. 317 note 2.

46 *Ibid.*, p. 320.

47 *Ibid.*, pp. 336–45.

48 Dispatch, 23 June 1610, *CSP Venetian 1607–10*, p. 516.

49 For the Creation ceremony see Cornwallis (Hawkins), *Account*, p. 24; Winwood, *Memorials*, III, pp. 179–81; Nichols, *Progresses*, II, pp. 327–31; dispatch of Correr, 16 June 1610, *CSP Venetian 1607–10*, pp. 507–8; HMC Various, III, pp. 259–63; *Proceedings in Parliament, 1610*, I, pp. 95–8; II, pp. 126–8. For the Prince's robes see PRO, SP 14/55, ff. 38–9; SP 14/57, ff. 144^v–45. See also the sermon by one of the Prince's chaplains, Daniel Price, *The Creation of the Prince, A Sermon Preached in the Colledge of Westminster, on Trinity Sunday, the day before the Creation of the most illustrious Prince of Wales*, London 1610: 'such a young *Ptolemy* for Studies and Libraries; such a young *Alexander* for affecting martialisme and chivalrie, such a young *Iosiah* for religion & piety'.

Generally for the Creation *fêtes* see David M. Bergeron, *English Civic Pageantry 1558–1642*, London, 1971, pp. 94–6.

50 For *Tethys' Festival* see: Nichols, *Progresses*, II, p. 360; Chambers, *Elizabethan Stage*, III, pp. 281–3; Orgel and Strong, *Inigo Jones*, I, pp. 191–201 (nos. 53–8); John Pitcher, '"In those figures which they seeme": Samuel Daniel's *'Tethys' Festival'* in *The Court Masque*, ed. David Lindley, Manchester U.P., 1984, pp. 33–46. Pitcher's article includes much dubious interpretation of the masque's numerological symbolism, difficult to sustain in the absence of details of the choreography or certainty on numbers, e.g. the text states that there were eight attendants on zephyrs, another source twelve.

The planning of the masque went back to December 1609, see the Countess of Hertford's letter to Viscount Cranborne, *HMC Hatfield*, XXI, p. 170; and February reference in Orrell, 'London Stage', pp. 165–6.

51 Orgel and Strong, *Inigo Jones*, I, p. 194; ll. 125–30.

52 This is listed amongst the Prince's jewels on his death, a 'very riche cros Sword all sett with Dyamants'; William Bray, 'An Account of the Revenue, the Expenses, the Jewels, &c. of Prince Henry', *Archaeologia*, XV, 1806, pp. 18–20.

53 Orgel and Strong, *Inigo Jones*, I, p. 194, ll. 139–40.

54 On which see Yates, *Astraea*, pp. 24–87.

55 Orgel and Strong, *Inigo Jones*, I, p. 194; ll. 142–7.

56 Orgel and Strong, *Inigo Jones*, I, p. 195; ll. 252–3.

57 See Roy Strong, *Portraits of Queen Elizabeth I*, Oxford, 1963, p. 138 (nos. 17–18); same author's *Artists of the Tudor Court*, exhibition catalogue, V & A, 1983, p. 123 (no. 197).

58 Strong, *Portraits of Queen Elizabeth I,* *op. cit.*, p. 75 (no. 72); same author's *Tudor and Jacobean Portraits*, London, 1969, I, pp. 104–7 (no. 2561).

59 Orgel and Strong, *Inigo Jones*, I, p. 196; ll. 367–8.

60 *Ibid.*, p. 195; ll. 311–12.

61 PRO, E 351/2794. For Drayton and the Prince see B. H. Newdigate, *Michael Drayton and his Circle*, Oxford, 1961, pp. 177, 197.

62 For the Creation Tilt see J. Stowe, *Annales*, London, 1631 edn, p. 991; Winwood, *Memorials*, III, p. 181; Nichols, *Progresses*, II, p. 260; *HMC Various*, III, pp. 260–63; Orgel and Strong, *Inigo Jones*, I, pp. 179–85 for designs for tilts and barriers.

63 Orgel and Strong, *Inigo Jones*, I, p. 184 (no. 47) for the caparison; p. 228 (no. 72) for the squire, previously assigned to *Oberon*. A third design for a lance bearer, *ibid.*, p. 184 (no. 48), may also be for the Creation Tilt.

64 See Strong, *The Cult of Elizabeth*, Appendix I, s.v. 1590 and 1599 for sources; *Complete Peerage*, IX, pp. 677–9.

65 Orgel and Strong, *Inigo Jones*, I, p. 181 (no. 46).

66 On the shepherd mythology see Strong, *The Cult of Elizabeth*, pp. 149–50.

67 For the fireworks and sea fight see Nichols, *Progresses*, II, pp. 322–3.

68 See D. H. Wilson, 'Summoning and Dissolving Parliament, 1603–25, the Council's Advice to James I', *Historical Review*, XLV, 1939, pp. 279–300.

69 Dispatch of 23 June 1610, *CSP Venetian 1607–10*, pp. 515–16.

70 For Oberon see: Chambers, *Elizabethan Stage*, III, p. 385–6; 'Oberon, The Fairy Prince', ed. Richard Hosley in *A Book of Masques*, ed. Allardyce Nicoll, Cambridge U.P., 1967, pp. 43–70; Orgel and Strong, *Inigo*

Jones, I, pp. 205–28 (nos. 63–73). I am indebted to the best discussion of this masque in Stephen Orgel, *The Jonsonian Masque*, Harvard U.P., 1965, pp. 82–91.

71 Orgel, *The Jonsonian Masque, op. cit.*, p. 84.

72 Orgel and Strong, Inigo Jones, I, p. 197; ll. 62–3.

73 *Ibid.*, p. 288; ll. 226–32.

74 See above, p. 109.

75 Orgel and Strong, *Inigo Jones*, I, pp. 210–14 (nos. 60–62). Dispatch of 25 November, *CSP Venetian, 1610–13*, p. 79.

76 For a discussion of this see Roy Strong, *Britannia Triumphans. Inigo Jones, Rubens and Whitehall Palace*, London, 1980, p. 25.

77 See John Peacock, 'Inigo Jones's Stage Architecture and its Sources', *Art Bulletin*, LXIV, 1982, pp. 199–205 on the designs for *Oberon* with some pertinent and other dubious sources for the architecture.

78 Orgel and Strong, *Inigo Jones*, I, p. 208; ll. 236–40.

79 *Ibid.*, I, pp. 208–9; ll. 219, 299, 351–2.

80 John P. Cutts, 'Le Rôle de la Musique dans les Masques de Ben Jonson et Notamment dans *Oberon* (1610–11)' in *Les Fêtes de la Renaissance*, I, ed. Jean Jacquot, CNRS, Paris, 1956, pp. 285–303.

81 W. H., *True Picture*, p. 31.

80 See David C. Prince, *Patrons and Musicians in the English Renaissance*, Cambridge U.P., 1981, esp. pp. 224–5 which lists the musicians in the household in the years 1610–12.

83 John Aplin, 'Sir Henry Fanshawe and Two Sets of Early Seventeenth Century Part Books at Christ Church, Oxford', *Music & Letters*, 57, 1976, pp. 11–24.

84 References in respect of music: PRO, SP 14/57 Privy Purse Expenses 1609–10, ff. 129, 135^V;

E 351/2794 Accounts 1611–12. For
the organ: Landesbibliothek Kassel, MS 68, f. 70.

85 Garganò, *Scapigliatura*, pp. 92–3;
Lotti to Vinta 4 October 1612
ASF 4190, f. 55.

86 On Notari see under debts, PRO
E 101/433 no. 15 'Angelo de Nota-
rie for Arrerages of his fee or pen-
cion and dispache awaye by order
of the Lordes Commissioners—l^li'.
See Ian Spink, 'Angelo Notari and
his "Prime Musiche Nuove"',
Monthly Musical Record, 86–7,
1956–7, pp. 168–77; Pamela J. Wil-
letts, 'Autographs of Angelo Notari', *Music & Letters*, 50, 1969,
pp. 124–6; Garganò, *Scapigliatura*,
p. 94.

87 For *Love Freed*, see '*Love Freed...*',
ed. Norman Sanders in *A Book of
Masques, op. cit.*, pp. 71–93; Chambers, *Elizabethan Stage*, III,
pp. 386–7; Orgel and Strong, *Inigo
Jones*, I, pp. 229–37 (nos. 74–6).

88 Orgel and Strong, *Inigo Jones*, I,
p. 231; ll. 95–7.

89 For *Love Restored* see Chamberlain,
Letters, ed. McClure, I, p. 328;
Chambers, *Elizabethan Stage*, III,
pp. 387–8; *Ben Jonson*, ed.
C. H. Herford and P. and E. Simp-
son, Oxford, 1967 edn, X,
pp. 531–7 for documentation; *Ben
Jonson, The Complete Masques*, ed.
Stephen Orgel, Yale U.P., 1969,
pp. 186–97 for the text; Jeffrey
Fischer, '*Love Restored*: A Defense
of Masquing', *Renaissance Drama*,
N.S., 8, 1977, pp. 231–44.

90 Nichols, *Progresses*, II, pp. 463–7;
Chamberlain to Carleton, 22 October, Letters, ed. McClure, I,
pp. 380–81; dispatch of 9 November, *CSP Venetian, 1610–13*,
p. 443.

91 Finnett to Trumbull, 23 October,
1612; Winwood, *Memorials*, III,
pp. 403–4.

92 Chamberlain to Winwood, 3 November 1612, *Letters*, ed. McClure, I,
pp. 383–4.

93 Cornwallis *Account*, p. 28.

94 Finnett to Trumbull, 23 October
1612; Winwood, *Memorials*, III,
pp. 403–4; Nichols, *Progresses*, II,
p. 463.

95 Dispatch of 16 November 1612,
CSP Venetian, 1607–10, pp. 446–7.

96 William Fennor, *Fennors Descriptions, or A Trve Relation of Certaine
and diuers speeches spoken before the
King and Queenes most excellent Maiestie, the Prince his highnesse, and the
Lady Elizabeths Grace*, London,
1616.

97 For the *Memorable Masque* see:
Chambers, *Elizabethan Stage*, III,
pp. 260–62; Jack E. Reese, 'Unity
in Chapman's *Masque of the Middle
Temple and Lincoln's Inn*', *Studies in
English Literature*, 4, 1964,
pp. 291–305; Orgel and Strong,
Inigo Jones, I, pp. 253–63; D. J. Gordon, 'Le *Masque Mémorable* de
Chapman' in *Les Fêtes de la Renaissance, op. cit.*, pp. 305–17 reprinted
in D. J. Gordon, *The Renaissance Imagination*, ed. Stephen Orgel,
University of California Press,
1975, pp. 194–202.

98 Orgel and Strong, *Inigo Jones*, I,
p. 261; ll. 595–603.

99 For the Inner Temple and Gray's
Inn Masque see Chambers, *Elizabe-
than Stage*, III, pp. 253–5; 'The
Masque of the Inner Temple and
Gray's Inn' ed. Philip Edwards in *A
Book of Masques, op. cit.*,
pp. 125–48.

100 *A Book of Masques*, p. 140,
ll. 288–97.

101 *Ibid.*, p. 139, ll. 273–6.

102 For Beaumont see Charles Mills
Gayley, *Francis Beaumont. Dramatist*,
London, 1914; Chambers, *Elizabe-
than Stage*, III, pp. 215–18.

103 Undated letter, BL Harleian
MS 7008, f. 23.

104 For Chapman and Prince Henry
see *DNB*; Chambers, *Elizabethan
Stage*, III, pp. 249–50; Wilson,

261

Prince Henry, pp. 74–5, 104–5, 144–5; Graham Parry, *The Golden Age Restored. The Culture of the Stuart Court*, Manchester U.P., 1980, pp. 66–7.

105 PRO, LC 2/4/6.

106 D. Jocquet, *Les Triomphes, Entrées, Cartels, Tournois, Cérémonies, et aultres Magnificences, faites en Angleterre...*, Heidelberg, 1613, sig. 11 ff. See David Norbrook, 'The Reformation of the Masque' in *The Court Masque*, ed. Lindley, pp. 98 ff. Mr Norbrook refers to a forthcoming article.

107 C. F. Ménéstrier, *Des Ballets Anciens et Modernes selon les Règles de Théâtre*, Paris, 1682, pp. 114, 123.

108 Orgel and Strong, *Inigo Jones*, I, pp. 241–52 (nos. 78–83).

109 *The Works of Thomas Campion*, ed. Walter Davis, London, 1969, p. 260 note 38.

110 Nichols, *Progresses*, II, pp. 527–41.

111 Jacques Vanuxem, 'Le Carrousel de 1612 sur la Place Royale et ses Devises' in *Les Fêtes de la Renaissance, op. cit.*, pp. 191–203.

The Prince's Collections (pp. 184–219)

1 For the history of collecting see F. H. Taylor, *The Taste of Angels*, London, 1948; Germain Bazin, *The Museum Age*, London, 1967, ch. IV.

2 See *Palazzo Vecchio: Committenza e Collezionismo Medicei 1537–1610*, Exhibition catalogue in *Firenza e la Toscana dei Medici nell'Europa del Cinquecento*, Florence, 1980, esp. pp. 245–50.

3 R. J. W. Evans, *Rudolf II and His World. A Study in Intellectual History*, Oxford, 1973, pp. 176 ff.

4 For the early history of the old Royal Collection see Oliver Millar, *The Tudor, Stuart and Early Georgian Pictures in the Collection of H.M. The Queen*, London, 1977, pp. 17–28.

5 On Anne of Denmark and the arts see: John Harris, Stephen Orgel and Roy Strong, *The King's Arcadia. Inigo Jones and the Stuart Court*, Arts Council Exhibition, 1974, pp. 95–8; Roy Strong, *The Renaissance Garden in England*, London, 1979, pp. 87–97; same author's *The English Renaissance Miniature*, London, 1983, pp. 169–70; same author's *Artists of the Tudor Court*, Exhibition catalogue, V & A, 1983, pp. 151–3. For Christian IV see Joakim A. Skovgaard, *A King's Architecture. Christian IV and his Buildings*, London, 1973.

6 The only account of Anne of Denmark's collection is in Millar, *The Queen's Pictures*, pp. 22–8.

7 Richard Haydocke, *A Tracte containinge the Artes of curious Painting Carueinge & Buildinge*, Oxford, 1598, preface.

8 *HMC Hatfield*, XXI, p. 39. The letter is calendared under March 1609 but it is endorsed 1610, which is surely the correct date.

9 For Robert Cecil's collection see E. Auerbach and C. K. Adams, *Painting and Sculpture at Hatfield House*, London, 1971, pp. 26, 92 (91), 93 (92), 93 (93), 95 (95), 96 (98), 97 (99), 102 (109), 105 (112).

10 PRO, SP 14/57 f. 133.

11 *Ibid.*, f. 134 15 March 1610: 'to my lady Cumberlands man with two pictures', £1; f. 134[V]: 'to S[r] Edward Cecyls man with a picture to his highness', 12sh.; f. 136: 'to M[r] Edmondes man with pictures to his highness', 10sh.; f. 137[V] 21 July 1610: 'to my lord of Exeters man with two pictures to his highness', £2; f. 137[V] 22 July 1610: 'to S[r] Noel Carons man with a picture to his highness', £1.

12 Sir Walter Cope to Carleton 26 January 1610/11, PRO, SP 14/61, f. 61.

13 The purchases may be grouped as follows: (i) from Philip Burlamachi: PRO, E 351/2794 1611–12: 'Burlmach for the Pictures that came from Venice', £480.17sh.4d.; (ii)

from Isaac Oliver (payments that cannot be categorized certainly as for pictures *by* him): PRO, SP 14/57 f. 134: 1 March 1610: 'to Mʳ Isaac the Paynter for the pictures made to his highnes', £ 18; PRO, E 351/2794 1611–12: three pictures, £ 32; 'one greate picture', £ 34; three other pictures, £ 30; 'one greate twoe litle pictures', £ 40.; (iii) from various Dutchmen: PRO, E 351/2794 1611–12: 'Vandellivell Duchman for the Pictures of vij Emperors', £ 10; 'one Clase a Duchman for Pictures' £ 70; 'twoe Pictures bought of a Duchman', £ 12; 'a littell Duchman for Pictures', £ 240.; (iv) from Martin von Bentheim, the painter: AO 1/2021 No. 1A: 'Martyn van Benthem for the pryse of certen pictures for the furnishinge of the gallerye at St James, by warrante under the privie seale dated the xxviᵗʰ of Aprill 1612, and his acquittance-xiˡⁱ', see E. Croft-Murray, *Decorative Painting in England 1537–1837*, London, 1962, I, p. 193.; (v) from Philip Jacob: PRO, E 351/2794 1611–12: for pictures, £ 10; for thirty alabaster pictures, £ 40.10. All these payments covering the period 1 October 1610 to 6 November 1612 are repeated in AO 1/2021 No. 2 and printed in *Extracts from the Accounts of the Revels at Court in the Reigns of Queen Elizabeth and King James*, ed. Peter Cunningham, London, pp. xiii-xv.

14 Dispatch of Correr 2 June 1610, *CSP Venetian, 1607–10*, p. 500.

15 J. G. van Gelder, 'Notes on the Royal Collection—IV. The "Dutch Gift" of 1610 to Henry Prince of "Whalis" and Some Other Presents', *Burlington Magazine*, CV, pp. 541–4. See PRO, SP 14/57, f. 136: 'to the Estates of hollands men with diuers pictures to his highnes', £ 8.

16 Oliver Millar, *Abraham van der Doort's Catalogue of the Collection of Charles I*, Walpole Society, XXXVII, 1960, pp. 187, 196; M. Russell, *Visions of the Sea. Hendrick C. Vroom and the Origins of Dutch Marine Painting*, Sir Thomas Browne Institute, Leiden, 1983, N.S. 2, pp. 162–4, 166.

17 Lotti to Vinta, 29 March 1610, ASF 4189.

18 Jean Alazard, *The Florentine Portrait*, London and Brussels, 1948, pp. 190 ff; and *Palazzo Vecchio: Committenza e Collezionismo Medicei 1537–1610*, p. 277 (no. 522).

19 De' Servi to Cioli, 23 June 1611, ASF 4189; most of this was published by Gargano, *Scapigliatura*, pp. 68–9.

20 Lotti to Vinta, 13 July 1611, ASF 4189.

21 J. Irene Whalley, 'Italian Art and English Taste. An Early Seventeenth Century Letter', *Apollo*, XCIV, 1971, pp. 184–91.

22 H. M. Colvin, John Summerson, Martin Biddle, J. R. Hale and Marcus Merriman, *The History of the King's Works*, IV, 1485–1660, London, 1982, p. 245.

23 W. B. Rye, *England as seen by Foreigners in the Days of Elizabeth and James the First*, London, 1865, p. 161; *Les Voyages du Sieur de Mandelso*, Leiden, 1719, p. 750.

24 Millar, *Van der Doort's Catalogue*, p. 8 (3).

25 *Ibid.*, pp. 227 (9).

26 *Ibid.*, p. 3 (nos. 7 and 10).

27 Landesbibliothek Kassel, MS Hass. 68, f. 70.

28 *Ibid.*, p. 185 (2).

29 Possibly 'A Battaile' listed at St James's, *ibid.*, p. 227 (37).

30 Oliver Millar, *The Inventories and Valuations of the King's Goods 1649–1651*, Walpole Society, XLIII, 1972, p. 305 (120).

31 'A lyeing entire figure of Prometheus done By Jaquama Palma the younger', Millar, *Van der Doort's Catalogue*, p. 226 (2); same author's *Queen's Pictures*, p. 28.

32 Millar, *Van der Doort's Catalogue*, p. 79 (16).

33 *Ibid.*, pp. 226–8.

34 John Walsh Jr., 'The Dutch Marine Painters Jan and Julius Porcellis: I. Jan's early career', *Burlington Magazine*, CXVI, 1974, pp. 654–62.

35 Millar, *Van der Doort's Catalogue*, p. 185 (3).

36 *Dutch Pictures in Oxford*, Exhibition catalogue, Ashmolean Museum, 1975 (9); C. Brown, *Burlington Magazine*, CXVII, 1975, p. 495.

37 Burton B. Fredericksen, 'E Cosi Desio me Meno', *The J. Paul Getty Museum Journal*, 10, 1982, pp. 21–38.

38 Sold Christie's 24 April 1981 (lot 141); E. R. J. Reznicek, 'Het begin von Goltzius's loopbaan als Schilder', *Oud Holland*, 75, 1960, pp. 42–3 fig. 7.

39 For the story of the bronzes see Katherine Watson and Charles Avery, 'Medici and Stuart: a Grand Ducal Gift of "Giovanni Bologna" Bronzes for Henry Prince of Wales (1612)', *Burlington Magazine*, CXV, 1973, pp. 493–507.

40 Lotti to Vinta 29 April 1610, ASF 4189; reminder by Lotti to Vinta of this request in a letter of 22 June 1610, ASF 4189.

41 The fifteen are listed in Millar, *Van der Doort's Catalogue*, pp. 72 (9), 92–6 (nos. 1–15). See Watson and Avery, *op. cit.*, pp. 506–7 for a collation of inventory references and the letters. Versions and variants of all these bronzes are discussed in *Giambologna 1529–1608. Sculptor to the Medici*, Exhibition catalogue ed. Charles Avery and Anthony Radcliffe, Arts Council, V & A, 1978.

42 Cioli to Vinta, 12 July 1612, ASF 4190, f. 50.

43 Millar, *Van der Doort's Catalogue*, p. 96 (32), 212 (31), 'A Bigg Horse By John de Bolonia'. Avery and Watson do not discuss these additional bronzes or how they were acquired.

44 *Ibid.*, p. 92 (4).

45 Orgel and Strong, *Inigo Jones*, I, p. 160, ll. 58–9.

46 Whalley, 'Italian Art and English Taste', *op. cit.*

47 Fynes Moryson, *An Itinerary*, Glasgow, 1907, I, p. 327.

48 Manfred Leithe-Jasper, 'Bronze Statuettes by Giambologna in the Imperial and other early collections' in *Giambologna*, ed. Avery and Radcliffe, *op. cit.*, pp. 51–9.

49 John Evelyn to Samuel Pepys, 12 August 1689, in *Memoirs illustrative of the Life and Writings of John Evelyn, Esq.,...*, ed. William Bray, London, 1819, II, p. 246.

50 *Archaeologia*, XV, 1806, p. 16.

51 Chamberlain to Carleton, 19 November 1612, *Letters*, ed. McClure, I, p. 391.

52 For van der Doort's life see Millar, *Van der Doort's Catalogue*, pp. xii-xvii.

52 BL Harleian MS 7009, ff. 1–2; AO 1/2021 No. 1A: 'Abraham Van der Dorte a drawer of pictures for his pencōn at l^{li} p anñ due to him for halfe a yeare ended at Mychas 1612—xxv^{li}'. Later in the same accounts £ 50 is given to him 'for a picture presented by him to the Prince' by warrant dated 1 March 1611/12. Annual salary, dated July 1612, of £ 50 p.a. listed in BL Harleian MS 7007, ff. 1–2.

54 Millar, *Van der Doort's Catalogue*, p. 26 note 2 (3).

55 PRO, E 357/2794.

56 PRO, E 351/2793.

57 *HMC Hatfield*, XXI, p. 352. See Horace Walpole, *Anecdotes of Painting*, ed. R. N. Wornum, London, 1849, I, p. 234 note 2.

58 Thomas Birch, *The Court and Times of James I*, London, 1848, I, p. 428.

59 Millar, *Van der Doort's Catalogue*, p. 74 (1).

60 *Ibid.*, pp. 135 note 1 and pp. 154–6

note 2. I have rendered the phonetics into standard English.

61 PRO, SP 14/57.

62 For a definitive account see *The Lumley Library*, ed. Sears Jane and Francis R. Johnson, London, 1956. See also Sir Thomas Smith, *Vitae Quorundam Eruditissirorum et illustrium Virorum*, London, 1707 edn, pp. 10–13.

63 A considered biography of Lumley is a *desideratum* but see E. Milner, *Records of the Lumleys of Lumley Castle*, London, 1904; L. Cust, 'The Lumley Inventories', *Walpole Society*, VI, 1918, pp. 15–35; Roy Strong, *The English Icon. Elizabethan and Jacobean Portraiture*, London, 1969, pp. 45–7.

64 D. Piper, 'The 1590 Lumley Inventory' *Burlington Magazine*, XC, 1957, pp. 224–31.

65 Frances A. Yates, *Theatre of the World*, London, 1969, p. 12; Chapter I, pp. 1–19 deals with Dee's library and its importance. See also for an account Peter J. French, *John Dee. The World of an Elizabethan Magus*, London, 1972, ch. 3.

66 On the building of the library see Colvin *et al*, *The History of the King's Works*, IV, ii, p. 245.

67 See *English Bindings in the Library of J. R. Abbey*, 1940 (no. 17); Howard M. Nixon, *Twelve Books in Fine Bindings from the Library of J. W. Hely-Hutchinson*, Roxburghe Club, 1953, pp. 10–12.

68 These are from PRO, SP 14/57 ff. 133ᵛ, 134. References to the presentation of books is frequent including: f. 129ᵛ 18 October 1609: 'to a frenchman that presented a booke to his highnes', £ 4; f. 131ᵛ 13 December 1609 to a stranger who presented a book, £ 4; 2 January 1609/10: to a poor scholar who presented a book, £ 2; f. 133ᵛ 14 February 1609/10: to one who presented a book, £ 3.

69 PRO, E 351/2794 also includes 'A Duchman presenting a Law Booke',

£ 15; 'One that presented a greate Dictionary', £ 20.

70 PRO, AO 01/2021 No. 1A.

71 Lotti to Vinta, 23 September, ASF 4189.

72 Landesbibliothek Kassel, MS 68, ff. 83–83ᵛ.

73 Garganò, *Scapigliatura*, pp. 68–9.

74 PRO, SP 14/57 ff. 129ᵛ, 133. For Gideon de Laune see George Corfe, *The Apothecary*, London, n.d., pp. 21–2.

75 Landesbibliothek Kassel, MS Hass. 68, ff. 61ᵛ–62.

76 Christopher Hill, *Intellectual Origins of the English Revolution*, London, 1972 edn, esp. pp. 213–19.

77 See Leila Parson, 'Prince Henry (1594–1612) as a Patron of Literature', *Modern Language Review*, 47, 1952, p. 503 for the payment on 3 May 1609 of £26.13.4d to 'Lidgate'; BL Harleian MS 7009, ff. 1–2 annual pension listed as from August 1611.

78 Frances A. Yates, *Theatre of the World*, London, 1969, ch. 1; Peter J. French, *John Dee. The World of an Elizabethan Magus*, London, 1972, ch. 4; John Dee, *The Mathematicall Preface to the Elements of Geometrie of Euclid of Megara* (1570), intro. by Allen G. Debus, Science History Pub., New York, 1975.

79 French, *John Dee*, p. 87.

80 W. H., *True Picture*, p. 31.

81 *Collectanea*, 1st series, ed. C. R. L. Fletcher, Oxford Historical Society, Oxford, 1885, pp. 274 ff. esp. pp. 277–8.

82 Frances A. Yates, *The French Academies of the Sixteenth Century*, London, 1947, p. 278.

83 'Project for an Academy Royal' in John Gutch, *Collectanea Curiosa...*, Oxford, 1781, I, p. 214.

84 For Drebbel see Rye, *England as seen by Foreigners*, p. 232, note 84;

F. M. Jaeger, *Cornelius Drebbel en Zijne Tidgenooten*, Groningen, 1922, pp. 28–30, 104–6, 125; Evans, *Rudolf II*, p. 189.

85 Tymme, *Dialogue*, pp. 60–63.

86 PRO, SP 14/57, f. 131ᵛ 18 December 1609, £ 20 'To Cornelius the Dutchman at his highnes command'; f. 134ᵛ 29 March 1610, £ 20 'to Cornelius the Dutchman at his highnes command'.

87 Rye, *England as seen by Foreigners*, pp. 239–40.

88 Dee, *Preface, ed. cit.*, sig. d.j.

89 David W. Waters, *The Art of Navigation in England in Elizabethan and Early Stuart Times*, London, 1958, pp. 525–6.

90 *Ibid.*, pp. 217–19.

91 *Ibid.*, pp. 219–30. E. G. R. Taylor, *The Mathematical Practitioners of Tudor and Stuart England*, Cambridge, 1954, pp. 44–8, 51, 136–7, 181–2.

92 PRO, SP 14/71, f. 79.

93 Waters, *Art of Navigation*, pp. 217–19; Taylor, *Mathematical Practitioners*, pp. 95, 129, 176.

Epilogue: Our Rising Sun is Set (pp. 220–225)

1 For accounts of his death see: Cornwallis, *Account*, pp. 31 ff.; Birch, *Henry*, pp. 332 ff.; *CSP Venetian, 1610–13*, pp. 447–8; Chamberlain, *Letters*, ed. McClure, I, pp. 384, 389; HMC Mar & Kellie, p. 46; *CSP Domestic, 1611–18*, pp. 154, 155, 161.

2 Dispatches of 29 November 1612, 29 December, 8 January and 11 April 1613, *CSP Venetian, 1610–13*, pp. 449, 469, 178, 521.

3 *Ibid.*, p. 472.

4 For discussions and lists of the memorial literature see: Nichols, *Progresses*, II, pp. 504–12; Wilson, *Prince Henry*, pp. 144–68; Ruth Wallerstein, 'The Laureate Hearse' in *Studies in Seventeenth Century Poetics*, Wisconsin, 1950, pp. 59–95.

5 Dorset to Edmondes, 23 November 1612, Nichols *Progresses*, II, p. 490.

6 Chamberlain to Carleton, 12 November 1612, *Letters*, ed. McClure, I, p. 390.

7 Jane Clark, 'The Buildings and Art Collection of Robert Dudley, Earl of Leicester (with notes on his portraits)', MA Report, Courtauld Institute of Art, University of London, 1981; Roy Strong, *The English Icon. Elizabethan and Jacobean Portraiture*, London, 1969, pp. 163–6, 346; same author's *The English Renaissance Miniature*, London, 1984 edn, p. 74.

8 There is a vast literature on Sidney, but for the visual arts see: Alexander C. Judson, *Sidney's Appearance, A Study in Elizabethan Portraiture*, Indiana U.P., 1958; Katherine Duncan-Jones, 'Sidney and Titian', *English Renaissance Studies Presented to Dame Helen Gardner*, Oxford, 1980, pp. I–II.

9 Essex and visual arts is touched upon in my *The Cult of Elizabeth. Elizabethan Portraiture and Pageantry*, London, 1977, pp. 56–83 and *The English Renaissance Miniature*, pp. 161–2.

10 Beaulieu to Trumbull, 12 November 1612, Winwood, *Memorials*, III, pp. 410–11.

List of Illustrations

Prince Henry in 1608. Reproduced by gracious permission of Her Majesty the Queen.

22   William Hole after a drawing by Isaac Oliver, *Prince Henry with the Pike*. Engraving. From Michael Drayton, *Poly-Olbion*, 1612.

23   Artist unknown, *Prince Henry wearing the suit of armour sent by Henri IV*. Painting. Dunster Castle, Copyright The National Trust.

24   Robert Peake, *Henry, Prince of Wales, and John, 2nd Lord Harington of Exton*, 1603. Painting. The Metropolitan Museum of Art, New York, purchased 1944, Joseph Pulitzer Bequest.

25   Riding House at Wolfeton, Charminster, *c.* 1610. From Royal Commission on Historical Monuments, *Dorset*, Vol. III, Pt. I, 1970.

26   Robert Smythson, Plan and drawings of Prince Henry's Riding School, St James's Palace, London, 1607–9. British Architectural Library, RIBA, London.

27   S.H.Grimm, *The Interior of the Riding School at Welbeck*. Drawing. British Library, London (Ms. Add. 15 545, f. 68).

28   John Smythson, Design for the Riding School at Welbeck, 1622. British Architectural Library, RIBA (Smythson Drawings 111/15 (3)).

29   Crispin van de Passe, *Frederick V, Elector Palatine, later King of Bohemia*. Engraving. The Folger Shakespeare Library, Washington, DC.

30   M.J. van Miereveld, *Maurice of Nassau*. Painting (detail). Rijksmuseum-Stichting, Amsterdam.

31   Henri IV as the Gallic Hercules. Engraving. Bibliothèque Nationale, Paris.

32   Marcus Gheeraerts the Younger, *The Princess Elizabeth*, *c.* 1611. Painting. Palazzo Chiablese, Turin.

33   Isaac Oliver, *Prince Henry*, *c.* 1612. Miniature. Reproduced by gracious permission of Her Majesty the Queen.

34   Inigo Jones, aged about forty, *c.* 1614. Engraving by Francesco Villamena.

35   Artist unknown, perhaps by Constantino de' Servi, Knight masquer perhaps in Campion's *Masque of Squires*, 1613. Drawing. Devonshire Collections. Trustees of the Chatsworth Settlement. Photo Courtauld Institute of Art, London.

36   Car of Venus in the *Sbarra* of 1579, Florence. Engraving.

37   The first intermezzo, 1589. The Harmony of the Spheres. Engraving by Agostino Carracci after Bernardo Buontalenti. Photo Soprintendenza per i Beni Artistici e Storici di Firenze.

38   Giovanni da Bologna's *Appennino* at Pratolino. Engraving by Stefano della Bella from Sgrilli, *Descrizione della regia villa*, 1742.

39   Project for a giant probably for Henry, Prince of Wales, at Richmond Palace, *c.* 1611. Engraving from Salomon de Caus, *Les Raisons des forces mouvantes*, Paris, 1624.

40   Fountain for Henry, Prince of Wales. Engraving from Salomon de Caus, *La Perspective*, 1611.

41   Wenceslas Hollar, *Richmond Palace*. Engraving, 1638. British Museum, London.

42   Robert Peake, *Henry, Prince of Wales*, *c.* 1604–10. Painting. Palazzo Chiablese, Turin. Photo Francesco Aschieri.

43   Hendrik Goltzius, *Manlius Torquatus*. Engraving from *The Roman Heroes*; *c.* 1586. Rijksmuseum-Stichting, Amsterdam.

44   Attributed to François Clouet, *Henri II*. Painting. The Metropolitan Museum of Art, New York, Bequest of Helen Hay Whitney, 1944.

255

45 Robert Peake, *Henry, Prince of Wales,* *c.* 1610. Painting. From the Collection at Parham Park, Pulborough, Sussex. Copyright reserved.

46 William Rogers, *George Clifford, 3rd Earl of Cumberland,* Engraving. British Museum, London.

47 Marcus Gheeraerts the Younger, *Unknown man 'à l'antique',* *c.* 1610. Painting. Stanford University Museum of Art, The Mortimer C. Leventritt Fund.

48 Isaac Oliver, *Prince Henry, 'à l'antique',* *c.* 1610–11. Miniature. Fitzwilliam Museum, Cambridge.

49 William Rogers, *Robert Devereux, 2nd Earl of Essex.* Engraving. British Museum, London.

50 Cornelis Boel, *Henry, Prince of Wales,* *c.* 1612. Engraving. British Museum, London.

51 Isaac Oliver, *Moses striking the Rock,* probably before 1586. Drawing. Copyright reserved. Reproduced by gracious permission of Her Majesty the Queen (Royal Library, Windsor Castle, RL 13529).

52 Isaac Oliver, *Nymphs and Satyrs,* probably after 1610. Drawing. Copyright reserved. Reproduced by gracious permission of Her Majesty the Queen (Royal Library, Windsor Castle, RL 13528).

53 Cornelis Boel, Title-page to the Authorized Version of the Bible, 1611. Engraving. British and Foreign Bible Society, London.

54 Inigo Jones, Design probably for Merlin in the *Barriers,* 1610. Devonshire Collections. Trustees of the Chatsworth Settlement. Photo Courtauld Institute of Art, London.

55 William Hole, Title-page to Chapman's *Homer, Prince of Poets,* 1610, dedicated to the Prince and perhaps after a design by Inigo Jones.

56 The Little Castle, Bolsover, Derbyshire, 1612–14. Photo National Monuments Record.

57 *Gallia,* Title-page to Pierre Matthieu, *L'Histoire de la France,* 1605. Bibliothèque Nationale, Paris.

58 William Hole, perhaps after a design by Inigo Jones, Title-page to Michael Drayton's *Poly-Olbion,* 1612. Engraving.

59 John Aubrey, Sketch of the classical portico added by Sir James Fullerton to Byfleet Lodge. Bodleian Library, Oxford (Ms Aubrey 4, f. 196).

60 Inigo Jones, Design for the tomb of the wife of Sir Rowland Cotton, *c.* 1608. British Architectural Library, RIBA.

61 The Cotton tomb as executed. Church of St Chad, Norton-in-Hales, Shropshire. Photo National Monuments Record, copyright reserved.

62 Michelangelo, Lorenzo de' Medici, Basilica of San Lorenzo, Florence. Photo Alinari/Brogi 55630.

63 Nicholas Stone, Monument to Francis Holles, *c.* 1622. Westminster Abbey, London.

64 Inigo Jones, The *Barriers,* January 1610: St George's Portico. Drawing. Devonshire Collections. Trustees of the Chatsworth Settlement. Photo Courtauld Institute of Art, London.

65 Inigo Jones, The *Barriers,* January 1610: the fallen House of Chivalry. Drawing. Devonshire Collections. Trustees of the Chatsworth Settlement. Photo Courtauld Institute of Art, London.

66 Inigo Jones, The *Barriers,* January 1610: Polish knight. Drawing. Devonshire Collections. Trustees of the Chatsworth Settlement.

67 Giulio Parigi, *Il Giudizio di Paride,* 1608. Engraving. Victoria and Albert Museum, London (E. 610–1949).

256

68 *Scena Tragica.* From Sebastiano Serlio, *Architettura*, Venice 1569. British Architectural Library, RIBA.

69 Inigo Jones, The *Barriers*, January 1610: Design probably for Prince Henry's helmet. Drawing. Devonshire Collections. Trustees of the Chatsworth Settlement.

70 Inigo Jones, The *Barriers*, January 1610: Design probably for the Prince's *impresa* shield bearing the figures of Minerva and Lady Chivalry. Drawing. Devonshire Collections. Trustees of the Chatsworth Settlement.

71 Inigo Jones, Design for tilt entry for Sir Richard Preston, at the Accession Day Tilt, March 1610. Drawing. Devonshire Collections. Trustees of the Chatsworth Settlement.

72 Nicholas Hilliard, Reverse of a medal of Elizabeth I, *c.* 1590. British Museum, London.

73 Marcus Gheeraerts, *Queen Elizabeth I: the Ditchley Portrait, c.* 1592. Painting. National Portrait Gallery, London.

74 Inigo Jones, *Tethys' Festival,* June 1610: River Nymph. Drawing. Devonshire Collections. Trustees of the Chatsworth Settlement. Photo Courtauld Institute of Art, London.

75 Inigo Jones, Creation Tilt, June 1610: Horse caparison. Drawing. Devonshire Collections. Trustees of the Chatsworth Settlement. Photo Courtauld Institute of Art, London.

76 Inigo Jones, Creation Tilt, June 1610: Mount and beacon for Lord Compton as a Shepherd Knight. Drawing. Devonshire Collections. Trustees of the Chatsworth Settlement. Photo Courtauld Institute of Art, London.

77 Inigo Jones, Probably for the Creation Tilt, June 1610: Design for a lance-bearer. Drawing. Devonshire Collections. Trustees of the Chatsworth Settlement.

78 Inigo Jones, *Oberon*, January 1611: Prince Henry as Oberon. Drawing. Devonshire Collections. Trustees of the Chatsworth Settlement. Photo Courtauld Institute of Art, London.

79 Inigo Jones, *Oberon*, January 1611: Attendant in Ancient British dress. Drawing. Devonshire Collections. Trustees of the Chatsworth Settlement. Photo Courtauld Institute of Art, London.

80 Inigo Jones, *Oberon*, January 1611: Costume design for a fairy. Drawing. Devonshire Collections. Trustees of the Chatsworth Settlement.

81 Inigo Jones, *Oberon*, January 1611: Project. Drawing. Devonshire Collections. Trustees of the Chatsworth Settlement. Photo Courtauld Institute of Art, London.

82 Inigo Jones, *Oberon*, January 1611: Oberon's Palace. Drawing. Devonshire Collections. Trustees of the Chatsworth Settlement. Photo Courtauld Institute of Art, London.

83 Inigo Jones, Design for the setting for the Queen's masque for 1611, Ben Jonson's *Love Freed from Ignorance and Folly.* Devonshire Collections. Trustees of the Chatsworth Settlement. Photo Courtauld Institute of Art, London.

84 William Hole, possibly after Constantino de' Servi, *Angelo Notari.* Engraving, intended as a frontispiece to his *Prime Musiche Nuove*, 1613.

85 William Hole, possibly after Constantino de' Servi, Title-page to Angelo Notari, *Prime Musiche Nuove*, 1613.

86 One of Cornelius Drebbel's perpetual motion machines. From Thomas Tymme, *A Dialogue Philosophical*, 1612.

87 Jacob de Gheyn, Abraham Gorlaeus. Frontispiece to his *Dactyliotheca*, Leiden 1601.

88 Jacob de Gheyn, Engraved gems set into rings. From Abraham Gorlaeus, *Dactyliotheca*, Leiden 1601.

89 Jacob de Gheyn, Engraved gems set into rings. From Abraham Gorlaeus, *Dactyliotheca*, Leiden 1601.

90 William Hole, *Prince Henry's Hearse*, 1612. Engraving. British Museum, London.

91 Hendrik Goltzius, Allegorical figure, possibly *Pictura*, 1610. Painting. Collection Armin Pertsch, Mannheim.

92 HP brandmark, from the reverse of ill. 91. Collection Armin Pertsch, Mannheim.

93 Artist unknown, *Castruccio Castracane*, one of the portraits of *uomini illustri*. Uffizi, Florence. Photo Alinari/Mannelli 753.

94 Artist unknown, *Zanobi di Strada*, one of the portraits of *uomini illustri*. Uffizi, Florence. Photo Alinari/Mannelli 741.

95 Artist unknown, *Old Woman Blowing Charcoal*. Painting. Reproduced by gracious permission of Her Majesty the Queen.

96 Artist unknown, *A boy looking through a casement*. Painting. Reproduced by gracious permission of Her Majesty the Queen.

97 Studio of Hendrik Vroom, *Battle off Gibraltar fought against the Spaniards*, 1607. Painting. National Maritime Museum, Greenwich.

98 Attributed to Hendrik Vroom or Jan Porcellis, *A Storm at Sea*. Painting. Reproduced by gracious permission of Her Majesty the Queen.

99 Artist unknown, *The Battle of Ravenna*. Painting. Reproduced by gracious permission of Her Majesty the Queen.

100 Hans Vredeman de Vries, *Christ in the House of Mary and Martha*. Painting. Reproduced by gracious permission of Her Majesty the Queen.

101 Attributed to Abraham Bloemaert, *The Parable of the Tares*. Painting. Private collection. Photo Ashmolean Museum, Oxford.

102 Hans Holbein the Younger, *Allegorical figure on horseback*, *c.* 1530. Painting. The J. Paul Getty Museum, Malibu.

103 Palma Giovane, *Prometheus*. Painting. Reproduced by gracious permission of Her Majesty the Queen.

104 Giovanni da Bologna, *Astronomia*. Bronze statuette, gilded. Kunsthistorisches Museum, Vienna (Sammlung für Plastik und Kunstgewerbe, 5893).

105 Giovanni da Bologna, *La Fortuna*. Bronze. Musée du Louvre, Paris (Département des Objets d'Art, OA 10598). Photo Musées Nationaux.

106 After Pietro Tacca, *Shepherd bagpiper, seated*. Bronze. Museo Nazionale, Bargello, Florence (464).

107 Workshop of Giovanni da Bologna, *Hercules wielding the club*. Bronze. Museo Nazionale, Bargello, Florence. Photo Alinari 32877.

108 Workshop of Giovanni da Bologna, *Nessus and Deianeira*. Bronze. Collection Cyril Humphris, London.

109 Giovanni da Bologna, *Hercules and the Centaur*. Bronze. Kunsthistorisches Museum, Vienna (Sammlung für Plastik und Kunstgewerbe 5834).

110 Workshop of Giovanni da Bologna, *Horse rearing*. Bronze. Reproduced by gracious permission of Her Majesty the Queen. Photo Courtauld Institute of Art, London,

111 Workshop of Giovanni da Bologna, *Horse pacing*. Bronze. Reproduced by gracious permission of Her Majesty the Queen. Photo Courtauld Institute of Art, London.